Methods in Caribbean Research

Methods in Caribbean Research

Literature, Discourse, Culture

Edited by
Barbara Lalla, Nicole Roberts,
Elizabeth Walcott-Hackshaw
and Valerie Youssef

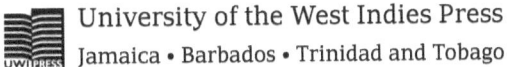 University of the West Indies Press
Jamaica • Barbados • Trinidad and Tobago

University of the West Indies Press
7A Gibraltar Hall Road, Mona
Kingston 7, Jamaica
www.uwipress.com

A catalogue record of this book is available from the National Library
of Jamaica.
ISBN: 978-976-640-348-5

Book and cover design by Maria Papaefstathiou
(e-mail: maria.pap@graphicart-news.com)

Printed in the United States of America.

Contents

Part 1
Research Methodology

Conceptual Frames

Methods of Research: Data Collection

Methods of Research: Application and Analysis

Part 2
The Research Process

Acknowledgements

The editors thank the University of the West Indies for the research grant that supported this work. They also thank Natasha Callendar, Zara Ali, Andra Ramdeen and Jessy Mitchell for assistance in collecting information for the work and formatting the manuscript.

Representation of culturometric self-norming – Leonardo da Vinci's *Vitruvian Man* (figure 3.1) and the culturometric family of research methods and techniques (figure 3.2) are adapted from the culturometric website http://www .culturometrics.org.

Introduction

Caribbean Research and Scholarship in Literature, Discourse and Culture

Barbara Lalla and Valerie Youssef

This book offers tools for Caribbean research in literature, discourse and culture and in the intersections of these disciplines. It provides guidelines for approaching research from inside or outside the Caribbean, on Caribbean topics or alternatively on non-Caribbean material from a Caribbean perspective. Thus, it considers available and appropriate methods for such research, and emphasizes the need to articulate relevant theoretical underpinnings for serious scholarship.

Qualitative versus Quantitative Research

Humanities research in the Caribbean today is usually regarded as qualitative and interpretive, owned as much by the subject of the research as by the researcher. Often it is gendered, participatory, multicultural and oriented towards social action. Often postcolonial and postmodern in orientation, its centre shifts and invites multiple interpretations.

This qualitative approach locates the researcher in relation to the research, and, to make the world that is to be investigated visible, the researcher frames observations within a set of theories. So used, these theories become tools for orienting the investigation, associable with a range of practices for transforming the world being observed into images, representations, recordings of selected oral texts, memoranda to the self and so forth. The relation between observer and observed is a crucial consideration, and interpretation may be negotiable rather than fixed. Such scholarship demonstrates concern for how experience is created and meaning derived or constructed, rather than concern for measurement, and research is value based rather than value free.

Nonetheless, twenty-first-century research does increasingly operate with mixed methodologies for effective results, using approaches which are pragmatic, fitted to the case at hand. It is important to note that a quantitative approach may be employed in historical, economic, demographic, socio-historical and archaeological research as well as in linguistics and cultural studies and, to a limited extent, in literary critiques. Corpus linguistics, for example, is used to describe and analyse language varieties more accurately, and specific Caribbean studies identify regional standards more robustly than other techniques (see, for example, Deuber 2010). Research on discourse now includes quantitative as well as qualitative critiques, recognizing that the numerical occurrence of linguistic features in a text may be significant to interpretation or may help to validate the text through precise depiction of some historical circumstance in its context. Successive repetition of memories recalled, for example, has been shown to mirror the individual's experiential evaluation of abusive behaviour in profound ways (Morgan and Youssef 2006, 89–90). Béatrice Boufoy-Bastick's culturometric analysis, described in this text as a possible model for assessing multiculturalism, is based on a qualitative questionnaire but uses statistical analysis to assess its results.

Researchers distinguish qualitative from quantitative research while recognizing the place of each in their work as well as the strengths and weaknesses of each. R. Burke Johnson and Anthony J. Onwuegbuzie (2004) argue cogently that the rigour of research which employs mixed methods is essential to better understandings of the complex phenomena we investigate. Many research topics draw on both objective and subjective approaches and are thereby enriched. The positivist defines an objective reality beyond the mind, while the interpretivist holds individual experience as paramount. When describing the slave trade, however, facts assembled from the archives inform our understanding of both objective and subjective reality. The data on boats, conditions, numbers of individuals packed into them and numbers who died, help to formulate both objective and subjective realities. In research on literature that explores the slave trade, such objective facts cogently inform subjective understandings.

All researchers seek verity and must determine appropriate ways of arriving at and substantiating their findings. Positivists who replicate an experiment countless times with identical results conclude that they have discovered an irrefutable truth (reliability). Interpretivists question ultimate generalizable truth since they view truth as individual and experiential. Interpretivist research, however, is enriched by the depth and diversity achieved through building the knowledge base. The scholar cannot discuss the perspective of V.S. Naipaul without having read his work extensively, as well as relevant commentary and information on his personal background; nor can the writer's style be usefully discussed without extensive study of his oeuvre. Reliability for the interpretivist researcher in this way resembles that of the positivist. Indeed, although some humanities scholars, and literary scholars in particular, still view research training with suspicion, Gabriele Griffin recognizes that the "cultural turn" in the social sciences has led to the increased influence of rigorous humanities methods on other disciplines and urges researchers in the humanities to reclaim these proudly (2005, 14).

Caribbean Research

What sets the Caribbean apart and justifies an application of scholarly method to its own needs? What defines the world of Caribbean letters? Why not merely apply established approaches to scholarship that work satisfactorily in Western metropoles?

Antonio Benítez-Rojo explains "that Caribbeanness is a system full of noise and capacity, a nonlinear system, an unpredictable system, in short a chaotic system beyond the reach of any specific kind of knowledge or interpretation of the world" ([1992] 1996, 295). To his way of thinking, "no perspective of human thought – whether pre-modern, modern or postmodern, can by itself define the Caribbean's complex sociocultural interplay. We need all of them at the same time". Caribbean scholarship then requires flexibility to accommodate these multiple perspectives if the interpretation is to encompass a truly Caribbean vision rather than an external view of our world. A "revolution of self-perception", in the words of Gordon Rohlehr, "grows increasingly more complex and multi-faceted. . . . It challenges conventional notions of history and is part of a vast world-wide movement to relocate the submerged cultures of the devastated in the kingdom of human and humane achievement" (1992, 15).

Because of the control that researchers exert over their material, it is sometimes argued that the "reality" they observe and record is to some extent of their own construction, and, in the Caribbean, researchers would prefer to define our understanding of the world and our views on the understandings of others, rather than have it handed down to us. Some researchers reject such self-awareness as navel-gazing, but a concern with the circumstances of interpretation in this particular politico-geographical situation makes the relation of observer and observed crucial. This does not preclude objectivity. Caribbean qualitative researchers are bound (professionally, intellectually and ethically) to clarify their positions from the outset. Modern research acknowledges that most study is influenced by beliefs, by theories the observer hopes to prove or disprove and by ideologies the interpreter accepts or resists. However, such research achieves objectivity by defining the researcher's position in relation to what is observed, achieves validity by substantiating claims and acknowledging contrary positions, and achieves reliability by consistently applying criteria for the judgments made.

Traditional Western ethnographic research distinguished what seemed strange and unknown from the valorized culture of the researcher. Fieldwork constituted a rite of passage for the researcher, whose findings were framed in imperialist ideology. Even researchers who tried to avoid this found themselves trapped in their own world views, their findings presented as eternal truths. Caribbean thinkers such as George Lamming reject early positions as contributing to a "terror of the mind" (2004, 7). Rex Nettleford demonstrates that Caribbean research interferes with traditional hierarchical relationships between superordinate and subordinate traditions in establishing an indigenization of values (1978, 181).

Within the Caribbean, we are particularly bound to engage with multiple and often conflicting ways of knowing. Indeed, Lamming suggests, "creative conflict is the dynamic which drives the Caribbean imagination" (36). In the case of the French Caribbean, for example, three major literary, ideological and cultural movements of Négritude, Antillanité and Créolité articulate multiple "ways of knowing" the Antillean condition. Aimé Césaire's Négritude emphasizes the need to valorize the region's African heritage. However, Négritude's monolithic, rooted nature could not encompass Édouard Glissant's broad, complex, rhizomatic vision of Caribbeanness or *Antillanité* (1981). The debate continues with Patrick Chamoiseau's concept of *Créolité* (Bernabé, Chamoiseau and Confiant 1989) and Glissant's unpredictable process of *creolization*, encompassing hybridization of cultures and languages and all that this might entail (1989). These "creative conflicts" reinforce the researcher's need for objectivity and sensitivity to the many facets of ideological complexity in the Caribbean. Any researcher would have to consider how socio-economic and political relationships with France have shaped these debates on the French Caribbean.

Caribbean research in literature, language and culture may address the officially English-, French- and Spanish-speaking Caribbean areas in which Creole and indigenous languages, often spoken by the vast majority of the population, are represented in the literature as defining the voice of the people. Such research may focus on one area or involve comparative critique of writing across languages. Caribbean criticism is called for, rather than uncritical adoption of some external framework for evaluating our own artistic achievements, even as this critical practice proceeds in full awareness of other existing theory.

Frequently overlooked when discussing research methods are research needs for creative writing itself, although such writing benefits from rigorous investigation of, say, setting or cultural background. Worldwide recognition of Caribbean letters suggests that our creative writers like those of other cultures ground their art in serious practice, so research approaches to creative writing in the Caribbean can be usefully described.

Caribbean language is so pivotal to its cultural practices, literature and discourse as to warrant rigorous observation beyond an interest in linguistic operations for their own sake. Caribbean linguistics, especially in areas such as sociolinguistics, illuminates diversity of expression regionally, nationally and individually and the sociocultural reasons for that diversity. Research in oral and written discourse also deepens understanding of Caribbean literary and cultural contexts and of the development of the discourse against a background of cultural collision, oppression and resistance. Moreover, our experience of such development, recent and vivid, places us at a vantage point for commenting perceptively on comparable circumstances in other cultures, circumstances less perceptible to scholars in, say, western European cultures who may, perhaps, be operating by hindsight. Significant Caribbean research is called for with respect to other discourses and cultures, in respect to such experiences as displacement, cultural collision, and so on.

Such research is conducted both by experienced and aspiring scholars, and, for this latter group, it is important to identify all that is required for postgraduate research, whether that be a research paper, a creative composition (suitable to an MFA) or more extensive study in a dissertation for a research degree. Whatever the scope of the research, it all moves from its definition of core issues and topic to a viable design that includes articulation of a conceptual orientation and methods by which data will be assembled and analysed.

This work is divided into two parts, the first relevant to both seasoned and less experienced scholars, including graduate students, and the second mainly to graduate students. In part 1, the first four chapters set out conceptual frames within which Caribbean research may be conducted. The need to establish a theoretical orientation and the nature of a specifically Caribbean criticism must be a crucial consideration for all researchers in the humanities and is the subject of chapter 1. Chapter 2 discusses the significance of the cultural turns in critical theory, and one approach for measuring cultural identity is proposed in chapter 3. Chapter 4 explores the role of linguistic enquiry in criticism, the nature of discourse analysis and the importance of these to interpretation.

The next three chapters address methods and approaches to data collection on Caribbean topics or on Caribbean perspectives on other literary cultures. Chapter 5 offers guidance on field methods and interviewing, making reference to accessible electronic examples of the latter. Detailed attention to the gathering and documentation of rare information follows in chapter 6, illustrated with one selected Caribbean repository. Chapter 7 explores research processes and methods for the creative writer.

The final five chapters of part 1 focus on the application of the methods enumerated and on the analysis for which the data is intended. Chapter 8 applies to oral performance in general but focuses on Calypso research, offering guidelines for probing the rich oral traditions of the Caribbean. Chapter 9 applies research methods to analysis of text and discourse, enabling the transfer of techniques between nonliterary and literary material. Chapter 10 explains the comparative approach and leads into a discussion of translation in chapter 11, while chapter 12 explores the applications of film studies to the reading of literature.

Part 2 of this book is devoted to guidance for the graduate student; chapter 13 focuses on the selection and definition of a topic, and chapter 14 on the preparation of a research proposal and the research habits required for professional integrity. Production of the dissertation or research paper demands analysis and cogent argument, so chapter 15 gives attention to the level of expression required in higher study, and chapter 16 describes the meticulous editing and proofreading expected in the written presentation of advanced research.

Throughout, the book invites its readers to engage with the particular promise and challenge of conducting advanced study in the context of Caribbean experience.

Part 1
Research
Methodology

This part of the study addresses conceptual frames, methods of data collection and methods of analysis. The relationship between theory and research is both symbiotic and dialectic. Theories are formulated through extensive research, and research projects require the support of a theoretical frame or model. This intersection between theory and research should promote debate, elucidation and even modification of the existing theory. If the fundamental aim of any research project is to add to the existing scholarship on the particular subject area, then it is through theory and analysis that this is achieved. Nick Nesbitt's *Universal Emancipation* (2008), for example, draws from the theories of Enlightenment thinkers like Spinoza, Rousseau, Kant and Hegel to explore the idea of universal emancipation and the Haitian Revolution, arguing that the Haitian Revolution concretized the abstract European philosophical notion of freedom and equality. In the process Nesbitt opens new approaches to interpreting events leading led up to the 1804 declaration of Haitian independence.

In focusing first on conceptual frames, this section of the book begins with Jennifer Rahim's overview of developments in Caribbean literary theory and criticism. Rahim leads us through the maze of theoretical, ideological and creative concerns in the region and demonstrates how interlocking theoretical frames of foremost Caribbean thinkers strive for a collective self-understanding.

To map points of convergence and divergence, Rahim draws on several scholars, theorists and Caribbean writers and notes tensions at the crossroads of politics and poetics or theoretical debates that promote either universality or insularity. She goes on to illustrate the need for new models and methods to reconceptualize Caribbean realities, and, by looking at both literary and theoretical production, she explores the idea of a Caribbean aesthetic, showing how the debates between writers and scholars describe the region's inescapable polymorphic nature. She considers the trope of travel through a wide lens that includes concepts of diaspora, nomadism and transnationalism, or transnationality, then leads us through the ideas of Caribbean feminist discourse, Caribbean female subjectivity and gender criticism. She then elucidates the notion of Caribbean resistance and counterculture, referring to Barbara Lalla's concept of a "maroon consciousness" in Jamaican fiction.

Paula Morgan introduces her discussion of cultural studies in Caribbean literary research with the fundamental idea that every engagement with a literary work is, in fact, cultural. Drawing on definitions of culture by Raymond Williams and George Lamming, she illustrates the problematics of defining the term *culture*, noting that, for researchers engaging in Caribbean cultural studies, there is no distinct methodology. Overviewing evolution and revolution in the field of cultural studies, Morgan points to the early movement away from a Eurocentric 1950s Marxist ideology and the influence of structuralism and poststructuralism in particular and discusses the process by which the widening landscape of cultural studies has interrogated and unmasked the Western canon. Morgan also draws our attention to the critical concerns of the politics of cultural representation. For measuring the flux and flow of cultural identity, Boufoy-Bastick proposes the dynamic concept of culturometrics, which she defines as a constructionist philosophy focused on who we are and how we change, whose central concept is cultural identity and central concern is its measurement. *Who we are* has a particular value in a particular context, so Boufoy-Bastick sees the importance of applying culturometrics to facilitate the uncovering of intrasubjectivities and to empower research subjects to a self-determined change in cultural identity. Trinidad's multiethnic community has proven to be a fertile ground for informing Boufoy-Bastick's concept.

The interplay of culture and discourse informs analysis of Caribbean literature where writing is definitively marked by regional linguistic characteristics, typically the Creole vernacular in interplay with the standard (official) language. Barbara Lalla and Valerie Youssef distinguish text and discourse to emphasize the significance of discourse analysis in extending the concept of the text to shared social realms that can be analysed as artefacts with their own integrity. Lalla and Youssef draw our attention to approaches, such as literary linguistics and critical discourse analysis, through which the researcher may interrogate the ideological perspective of the writer and the enactment of power through discourse. The problematic concept of representation and "authenticity" in Caribbean literary discourse is also explored.

In most areas of study data collection is primary – a means of coming to an understanding of our topic of research, of setting out to answer our research questions, of proving or disproving our hypotheses or questions in fieldwork of the types described by Youssef. For the literary scholar, the texts to be studied represent the primary data, and further data collection elucidates our object of study. For the creative writer, whom Elizabeth Walcott-Hackshaw and Barbara Lalla address, data collection helps build a fictional picture rooted in reality. Data-collection techniques of qualitative research allow us to systematically collect information about our objects of study (people, objects, phenomena) and about the settings in which they occur.

Strategies for collecting accurate information and gathering sound content must be carefully defined for a solid study to be achieved. These strategies may include using available (but potentially hidden) information found in texts like newspaper articles, other print media, speeches, diaries and so on; historical documents or archival sources; nonwritten sources like artefacts; and visual sources like pictures, films, cultural forms and practices. Glenroy Taitt particularly speaks to the collection of elusive and transient data through the example of one Caribbean repository. Data collection also proceeds through observation (collection of field notes on a situation or setting), participant or nonparticipant observation, interviewing, questionnaires, focus group discussions and tracing of archival data, such as Youssef, Morgan and Lalla describe.

The completeness of data collected is pivotal. Whether scanning archives or setting up interviews, researchers ensure the fullest possible set of data or a representative subset. Ideally, researchers share a transformative agenda to create work "that may change the lives of the participants, the institutions in which individuals work or live, and the researcher's life" (Creswell 2003,

9–10). This common goal of coming to better terms with our world demands quality data collection.

Caribbean research involves not only the collection of data from or pertaining to the Caribbean but approaches to data analysis and to applying the resulting information to a range of inquiries – to pursuing, where possible, peculiarly Caribbean insights. In a discussion of Caribbean oral tradition that focuses on calypso, Louis Regis discusses methods of collection and approaches to analysis of material for which no long-established practices of academic enquiry exist. His findings may be widely applied, for example, to investigations of postcolonial resistance, of race and ethnicity in cultural expression, and of discourse in performance poetry that includes rap and reggae as well as calypso.

With a view to analysing the written text, Youssef and Lalla discuss analysis of scribal discourse for depth of interpretation. Discourse analysis, for example, of natural speech and conversation, illuminates operations in Caribbean speech, offers the literary critic a technical approach to dialogue and direct speech, and reveals cultural differences between speakers in different language situations or social contexts. In the multicultural and multivocal Caribbean, research frequently involves work on intersecting texts, work on similar topics or in identical genres but in different languages, or work eclectically combining approaches or manoeuvring between disciplines. Walcott-Hackshaw explores the comparative approach to literary interpretation – clearly applicable not only to investigation that overtly compares works in different languages, authors, genres or theories but also to studies that refer to counterdiscourse, intertextuality and other concepts to which comparison is intrinsic. Translation also being implicitly comparative, Jairo Sánchez-Galvis's presentation of models, methods and applications of translation complements those of comparative critique in supplying an essential resource for study of discourse in the multilingual Caribbean. Finally, in exploring interfaces between discourses and between disciplines that speak to the multicultural world of Caribbean letters, Jean Antoine-Dunne considers intersections between film and literature in Caribbean research. Throughout, the reader is encouraged to consider the widest possible application of each method employed or discussed.

conceptual
frames

Chapter 1

Issues and Developments in Caribbean Literary Theory and Criticism

Jennifer Rahim

Caribbean Theory and Criticism: Interlocking Terms

Terms like *Caribbean literary theory and criticism* are somewhat troublesome, even if necessary, descriptive categories; in fact, some may consider them anomalies for at least two reasons. First, like so many contemporary theoretical models and critical practices such as (post) feminism, postcolonialism and postmodernism, one is almost always speaking not just in plurals – that is, *theories* and *criticisms* – one is also acknowledging the presence of embattled and unevenly weighted interdependencies. One may even be speaking with a forked tongue, given the complicated and shifting politics of ethnic and ideological affiliations that impact ways of thinking and reading Caribbean cultural realities and productions. Multiplicity, confluence, paradox, contestation and therefore inevitable change are native to the ever-evolving theoretical paradigms and critical methods they represent and agendas they serve.

The region shares a colonial history marked by the "trauma of transportation" (Hall 1991, 4), violent displacement and relocation. Cultural loss and fragmentation impacted a broad cross-section of peoples, the largest being the enslaved Africans. (See also Ramchand [1970] 1983; and Edwards 2001, 31–32.) At the same time, this turbulent origin is a story of resistance, survival and retention that wrought remarkable cultural transformations and, with them, the need for new epistemologies and methodologies malleable to the hybrid ethic of strategic relation and exchange that defines Caribbean culture. The significant geographical, linguistic, political and demographic diversity, however, makes it foolhardy to speak reductively of a single Caribbean. Further, for those nervous about prematurely putting up defining fences, or any at all, the notion of a Caribbean theory and criticism may seem somewhat reductionist and insular. Yet, from another perspective, such an umbrella concept may suggest the suppression of the particularities of individual island nations – what distinguishes Jamaica's culture and literature from Trinidad's, for instance. Preferable for some may be terms that appeal to a broader network of geographies, histories and cultures. Michael Dash, for instance, prefers *New World*, which is neither "polarizing" nor "exclusivist" but "concerns itself with establishing new connections" (Dash 1998).

This striving for a collective self-understanding that marries sameness and difference, location and translocation, is especially critical in a Western literary academy where particularly the postcolonial school has notoriously excluded seminal aspects of the region's literature and thought from its ambit of concerns. There is now what may be considered a belated recruitment of the Caribbean's hybrid and Creole poetics by metropolitan scholars in search of theoretical models to address the kinds of accelerated cultural plurality and confluence with which the region has had to creatively engage from its inception. Also significant to the relationship of the Caribbean literary scholarship with "mainstream" literary theory and criticism is, as Dash warns, the current "postmodern flood of metanarratives" whose impulse is to "sweep away all boundaries" (1998, 2; and see Khan 2001; and Rampersad 2002). The problem in this regard is that postmodern relativity with its seemingly unanchored flows can, on the one hand, appear counterproductive to the region's efforts to gather and reconstruct its "scattered skeleton". On the other, there is the longstanding concern with absorption by the cannibalizing and universalizing tendencies of "foreign" theory. Yet it is also true that the practice of Caribbean theory and criticism has garnered enough authority to adopt a "take it or leave it" attitude (2008, 22) as Barbara Lalla claims in the case of postcolonialism, a stance that invites the reconsideration of those fears of replacement or displacement.

The second challenge surfaces when one considers that many foundational theorists and critics of Caribbean literature and culture are also creative writers.

Derek Walcott, Wilson Harris, Kamau Brathwaite, Édouard Glissant, Antonio Benítez-Rojo, Erna Brodber, Earl Lovelace and Sylvia Wynter have to various degrees theorized Caribbean culture and literature as well as functioned as literary critics. The Caribbean is by no means unique in this regard. The scenario, however, does introduce an interesting circumstance in which, at the outset at any rate, literature seems to be well placed at the centre of theory and criticism. Literature, in this context, both leads literary scholarship, for better or worse, and makes disciplinary boundaries more porous. This interdependency is not an undesirable situation. In fact, some may consider it an ideal. Literary scholarship is prevented from becoming esoteric and rootless, as thought and practice, concept and method are shaped by cultural production itself. Conversely, such neighbourliness can result in theoretical and critical approaches that become mired in narrow personal or group politics – their ideological agendas and limitations. Caribbean literary scholarship has had its fair share of those wars of affiliation, in which writers and critics alike have been ensnared. The 1970s Walcott versus Brathwaite debate is an example and is consolidated in Patricia Ismond's comment that Walcott found his "strongest convictions about the route of renewal through assimilation and indigenization" to be incompatible with Brathwaite's "African-rooted" "black aesthetic" (2001, 116).

Acknowledging this tension between ideology and aesthetics, or, if you will, different takes on Caribbean poetics, is not saying that an ethnically purged or apolitical approach to literary scholarship is more desirable. It has long been established that the liberal humanists' claim to depoliticized objectivity is not possible – nor is it desirable. Feminist scholarship following the materialist lead of Marxist thought has made it unquestionably clear that we are all circumscribed by politics. Similarly, as Edward Said so forcefully elucidates, "Critics are not merely the alchemical translators of texts into circumstantial reality or worldliness; for they too are subject to and producers of circumstances, which are felt regardless of whatever objectivity the critic's methods possess" (1983, 35). Further, to simply operate from a prescriptive paradigm that literature precedes theory and even criticism is not a watertight position. After all, with the literature-theory-criticism constellation, one is inevitably enmeshed in a chicken-and-egg aporia. The exact chronology of Brodber's novel *Louisiana* (1994) and her nonfiction *The Continent of Black Consciousness: On the History of the African Diaspora from Slavery to the Present* (2003) may be of less importance than the ideological intersections between them; likewise, whether the cross-cultural imagination explored in Harris's novels predated or accompanied his numerous essays. In both cases, it is not unlikely that the process is in some way interdependent. The same is true for the literary theorist or critic. Ideology, which is always historically and environmentally located, inevitably impacts on the theoretical perspective one offers or the methodology one adopts. Nevertheless, a literary criticism worth its salt must be guided by the literature, and must be illuminated by enabling theorizing on its aesthetic and thematic concerns. Critical practice must also be free enough to honestly evaluate its own quality and, when necessary, challenge its politics to move beyond pet peeves.

The fundamental interconnectedness between creative production (on the one hand) and theoretical and critical practice (on the other) cannot be under-rated. This is especially true for an ethnically diverse and eclectic civilization like the Caribbean, where any reflection on literary theory and criticism is inevitably an engagement with the politics of poetics which is tethered, sometimes uncomfortably, to the issue of cultural identification. Unavoidably, therefore, the touchy practice of cultural and intellectual syncretism arises. There is no denying that hybridity is the outcome of turbulent histories of contact and accommodation – tensions associated with problems and pos-sibilities, depending of course on where one puts down one's aesthetic and, by extension, one's ideological bucket. Walcott's almost agonizing yet illuminating preoccupation with "making style" ("Mas' Man") (1981, 31) and Brathwaite's much-quoted metaphor, "the hurricane does not roar in pentameters" (1986, 265), differently capture the aesthetic conflict that has ensued at the deepest levels of imagination and being.

Aesthetic Rehousing: Remaking Models

The collision of cultural differences impacted the region's writers, no less than its theorists and critics, and can perhaps be described as a kind of aesthetic and epistemological unhousing. All have been affected by the radical trauma of displacement from multiple ancestral homes and forced resettlement in strange landscapes and under new social arrangements. As a result, a complicated matrix of influences developed involving the intellectual and cultural traditions of the colonial hierarchy and those of the colonized. These accumulated influences created a situation in which "new" models and methods were needed to think and read Caribbean realities, its identities and (counter)discursive practices. Along with the trauma of encountering the oppressive "monumental architecture of the old world" came an opportunity for re-creation – the reason Wilson Harris aptly describes Caribbean peoples as occupying "an architectural age" (1967, 13), one that is very much still in the making. This new architecture of course began to shape itself over a long period of negotiated accommodation. In the sphere of cultural production and performance, this involved the transgression and defamiliarization of "received codes", assimilation and reinscription manoeuvres evident, as Lalla argues, in the case of the Caribbean literary canon (1996, 4). The same can be said of the region's carnivalesque traditions. To varying degrees these processes have been and continue to be tense and celebrative, anxious and transgressive, but ultimately always transformative.

The dilemma of being caught between displacement and re-creation is well allegorized in Caribbean literature via the recurrent motif of stifling households and incidents of escape from debilitating matriarchs or motherlands – not just for survival, but for the reconstitution, even reinvention, of the very self. V.S. Naipaul's *A House for Mr Biswas* ([1961] 1966), George Lamming's *In the Castle of My Skin* (1979), Merle Hodge's *Crick Crack, Monkey* (1970), Jamaica Kincaid's *Annie John* ([1985] 1997) and *Lucy* (2002) and Lawrence Scott's *Aelred's Sin* (1998) suggest the complicated range of that experience of spatial and ideological rupture. The reality, however, as Jamaica Kincaid's *Lucy* realizes, is that the act of leave taking is fraught with ambivalence since complete breaks are impossible. This is because home, as Edward Baugh argues, is not merely a "geographical site" but is mapped on the heart (2010, 18). Moreover, severing ties may perhaps not even be desirable, given that the DNA of the Caribbean is inescapably an aesthetic hybridity that is attributable to many ancestors and is rooted but also en route.

The articulation of a Caribbean aesthetic therefore almost always involves wrestling through various stages of discomfort and readjustment, anxieties of influences and strategic assimilations that come with being located in between worlds. This double consciousness, and in many cases multiple consciousness, is a trait colonialism bequeathed to all its subjects. Martinican poet–politician Aimé Césaire, one of the most rooted of Caribbean poets, therefore admits to Stuart Hall, "I am . . . French, my mind is French" (1991, 7). This doubleness, however, is historically conditioned and so experienced differently by later writers, but it has never been indicative of a rootless condition typified by the contemporary postmodern nomad, anchorless and bereft of moorings. It is rather the situation of being caught up in the fertile volatility of shifting cultural ground and inevitable transformations. The sometimes contentious cultural negotiations, sometimes satirical ideological battles – which are ignited not only by groups contesting for political and sociocultural space but also (un)consciously by individual writers – signal this unsettled condition. It is a condition generated by the confluence of natal and adopted traditions set in motion by Europe's expansion into the New World and continued into the period of independence but with difference agendas. The first forced contexts of acculturation had been anything but a pure mimicry of the European cultural traditions or the absolute suppression of African or Indian ones. Rather, they were initially exercises in "cunning assimilation" (Walcott 1998, 43) or "creative imitation" (Brathwaite 1974, 16). The politics of these strategically negotiated confluences of differences, however, tell their own histories of cultural ambivalence, violent dismissals and omissions. Such histories caution against any simplistic celebration of redemptive hybridities, although eclecticism and transformation engendered by exchange are foundational to the region's cultural dynamics and informed the rhetoric of nationalism.

It is no overstatement to say that this borrowing by creators as well as scholars has sometimes had volcanic outcomes. These explosions have come about mostly because both the issue of Eurocentric or foreign intellectual and cultural influences and the desire to privilege indigenous or nativist tropes and discourses have been closely aligned to anticolonial protest and decolonization or to nationalist aspirations. An instructive foundational debate related to this tension erupted in the 1970s between Kenneth Ramchand and Sylvia Wynter. That exchange is best consolidated in their respective essays "Concern for Criticism" (1970) and "Creole Criticism: A Critique" (1973). Norval Edwards ably unpacks the core of Wynter's "blistering" rebuttal of Ramchand's claim that she, along with Brathwaite and others practised a "brand of pseudo-criticism, 'neo-African theory' that reduces criticism to socio-political commentary" (Edwards 2001, 31). Edwards notes that in her counterattack Wynter classifies Ramchand's preference for the "objectivity" of a Leavisian close-reading practice as "Creole criticism" (19). This, she explains, is a critical approach that suffers the deficiency of being susceptible to blind mimicry of the Western modes of knowledge and methodologies and is thereby acquiescent to its status quo. She therefore locates Ramchand on the opposite end of her "challenging criticism" (19), a politically conscious reading practice that is oriented towards the "disenchantment" of subject societies from the West's Eurocentric cognitive norms (20).

The Ramchand/Wynter debate speaks directly to what can be called the ethnocentric and "anxiety of influence" caveats that have dogged Caribbean literary and cultural discourses. Perhaps they are in some ways both right in their analysis and accusations. What we know about the Caribbean's decolonization or indigenization journey is that long and varied debates have interrogated the notions of "authenticity" and belonging that represent different intellectual and cultural paths. At stake is the articulation of the very nature of Caribbean identity, which is itself something of a misnomer, as multiplicity, cross-fertilization and ongoing formation have made it impossible to contain what it means to be Caribbean in any one paradigm of consensual representation or aesthetic practice. The region's ethnic groups, ideological affiliations and agendas are far too diverse. The terrain of identity and identification practices in which the activity of making theory and doing criticism operate is far too invested in the varied performances of our desired Caribbeans of the imagination. Variance does not necessarily suggest shared experience. Edward Baugh, in his essay "Literary Theory and the Caribbean: Theory, Belief and Desire, or Designing Theory", hits on this rather intriguing conundrum when he writes: "All theories are designs. They make patterns of things, even chaos. They are also designs in that they have designs on us. The design is that theory is a projection of the theorist's belief, and belief is a function of desire" (2006, 57). The implication of course is that the field called Caribbean theory and criticism is as complicated and changing as its identity politics.

Root and Route: Two Primary Models

Baugh brings both these realities home in his wide-ranging taxonomy of telling metaphors spun by writers and theorists alike to represent the region. There is the ever-present image of the sea shared by many such as Walcott, Brathwaite and Benítez-Rojo; Glissant's root/rhizome; Benítez-Rojo's carnival and Curdella Forbes's hermaphrodite. There are also tropes that include Kamau Brathwaite's jazz novel, Kwame Dawes's reggae aesthetic, Evelyn O'Callaghan's dub/version. Others can also be added: Wilson Harris's womb of space and carnival theatre, Funso Aiyejina's novelypso, Earl Lovelace's bacchanal aesthetics, Gordon Rohlehr's mulatitude aesthetics, Barbara Lalla's maroon consciousness, Vijay Maharaj's katha, Shalini Puri's dougla poetics and, of course, the widely deployed Creole model as the "master" symbol of the region. This no doubt incomplete range of metaphors consolidates something of the two main ideological camps that represent, in different ways, the search for theoretical and critical methods for articulating an indigenous aesthetic.

Baugh utilizes Glissant's "root/rhizome contrasts" as a rubric for classifying the main literary approaches to theorizing the Caribbean (Baugh 2006, 58). There have been, however, many ways of identifying these contrasts to which are also linked philosophical standpoints, theoretical concepts and critical practices. Given the region's history, always central to these manoeuvres has been the need to rearticulate Caribbean identities against colonial systems of control and subjugation, their abuses, negations and misrecognitions. Always critical has been the assertion of a consciousness, a philosophy of being native indelibly linked to nationalist cum regionalist sensibilities. Paget Henry, whose commitment is to an ethnically delimited paradigm called Afro-Caribbean philosophical thought, speaks, for instance, of two traditions: the poeticist and historicist schools (2000, 6). The former, which includes thinkers like Walcott, Harris, Césaire, Glissant, Wynter and Rex Nettleford, is defined by its "reconstructive, transversal tendencies" (Henry 2000, 90) and by a preoccupation with the recovery of self as the first step to social reform. The latter tends towards institutional reform via insurrectionist pan-Africanist, Marxist and historicist approaches (Henry 2000, 6) and is represented by C.L.R. James, George Padmore, Marcus Garvey and Frantz Fanon. Henry, however, admits that his dualistic matrix has its own habits of crossing. He notes, for example, that Césaire and Fanon straddle poeticist and historicist schools. These incidentally intersect in some respect with Baugh's root/rhizome streams.

Yet, even as streams or traditions can be named and classified, it is perhaps better to think of these as representing dominant traits rather than functioning as absolutely pure or static paradigms. In other words, they are best approached as crudely generalized ways of classifying very complexly structured ideological positions. As the root image suggests, such approaches symbolized by marronage or kumbla-type theoretical models, typically conflate nationalism with an Afro-Caribbean aesthetic. They are primarily concerned with ancestral origins, natal connections, cultural specificities and their rebellious retentions in the context of colonial domination and cultural resistance. Such concerns are intricately tied to their seminal role in the decolonization agenda and thrust towards political independence. Key trends in this regard are the 1930s emergence of the Négritude movement and, in its aftermath, pan-Africanism, which swept the Caribbean and the United States from the 1940s onwards, culminating in the Black Power movement of the 1960s and 1970s. Such sociopolitical movements provided an anticolonial ideological framework that necessarily foregrounded black consciousness as a basis of resistance iconized in the figure of Caliban, the disenfranchised "abhorred" slave of Shakespeare's *Tempest*.

If one were to designate inhabitants to this household dubbed root approaches, one would have to return to the 1960s' and 1970s' culture debates, where Ramchand, for instance, identifies Wynter, Brathwaite, Gerald Moore and others with a critical "tradition" marked by "socio-political and racial-cultural generalisation" that represented a "neo-African theory". One also has to revisit Walcott's "Muse of History" where he discusses the limitations of an "extremist" "purist" approach to writing and West Indian identity and creative writing (Walcott 1998, 56; Ramchand 1970). If such errors are generated by fixating on history as factual recall and ultimately lead to the stagnation of imagination and spirit in recrimination and victimhood, as an alternative Walcott offers the narrativization of history as myth. The mythic approach celebrates "cunning assimilation" (1998, 43) as the basis for reinvention and the newness it generates as a truly New World ethic/poetic. The concept *root*, as it is loosely used or interpreted in Caribbean literary and theoretical discourse, has therefore come to mean an aesthetic and methodological orientation that is predominantly guided by appeals to "folk"-based, localized or Afro-diasporic features of resistance and by the retention of cultural essences or traditions. The reductive impact on how concepts like nationalist or regionalist, "nativist" or "indigenous" aesthetics are defined is almost unavoidable. Brathwaite's *Roots* (1986) or Dawes's attempt to deploy reggae as an interpretative methodology in *Natural Mysticism: Towards a New Reggae Aesthetic* (1999) and Carolyn Cooper's study of Jamaican popular culture in *Noises in the Blood* (1993) may therefore be tenuously identified as tenants in the "root" household.

Although essential to the politics and poetics of Caribbean resistance in the wake of colonial rule, the concept *root* can be misread as supporting an insular, separatist and essentialist interpretation of culture and identity. Names like James, Lamming, Brathwaite and Rohlehr are typically associated with nationalist, regionalist, socialist, historicist and Marxist orientations, given that they actively interface literary production with the histories and socio-economic conditions that shape writers and their societies. What this is sometimes reductively or simplistically taken to mean is that they promote a black nationalism or regionalism, when the reality is that their politics is very much more complicated. Rohlehr's discussion of Lamming and Brathwaite – significantly two of the leading proponents in the 1960s and 1970s of a black nationalist aesthetic – is very useful for avoiding such traps. According to Rohlehr, for these writers to be nationalists is not necessarily synonymous with being "narrow-minded patriots who cannot see beyond their island's one hundred and sixty square miles" (2007a, 395). This is because to be nationalist is also to be regionalist or Caribbean. Importantly, he goes on, such regionalism is a complexly woven internationalism since it translates to an "unremitting effort to understand the complex webs of culture and identities that have emerged out of the various diasporas – that have contributed to the making of Caribbean civilization" (Rohlehr 2007a, 406).

Further, as Sandra Pouchet Paquet argues, writers and thinkers can and do evolve. In her cogent analysis of Lovelace's essays published from 1967 to 2000, Pouchet Paquet traces a movement towards "a model of identity that valorises the heterogeneity of Caribbean cultures, by embracing their multiple origins and challenging an Afrocentric politics of privilege and purity" (2008, 69). Therefore, when Aiyejina interprets Lovelace's "bacchanal aesthetics" as "the aesthetics of the crossroads or the crucible" ([1998] 2003, xv), that more cross-cultural consciousness the novelist articulates in his March 2000 speech ("In the Voice of the People") has to be historicized in relation to his ideological evolution on issues about race and society. Pouchet Paquet actually hits on the major caveat associated with the interpretative practices of so-called root models, that is, their privileging of an ethnocentric politics or poetics. To counteract the suppression of Caribbean diversity that resulted, there has been a concerted turn from the Afro-Creole, pan-African discourses of the pre-1970s toward "imagining" the region as cross-cultural or Creole-becoming.

Dash, for instance, sees Glissant's concept of Caribbeanness or *Antillanité* as a kind of Bakhtinan heteroglossia that brings together streams of associations in an ongoing re-creative process. The literatures of the Americas therefore display this polymorphous and unfinished dynamic typical of the cross-cultural imagination. The emphasis is on inter-relationship, a multiplicity of roots and openness – features that more and more reflect the new universal cultural order. Dash therefore writes that "the Caribbean condition is increasingly becoming a global phenomenon. . . . Archipelagos of culture are being created throughout the world" (Dash 1999, 196). The antitotalitarian, nonhierarchical historicity and transversal or cross-cultural poetics articulated in Glissant's *Caribbean Discourse* therefore represents, according to Dash, a shift from "the reduction of Caribbean history to a racial melodrama of revenge or remorse" (1989, xi), the "monomania of Caliban" (xiii) and the "simplifications of the negritude movement" (xv). Ethnocentrism, however, is but one "detour" Glissant rejects. In *The Other America* Dash expands this to include all epistemological "detours" since they are "invariably characterized by a nostalgia for pure origins", whether they are "metropolitan in the assimilationist *detour*, African in the *detour* of negritude, or national in the *detour* of the myth of *marronnage*" (1998, 11). All of these modes of thought, for Glissant, distort and so distract from the dynamic, not static or monolithic, relational nature of Caribbeanness which seems to escape absolute containment.

In this frame of thinking, the focus is on diversity and heterogeneity. Caribbean cultural dynamics are seen to either pre-empt or intersect with the decentring logic of poststructuralist and postmodern theories. It should be noted, as mentioned earlier, that not all are comfortable with such associations. Nevertheless, Stuart Hall evokes Derrida's difference/differance as a means of reading the dynamic " 'doubleness' that marks the region's similarity and difference" (Hall 1994, 396). Models oriented to multiplicity, eclecticism and creolization are therefore naturally less troubled by cultural and intellectual interdependencies. Similarly, but with the emphasis on critical analysis, Glyne Griffith sees in Derrida's deconstruction a useful methodology for critiquing how the "narrative and epistemological structures" of West Indian novels "participate in and resist imperialist ideology" (1996, xiii). Moreover, heterogeneity as a cultural mechanism reinforces the ways in which mimicry and syncretism creatively transgress codes of privilege and borders of difference to produce new cultural forms and identities. Benítez-Rojo, for instance, utilizes postmodern chaos theory to discuss Caribbean cultural production as a synthesis of diverse cultural fragments and histories, "suspended in a soup of signs" (1992, 2). This radical diversity of "partials" is manifested in the creative recalibration of violently instituted binaries such as happens in the region's Carnival and polyrhythm musical expressions and linguistic practices. Following in this mode, he defines a Caribbean narrative as "a text that speaks of a critical coexistence of rhythms, a polyrhythmic ensemble" (1992, 28).

Much of Caribbean literary and cultural scholarship, taking the lead from the cultural processes in the region, invests extensively in hybridities. Caution, however, is always advisable since these paradigms can mask and perpetuate their own politics of exclusion and domination. Very pertinent therefore is Shalini Puri's warning against the benevolent appearance of "nonthreatening hybridities" such as "callaloo, the creole, and the mestizo", often sanctioned by Caribbean nationalisms, but nevertheless masking and redeploying colonial hierarchies of difference (2004, 45). Even Benítez-Rojo points to this deficiency in the misreading of *mestizaje* as a "synthesis" when it is in fact a union that "sees in the biological, economic, and cultural whitening of Caribbean society a series of successive steps toward 'progress'" (1992, 26). Like root models that tend towards monolithic, purist or extremist ideologies, hybrid paradigms (as Puri warns) can be as obsessed with assimilationist or universalizing agendas. Creolization, in particular, has been harshly criticized by some theorists. In addition to Puri, Aisha Khan (2001) and Sheila Rampersad (2002) point to the omission of the East Indian presence in Brathwaite's foundational model where the black–white norm is the focus. This type of paradigm has also been accused of enforcing a "one-way accommodation" that privileges the Afro-Creole com-ponent. Dougla poetics has therefore emerged as a significant development in theorizing creolization, drawing scholarly attention to lateral creolization processes between East Indians and Africans in the Caribbean diaspora. This trajectory of confluence is evident not only in biological mixing but in a range of cultural expressions that includes calypsos and literary texts. Puri is careful to state, however, that dougla poetics is not a panacea for interracial tensions between its representative groups. It is a theoretical and critical methodology that provides a useful vocabulary for reading a political identity in which contestations for national space are projected through not just racial but also gendered categories. From the late 1990s, therefore, one saw an increase in scholarly attention directed to the sensitive lateral creolization tensions and creative energies generated from the interface between the Indian and African Caribbean communities, apparent not only in biological mixing and national politics, but in popular culture and creative writing. Significant contemporary examples in this regard include calypsos such as Brother Marvin's controversial song "Jahaji Bhai" (1996) and Machel Montano and Drupatee Ramgoonai's "Real Unity" (2000), as well as novels such as Merle Hodge's *For the Life of Laetitia* (1993) and Joy Mahabir's *Jouvert* (2006).

Although the agenda of Europe's imperial project was to globalize itself, the violent arrival of the Old World in the New ushered in a modernity characterized by a culture of radical relation and amalgamation out of which have come unpredictable and unique transformations. To use Harris's formulation, the New World, of which the Caribbean is its most compressed and fertile theatre, is the "womb" of an "unfinished genesis" in which bridges of "involuntary associations" have been and continue to be erected across apparent disparities in cultures (Harris 1999, 239). The Haitian deity of the crossroads, Legba, and the Greek god of creativity, Hephaestus, are his examples of such links. Harris, of course, approaches this cross-cultural ethic or poetics as an "arts of imagination" (1999, 156) by appealing to the deeper unity of an ontologically shared archetypal consciousness. In this regard, Edwards suggests that Harris's emphasis on the primacy of the imagination as a regenerative resource has an affinity to the Romantics (2008, 26). Further, apart from his insistence on including the overlooked influence of the "Amerindian omen" in theorizing the Caribbean, Harris's poetics, for some, evokes in Jungian fashion the archetypes of the collective unconscious and the phenomenological school of Hegel and Heidegger (Henry 2000, 92).

Illuminating the complex architecture of human consciousness has been the persistent obsession of Harris's fiction and nonfiction works. He is convinced that imagination is the universal fabric of "spirit" that makes possible "quantum" leaps across "chasms" of "ghetto-fixated habit[s]" of perception and "perverse commitment[s] to privileged frame or family" such as those institutionalized by the violent constructs of debased and *sanctified* otherness under colonial rule (Harris 1999, 238). Harris then is after the renewal and transformation of the very ego/self which he articulates as a creolization of consciousness, that is, the "cross-cultural regeneration of the heart and mind of an age" that in its current capitalist and sectarian ethos perpetuates all forms of violence (p. 247).

The unhappy fault of categorizing conceptual frameworks, perhaps for convenience, in terms of dyads such as root/rhizome contrasts is that either side is susceptible to the polarization of differences in hierarchical ways. Baugh, of course, does no such thing when he identifies these variants even though he clearly states his preference for the rhizome model. However, it is useful to be aware of the pitfalls in seeing Caribbean cultural or intellectual models in terms of opposing categories or camps, however they are named. Caution must always be exercised against simplistically adhering to polarized categorizes, fixed according to totalizing frames of reference such as the folk/grassroots and the middle class/elite, "great" and "little" traditions, oral or scribal discourse, and so on. Even hybridity itself can become a totalizing model that represses some of the very differences or elements it claims to include. This has happened in nationalist discourses that evoke the hybrid nation such as Puri argues in the case of the "Mother Trinidad" construct employed by Eric Williams (2004, 47–48).

An excellent means of demonstrating the problem of uncontainability that any binarized approach to theorizing of the Caribbean will inevitably encounter can be appreciated with reference to Lalla's *Defining Jamaican Fiction: Marronage and the Discourse of Survival* (1996). It should be noted that Lalla's critical practice interfaces literary criticism with linguistic and discourse analysis, an application that she has helped to pioneer in Caribbean literary scholarship. Her use of the rebellious Maroon as a countercultural perspective for reading the alienated persona in Jamaican fiction is significant. It is mobilized as an interpretative lens to discuss what she calls the "maroon consciousness" (Lalla 1996, 206). She applies this to a number of dissociated characters in Jamaican fiction who, like their Jamaican authors, come from a variety of backgrounds. However, while they all share marginal perspectives and positions that challenge the status quo, she notes that they are not equally successful in moving their condition of "marronage beyond alienation toward integrity" (p. 206).

Clearly, this application raises the important question about how, in the context of Caribbean diversity, a concept like *native/indigenous* or even *root* is defined since, in Lalla's usage, the figure of the Maroon defines a "perspective" or "consciousness" that evokes but ultimately transcends its original geo-historical and racial characteristics. The wider applicability of the metaphor, as Lalla demonstrates, is most powerfully encoded in language use and code-switching habits of Caribbean speech that cannot be easily reduced to ethnicity or class, given the operation of a language continuum. Further, she writes of Jamaican fiction that, in its "resistance to canonism", there is definitely a "commitment or impulse to break parameters of thought prescribed by epistemes . . . [, however;] at the same time, not all Jamaican writing, either creative or critical, is impelled by anti-imperial rage". Nevertheless, she adds, a "number of Jamaican writers are quietly engaged in their own indigenous creations" (Lalla 1996, 5). The point is crucial on two counts. First, it rescues Caribbean literature and theory from a purely oppositional resistance model. Second, it suggests that the assertion of an indigenous aesthetic or critical practice is not necessarily enforced through violent ruptures with the canons of "empire" or "Western" theory. Resistance in this frame is redefined as a dialogic give and take with the other, not a one-way process that dismisses unwelcomed difference. Cultural assertion is therefore a process of negotiation with varied streams of influence manifested, for instance, in how (Jamaican) literature "transgresses and defamilarizes some received codes but confirms and reinscribes others" (p. 4). Such an approach is less anxious about consorting with mainstream "Western" academic scholarship, less spooked by fears of intellectual assimilation "from foreign" – and this in itself is a display of cultural and intellectual confidence.

If a tendency can be discerned in Caribbean discourse that equates resistance with the African presence, it justifiably emerges from the region's history of plantation slavery and the primacy of this group in the liberation struggle. The difficulty arises, however, when revolt is reductively normalized on the basis of race along with associated categories such as the *folk* and the *working class*. This only flattens the complexity of the Caribbean's social codes and political affiliations. Terms like *indigenous* and *native* are understandably tricky, being so integral to the region's intensely politicized identity debates. Gordon Rohlehr notes that "the tension between folk/grass-roots/proletarian and generally black and 'mulatto'/mestizo/bourgeois/Euro-centred aesthetics, has been generated by, even as it has itself engendered radically antagonistic notions about art, culture, and creative possibility" (2006, 255–56). These unevenly valued competing traditions can generate a misleading simplification of groups most commonly represented by the so-called grass-roots and middle-class divide. Lalla captures this tension: "The intersection of social parameters with racial parameters has naturally associated social protest with the lifestyle of the black urban poor and equated realism with the portrayal of the slum. In general, this phenomenon has excluded coloureds from consideration or predetermined their treatment" (1996, 184).

Rohlehr's concept of an "aesthetic continuum" provides a useful interface with Lalla's viewpoint. According to Rohlehr, the region's writers and creators compose a multifarious and often embattled ideological and stylistic field characterized by an open-ended interplay of "forms derived from the oral paradigm, and forms suggested by various aspects of Modernist aesthetics". Therefore, "the notion of an aesthetic continuum allows us to understand and accept both types of writer" (Rohlehr 1992b, 60). Like Lalla, he notes that "some writers are able to accommodate both extremes with relative ease", while "others have been involved in an intense dialectic in which the extremes appear as thesis and antithesis" (p. 60). Attentiveness to the range of competing influences facilitates inclusiveness, acknowledges interdependence and guards against "the folly of seeking to impose on our restless and varied sensibilities rigid monolithic notions of shaping" (p. 60). Rohlehr's carefully historicized analysis of the turbulent aesthetic journey of the Caribbean's "cultural mulat-toes", beginning in the 1940s and continuing to the 1990s, witnesses to a slow evolution of attitude and sensibility in relation to their hybrid heritage. The movement, he argues, is towards a deeper, more accepting sense of "intercon-nectedness", expanding from an originating Afro-Creole/Euro-Caucasian dyad to include a range of Old and New World influences representative of the "'new space' within which the Caribbean sensibility now dances" (Rohlehr 2006, 298).

The sustained sensitivity to the region's intricate creative sensibilities that marks Rohlehr's critical practice prompts Lamming's compliment that, like his countryman Walter Rodney, he has never succumbed to the "virus of ethnocentricity" (Lamming 2009, 25). Indeed, the overall temperament of Rohlehr's critical "art" can be described as a companioning dialectic with its primary source, the literature and culture. In this he has been faithful to mapping the interrelationship shared by "content, context and imagination" (Rohlehr 1992b, 60), which is not always reducible to ethnic, class, gender or other such categories. Therefore, if it is at all possible to name the ethic that informs Rohlehr's critical practice, it is perhaps to his criticism of Brathwaite's poetry, the writer he has most closely accompanied, that one must turn. The claim he makes for Brathwaite's "apocalyptic" poetics as an investment in the human capacity and will to mobilize the "renewal of a dehumanising history"

(Rohlehr 1992b, 255) is not dissimilar to his own. His therefore can be dubbed an apocalyptic criticism of challenge and transformation committed to tracing human patterns of experience and response in the context of Caribbean history and its cultural evolution.

Theorizing the Poetics of Travel

A seminal preoccupation of contemporary cultural discourse is travel. Movement undoubtedly marks the current global order. Temporary and permanent relocations have engendered, with increased occurrence, the condition of rooted and multiple ways of belonging. As a result concepts like diaspora, nomadism, transnationalism and postnationalism have gained significant currency as models for analysing these rapid and dramatic changes in identities, nationalities and cultural expressions. Again, the Caribbean seems to have had the jump on another hub word, *transnationality*, which speaks to a global arena of shifting boundaries and porous borders. After all, ours is a civilization whose evolution is a long story of coerced and necessary relocations. The very geographical configuration of its chain of islands conjures the image of a "meta-archipelago" whose virtue is that it has "neither a boundary nor a center" (Benítez-Rojo 1992, 4). Rohlehr captures the nature of the region as a culture forged by crossings of all kinds: "Caribbean cultures have been the products of the incessant movement of people back and forth, along new middle passages of necessity. Such movement has led in turn to the constant legal or illicit penetration of every sort of frontier, whether national, geographical, cultural, ethnic or religious. Caribbean identity is about transgression" (2007, 406). This defiant and essential, even natural, traversing of borders describes a lived experience of "nation" that according to Lamming is "not defined by specific territorial boundaries" (1995, 32); open ended, not fixed and closed space; always in motion like its closest neighbour, the sea. Even the region's literary tradition was, at the beginning, facilitated by travel, as early writers found it necessary to settle in the mother country in order to make a life of writing. Lamming's *The Pleasures of Exile* ([1960] 2004), for instance, interrogates, among other things, the trope of the traveller. There he asks the provocative question which circulates, perhaps unawares, in much of current cultural discourse: "How and where is the Caribbean?" The answer, of course, is echoed in his own exclamation, "And always the sea!" (Lamming 2004, 16–17) – that literal and symbolic highway of multiple departures and arrivals. According to Pouchet Paquet, *The Pleasures of Exile* "provides an interpretative model that illuminates and contextualizes issues around the production of literature as a national enterprise in relation to postcolonial formations of identity, race, ethnicity, and cultural hybridity" ([1960] 2004, xxiv) and so "anticipates the postcolonial critic's preoccupation with the politics of migration, cultural hybridity, and the prerogatives of minority discourse" (viii). Her own essay "The Thematics of Diaspora and the Intercultural Identity Question" seems a theoretical expansion of Lamming's engagement with the polemical "pleasures" of the Caribbean's "cultural hybridity". She contends that a critical methodology is needed to address the fact that "a Caribbean literary culture, broadly or narrowly defined, enjoins transnational affiliation rather than national solidarity" (1998, 229).

The Caribbean literary canon is indeed well represented by texts that explore the trope of the journey, literal or imaginative, along with the challenges of living in between worlds not only in England but in the much expanded Caribbean diaspora in United States and Canada and beyond. Jamaica Kincaid's *Lucy* (2002), Edwidge Danticat's *Breath, Eyes, Memory* (1995), Ramabai Espinet's *The Swinging Bridge* (2003), V.S. Naipaul's *The Enigma of Arrival* (1987) and Cristina García's *Dreaming in Cuban* (1994) represent this very prolific narrative trajectory. Pouchet Paquet therefore sees the need for a method of reading Caribbean culture and by extension its literatures that attends to its thematic of diaspora which "highlights the Caribbean text as a product of heterogeneous legacy" (1998, 230). Such a methodology, she argues, "privileges intercultural identity as a transnational phenomenon that reaffirms established colonial links between Caribbean literary production and the metropolitan centres of Europe and continental America" (Pouchet Paquet 1998, 229). In a slightly similar vein, O'Callaghan therefore stresses the necessity to establish "criteria for criticism" to deal with the newer body of Caribbean writing which she distinguishes from an earlier phase of exile writing, such as Samuel Selvon's *The Lonely Londoners* ([1956] 1985), that represent the environmental and cultural estrangement of immigrants to the mother country in the post–World War II period. She sees the more recent texts as exhibiting a condition of "in betweenity" not solely marked by displacement and nostalgia. As such, their governing sensibility is "dicultural (or transcultural): as much at home in Britain or the United States as in Guyana or St Kitts or Antigua and crucially formed by the connections between the two worlds" (O'Callaghan 2001, 78).

Not all may be sold on what can appear to be the compression of the nation and transnation because such a manoeuvre can seem to play into the postmodern obsession with movement that undermines the reality of place and the locatedness of home. In global discourses that promote the notion of a new borderless world where there is no "elsewhere", nation state has become something of an anomaly. The challenge, however, of theorizing the Caribbean transnational remains in striking a balance that maintains the integrity of place and its specificities while being faithful to the Caribbean's ethic of movement and multiple dwellings. Alison Donnell (2006) makes an important point in this regard. She argues that, while the much-popularized "theoretical orthodoxies" inspired by Paul Gilroy's (1993) Black Atlantic model provide a much needed "redress to the claims of nationalism", they also create "an equally forceful sway, diverting attention away from increasingly marginal texts focussed on the located and the local" (Donnell 2006, 77). Donnell there-fore advocates the redirection of the critic's gaze to the literature of the nation and its located poetics, where she argues one finds a Caribbean model of the Black Atlantic that not only challenges the ship "chronotope" but demonstrates that "the nation is not the opposite of the transnation" (2006, 95). Neil Larsen is in this case right on target when he cautions that the postmodern hype about movement and transnationality "does not warrant, as is sometimes thoughtlessly claimed, the summary disposal of the national as a critical, or literary-historical category" (2001, 48).

The nation and its literature remain vital entities and are perhaps the best-positioned sites for recalibrating the politics of diasporan discourses. These have traditionally emphasized movement towards and relocation in northern metropolitan centres. Further, this trajectory, through which Caribbean trans-nationality has been theorized, has been staged as a progressive identity and even creative space, as opposed to the misconstrued insularity that attends the rootedness of the national with the latter betraying what it means to be fully Caribbean – never, by the way, the other way around. Glissant's notion of the itinerant imagination seems critical here, for it invites a shift from fixed and closed root models of identity and creative processes towards "errantry" founded on his conviction that "identity is no longer completely with the root but also in Relation" ([1997] 2000, 18). At the same time, however, the openness of rhizomatic thought is not without the insistence on the strategic preservation of "opacities" (Glissant [1997] 2000, 60) forged from rootedness. So, for Glissant, the interdependencies of the relational cannot function without the force of specificity in communities/societies whose "solid rootstock" is vulnerable to erosions by "a masked colonization" ([1997] 2000, 144). In an age where transculturality and transnationality now replace the traditional concept of pure race/nationality/culture, such a stance guards against the dilutions of cultural relativism or from being "arrested in undifferentiated conglomerations" (Glissant [1997] 2000, 141–42). But one cannot affirm this right to "specificity" even in the play of relations without a reminder of the violence and myopia that rigid localisms can breed and of which Glissant is all too aware. His thought therefore stands against all reductive "generalizations" that absorb or oppress "singularity" against the refusal to surrender to the ultimate "disindividuating system" of Relation which allows us to find "ourselves there along with others" ([1997] 2000, 195).

Gender and Sexuality

In "Acts of Possession: The New World of West Indian Writers", Kenneth Ramchand (1991) marks a key change in the West Indian literary landscape with the arrival of women writers. The "female perspective" offered by these texts which began appearing from about the 1970s changed not only the masculine face of the canon but, according to Ramchand, revitalized it (1991). Importantly, the rise of Caribbean women's writing dovetailed with the second wave of the women's movement in North America and Europe in which gender inequalities were given unprecedented attention. It would, however, take two decades for Caribbean criticism to enter the feminist dialogue and for gender to become a major theoretical site and interpretative imperative for reading women's literature as well as for rereading the "master" texts of the Caribbean canon. Literary scholars began to analyse how women's literature changed the contours of that tradition, to explore the stylistic and thematic interests of women writers, to engage with the politics of gender represented in that literature and to attempt to articulate the intersections and divergences of Caribbean women with the mainstream Western feminism and black American *womanist* agendas. Edited collections by Boyce Davies and Fido (1990) and Cudjoe (1990) signal these developments.

Seminal in this re/evolution is O'Callaghan's *Woman Version: Theoretical Approaches to West Indian Fiction by Women* (1993). She advances a theoretical model for reading Caribbean women's writing that draws on the reggae concept of *version*. As such, their narratives operate as a kind of "remix or dub version, which utilizes elements from the 'master tape' of Caribbean literary discourse . . . announces a gender perspective . . . and generally alters by recontextualization to create a *unique* literary entity" (1993, 11). The turn to gender criticism especially gained momentum from the burgeoning field of Caribbean feminist discourse in which Christine Barrow, Patricia Mohammed, Rhoda Reddock and others made key contributions with edited collections like *Caribbean Portraits: Essays on Gender Ideologies and Identities* (1998), *Gendered Realities: Essays in Caribbean Feminist Thought* (2002) and *Interrogating Caribbean Masculinities: Theoretical and Empirical Analyses* (2004).

As an interpretative method, the focus on gender facilitates discussions of the ways in which Caribbean female subjects are displaced in the political and socio-economic structures of the (post)colonial trans/nation; how language, race and sexuality are deployed by patriarchal and imperial discourses to institutionalize gendered oppression; and the role of aesthetic form and narrative strategies in reconstituting oppressive gender constructs. Although her focus is on black women's subjectivities, Patricia Saunders's (2007) claim that the writing of Caribbean women has moved against the function of masculinity as a "stabilizing" discourse transcends race and ethnic markers as well as geographical location. In fact, her argument that these writers have been "remapping literary and discursive landscapes providing alter/native narratives about exile and migration of female subjects" (Saunders 2007, 154) draws attention to the gendered nature of travel and immigration which, as Pouchet Paquet demonstrates (1998), have become key theoretical and critical sites of inquiry.

Like the preoccupation of early writers with a black nationalist aesthetic, the historical evolution of women's writing was such that attention naturally went to Afro-Creole female's subjectivities, with some theorizing of the "white" Creole woman drawing largely on Ramchand's adaptation of Fanon's concept of the "terrified consciousness" (Ramchand [1970] 1983, 224–25). Much has been said about the Afro-Caribbean woman, but Wynter's "Beyond Miranda's

Meanings: Un/Silencing the 'Demonic Ground' of Caliban's 'Woman'" is unparalleled for its powerful analysis of the role of colonial discourse in silencing and suppressing black female identity (1990). With the much later appearance of work by women of East Indian descent such as Trinidadian writers Lakshmi Persaud's *Butterfly in the Wind* (1990) and Ramabai Espinet's *Nuclear Seasons* (1991), a new critical trajectory opened up, making the black paradigm inadequate for theorizing the Caribbean woman's condition. A broader reading of Caribbean women's marginalization was needed as a result of the literature's engagement with the experiences of Indo-Caribbean women. This also implied giving consideration to the constructions of Indianness in the context a colonial patriarchy, an Afro-Creole nationalism and an East Indian masculinist hegemony. Rosanne Kanhai's *Matikor: The Politics of Identity for Indo-Caribbean Women* (1999) represents this expansion which was also a demand for a more inclusive feminist discourse. Just as the matikor image suggests a focus on the ethnic specificities of the East Indian female, Puri's reading (2004) of Espinet from the perspective of a "dougla feminism" indicates the emergence of a cross-cultural indigenous feminist theorizing and critical practice (Donnell 2006, 177).

Feminist discourse was understandably woman centred, concerned with Caribbean's women's experiences at home and abroad, their socio-economic struggles and strategies of resistance against imperial and patriarchal structures. The international shift in scholarship from feminist to gender criticism demanded that men's experiences be brought into the picture to readdress the female bias. A retheorization of gender inequality based on a decentred reading of power challenged the traditional stereotyping of gender differences. Also, the radical theorizing of sexuality engaged by gay, lesbian and queer theorists introduced dialogue on the politics of difference related to nonheterosexual identities. This dialogue, and the essentialist and biological approach to the gender/sex matrix were major interventions into the heterosexual presumptions of traditional feminism. Michel Foucault, Judith Butler and Eve Kosofsky Sedgwick produced the most influential work on body matters. Caribbean critics interested in the politics of sexuality drew on their work.

Gender and sexuality became important themes in Caribbean criticism and for theorizing the canon. Belinda Edmondson's *Making Men: Gender, Literary Authority, and Women's Writing* (1999), for instance, directs attention to the role of a colonially "made" masculinity in the authorization of West Indian national narratives written by male writers in exile. An unstated gender bias, however, meant that the same discursive privilege was not extended to women writers who had immigrated. From another perspective, Forbes's (2005) examination of gender representation in the work of early West Indian male authors is an effort to move the gender debate from the "deadlock of oppositional masculinist/feminist discourse". She therefore leans towards a more decentred critical methodology, using the "trope of hermaphroditism" to reread gender representations in West Indian canon (Forbes 2005, 24). However, if gender remained largely unread until the 1980s given the literary academy's preoccupation with the (masculinist) "national imperative" (Forbes 2005, 5), even more so was sexuality suppressed in a canon that traditionally shied away, both creatively and critically, from engaging the topic, which inadvertently normalized a heterosexual nation body. Ian Smith's 1999 essay "Critics in the Dark" therefore argues that Caribbean "critical geography seems to have no place to situate sexuality, specifically the homoerotic, within a postcolonial discourse" (p. 4). Then expanding the applicability of Butler's sexuality theory, Richard Clarke's essay "Androgyny and Miscegenation in *The Crying Game*: The Case for a Performative Model of Gender and Race" makes a compelling case for analysing the tensions that visit Butler's concept of "performativity" (2002).

But this focus on sexual orientation was primarily prompted by a new spate of literary texts such as Shani Mootoo's *Cereus Blooms at Night* ([1996] 2001) and *Valmiki's Daughter* (2008), Lawrence Scott's *Aelred's Sin* (1998), Jamaica Kincaid's *Lucy* (2002) and *My Brother* (1997), Patricia Powell's *A Small Gathering of Bones* (1994) and Michelle Cliff's *No Telephone to Heaven* (1987). Their frank explorations of the interface between sexual orientation and national identity thereby challenged the heterosexual orthodoxy of Caribbean nationalisms and invited theorizing on sexuality and narrative strategies for writing sexuality, gender and performance, the poetics of the closet, and the politics of belonging and leave taking. For example, in "'Compulsory Heterosexuality' and Textual/Sexual Alternatives in Selected Texts by West Indian Women Writers", O'Callaghan considers the possibility that West Indian women writers are party to "an unthinking naturalisation of 'compulsory heterosexuality'" (1998a, 298). The un-welcomed status of the homosexual in the island nation that this trend implies is corroborated by the parallel she discerns between immigration and writing the homoerotic. She therefore argues that the "more tolerant attitude towards gays as well as the presence of feminist and lesbian publishing outlets" makes explorations of the theme possible (1998, 302).

Conclusion

There have always been varied approaches to Caribbean theory and criticism. The aesthetic wrangling that characterized the region's literary and cultural scholarship from its outset emerged from a trend of thought that compressed national belonging and native authenticity with an ethnocentric expectation that privileged the dominant Afro-Creole component. The notable shift to heterogeneity in the post-1970s period was therefore an attempt to adjust some of the exclusions resulting from the understandable emphasis on race and ethnicity that characterized the decolonization exercise and the literary nationalism that accompanied it. There is no question that race remains an indelible marker of identity in the dialogue on Caribbean cultural identity, creative expressions and the politics of belonging, all of which directly impact agency in the context of the sociopolitical and imaginary nation space. While they are not immune to practising their own brand of hierarchical or exclusory habits, rhizomic paradigms discourage separatist or essentialist thinking along the oppositional resistance models that can partner with them. They seem to better facilitate the Caribbean's fragmentary and eclectic cultures, sensibilities and imaginative landscapes as well as demonstrate that race, particularly in the Caribbean, cannot be mobilized merely as a biologically fixed or purist ethnic category. Neither Europe's totalitarian, linear and realist models nor the nativist ones that replicated that Manichean thinking (but in the name of resistance to its biases) adequately responded to the complexity of the region's ongoing cross-cultural genesis.

Caribbean literary scholarship has certainly come into its own, with a rich resource of indigenous concepts and procedures that are even attracting the interest of academics outside its borders. Moreover, the region's maturity is evident in its development as a site for reading the other. Lalla's *Postcolonialisms: Caribbean Rereading of Medieval English Discourse* (2008) is a tour de force of the interpretative reversal, intellectual independence and cultural agency this represents. The Caribbean first received the British canon as the literature of empire and was also the subject of its gaze. Lalla reverses this axis of power as the vernacular literature of the English medieval period is now reread, a little ironically, from the lenses of the ex-colonized as a postcolonial "situation" (2008, 20). There is, as expected, more confidence than in the past with borrowing and adapting "Western" concepts and methodologies to read cultural phenomena or with simply exercising the choice to leave them alone. An interesting development that accompanies the current surge in Caribbean film production and film studies is Jean Antoine-Dunne's (2010) discussions of montage film techniques with reference to writers like Naipaul and Walcott. Additionally, Paula Morgan and Valerie Youssef's (2006) exploration of literary violence with the help of discourse and trauma theories in *Writing Rage: Unmasking Violence through Caribbean Discourse* speaks to the region's immediate need to confront this social crisis.

Postcolonial and postmodern intersections with Caribbean concerns and practices are common enough. Yet, even as similarities are noted and adaptations developed, there is significant distinction to the Caribbean postcolonial or postmodern, for instance, to eliminate reading their elements as mere mimics of their Western counterparts but rather as having pre-empted them. Dash therefore suggests that the world is becoming more Caribbean: "the Caribbean condition is increasingly becoming a global phenomenon" (1999, 196). Forbes articulates this scenario slightly differently when she writes that "the Caribbean text and Caribbean culture as a whole have become a site of appropriation for postmodern theory", that is, "as a prototype of the kind of identity and relationality to be desired by the globalized 'postmodern' world" (2005, 24). From both these perspectives, it seems that the postmodern Caribbean offers itself as sort of instructive site for a world that is now grappling with becoming postmodern. Yet, at the same time, it would be a mistake for the Caribbean and the New World in general to disregard the relationship between epistemological dissemination and the geo-politics of influence, as thought too can be (re)colonized or appropriated in the service of the powerful.

No doubt there will be different takes on what represents intellectual and cultural sovereignty. This is to be expected, given the Caribbean's inherent diversity. But this free dialogue with differences is precisely what fuels the enriching creative tensions necessary to its cultural dynamism which, at its best, is at the service of humanizing (r)evolution. Baugh articulates the matter so well when he notices that "all the theoretical models . . . grapple, in different ways, and perhaps with different degrees of success, with the fact of violence and the challenge of how not to perpetuate it" (2006, 60). If history has, to various degrees, unhoused all the peoples that compose Caribbean civilization, the task of literary theory and criticism is to co-partner with its creative writers in constructing a house with rooms enough for us all. The critic's mandate is therefore not merely to elucidate the text but to also challenge and so deepen the humanization of worlds.

Chapter 2

A Cultural Studies Approach to Caribbean Literary Research

Paula Morgan

L iterature is *mimetic* and *paradigmatic*: it reflects life scenarios and creates life models. Since life unfolds temporally and spatially within sociocultural and geopolitical contexts, every engagement with a literary text is a cultural engagement. We understand this when we read a historical text and find ourselves immersed in representation of the past as a distant land. The cultural values and forms – language, customs, norms and ideologies – seem odd and antiquated and may even appear inaccessible and in need of interpretation. An encounter with a "foreign" text also takes us to a distant land – this time through an engagement with cultural, ethical, linguistic and geographical differences which challenge our established and normative notions and which demand flexibility and sensitivity if we are to imaginatively enter into its world.

A cultural studies approach to literary studies identifies every text and fictional scenario – historical or contemporary, foreign, global or local – as a cultural engagement. It locates even writing, publishing, reading and interpretative practices within sociocultural contexts which, in turn, are deeply rooted in broad frameworks of power relations, the representation and creation of ideologies, hegemonies and modes of compliance, and resistance to the same. Such a reading of literary texts deliberately goes against the grain of conventional representational paradigms seeking access to culturally repressed and silenced ontologies and epistemologies. It also interrogates received cultures of reading and readers' investment in particular interpretive frameworks. To greater appreciate a cultural studies approach to literary texts, it is necessary to define culture and to delineate cultural studies as a field of enquiry.

Notions of Culture

Simply put, cultural studies is the study of culture. All notions of simplicity evaporate as soon as one tries to determine what culture is. Terry Eagleton in *The Idea of Culture* (2000) declares *culture* one of the slipperiest terms in the English language. Its etymology is derived from *coulter*, which means the "blade of a ploughshare", and is reflected in the current usage of the term agriculture. Its Latin root, *colere*, suggests a range of meanings including "cultivate, inhabit, protect and honour with worship". The notion of inhabiting evolved to incorporate connections to *colonus* and thereafter to colonization. The aspect of worshipping and protecting led conversely to the term *cultus* and thereafter to cult. Culture in the modern age came to mean transcendence. The evolving definitions of the term *culture* reflect significant historical transitions from rural to urban lifestyles as well as philosophical issues related to tensions between given and created, freedom and determinism, agency and endurance, change and identity, realist and constructivist. According to Raymond Williams, "The complex of senses within the term culture indicates a complex argument about the relations between general human development and a particular way of life and between both and the works and practices of art and intelligence" (1983, 88).

Caribbean theorists have insisted on material bases and the integrated nature of cultural forms. In the essay "Culture and Sovereignty", author and cultural critic George Lamming explains why notions of culture have never lost their connection with nurturing, feeding and cultivation, "whether it be a body or mind" that is under consideration:

> The first and essential meaning of culture is, therefore, the means by which men and women feed themselves; clothe and shelter themselves; the means whereby they achieve and reproduce their material existence. No food, no life. No food: no book, no religion, no philosophy, no politics, no performing arts. No one is exempt from the demands of material life. So we need to

understand therefore, why the farmer and fisherman are cultural workers, and that all questions relating to social transformation are cultural questions.

Secondly, we mean by "culture" the variety of ways in which men and women interpret and translate, through the imagination, the meaning of that material existence in the light of their experience: religion, philosophy, art and the institutions which mediate their daily lives. (1992, 283–84)

For the purpose of this text we will adopt a broad-based definition of *culture* as a grounded way of life and as the arts. We will also critique the manner in which the concept of culture as universal civilization/civility was deployed as pivotal to the imperial project of yoking the mind of the oppressed to cultural denigration and mental servitude.

Given that contestations of culture, power, representation, race and identity have been at the bedrock of Caribbean social and literary enquiry, it is not surprising that Caribbean scholars and thinkers have played a key role in establishing the conceptual parameters and the global reach of the field of cultural studies. George Lamming, Rex Nettleford and Gordon Rohlehr, with their decades-long engagement with the decolonization movement and the attendant recuperation and valorization of the Caribbean person, social formations and cultural forms, have made significant inputs into the field of cultural studies. In terms of the international tertiary focus on this now popular field, Caribbean-born scholars Stuart Hall and C.L.R. James have been highly instrumental in conceptualizing and defining the primary concerns of cultural studies. Hall, writing out of his lived experiences of Caribbean birth and parentage and British residence, lends penetrative insight into the processes by which identities are discursively constructed and enunciated in specific historical and institutional sites ("Who Needs Identity"). As early as 1963, James in his classic *Beyond a Boundary* (1963) presents a socio-historical appraisal of West Indian cricket which achieved groundbreaking creative synthesis between his ordinary lived experience of growing up in Tunapuna, Trinidad, and the global social dynamic which it served to illustrate. In the autobiographical account of his childhood and youth, James conceptualizes cricket as "first and foremost a dramatic spectacle. It belongs with the theatre, ballet, opera and the dance" (p. 196). Crashing the divide between high and low culture, Eurocentric hegemonies and lower-strata Caribbean self-fashioning and performance, James reads the game as a pivotal West Indian cultural practice and marker of cultural identity, located at the nexus of colonial rule and class antagonism.

Despite the immense popularity of cultural studies as a whole and Caribbean cultural studies in particular, it is not an easy field to delineate. It offers neither a clear, easily defined field for investigation nor a set of defined methodologies. From the earliest research in the field (traditionally identified as Richard Hoggart's *The Uses of Literacy* [1957]), cultural studies has been concerned with the interface between individual everyday symbolic and expressive life practices and the large network of social, class-defined, gendered, national, institutional and other engagements.

Cultural Studies: Theoretical Streams and Orientations

Cultural studies first emerged in Great Britain in the late 1950s and found an institutional axis in the Birmingham Centre for Contemporary Cultural Studies. Its first theorists groped towards the field of cultural studies in response to disappointment with classical Marxism of the 1950s, attendant upon its Eurocentric inclination and insistence on an economic base for cultural superstructures. The quest of New Left intellectuals at the institution – including Williams, Hoggart and Hall – for new ways of knowing and theorizing led to the emergence of cultural studies. The concerns of the British school of cultural studies from its inception were influenced by the Marxist theoretical agenda – power relations, "the global reach and history-making capacities of capital" and the production of critical knowledge as a practice. Cultural studies spoke into the gaps and silences left by some of the evasions of Marxism – culture, ideology, language and the symbolic potentials of capital flows (Hall and du Gay 1996: 264–66).

In his essay "Cultural Studies and Its Theoretical Legacies" ([1996] 1997), Hall defines cultural studies as an essentially unstable discursive formation constituted of multiple "discourses ... histories ... trajectories ... methodologies and theoretical positions, all of them in contention" (p. 263). As an open-ended project, the field of cultural studies is both aggressively multidisciplinary and resistant to policing and closure. Its theoretical and conceptual influences are numerous. Hall cites the foundational impact of Gramsci's notions of *situated knowledge* and the *organic intellectual*. The former refers to knowledge which is situated in and applicable to specific and immediate political or historical circumstances and hegemonies. The latter is defined in opposition to traditional intellectuals who perceived their class as above the rank and file and their pursuits as far removed from daily life; Gramsci identified the organic intellectual as emerging from the working class with the capacity to engage social life and analyse the culture of the masses, thereby creating a counterhegemony to disrupt the prevailing social order. Gramsci points to two tasks faced by the organic intellectual: to travel to the forefront of intellectual theoretical work and to transmit those ideas to those who do not belong to the intellectual class. Not a simple agenda and one with which cultural studies as an intellectual field grapples on a daily basis.

Cultural studies as it proceeded on its intellectual project was interrupted, so to speak, by two other theoretical streams. In the 1970s, feminism significantly impinged upon cultural studies, as documented by Charlotte Brunsdon's essay "A Thief in the Night: Stories of Feminism in the 1970s at CCCS", so much so that it altered the manner in which one could use terms such as *power* and *hegemony* within the field (Brunsdon 1997, 276–86). Feminist scholars asserted "the personal is political", "sisterhood is global" and gender and sexuality are pivotal to the understanding of power (Hanisch [1969] 1979; Morgan 1984; Brunsdon 1997). Their scholarly concerns brought into prominence the issue of gendered subjectivities. This occurred alongside resurgence of interest in the frontier between social theory and theory of the unconscious – psychoanalysis. Hall, in "The Meaning of New Times", comments on the impact of this parcel of theoretical insights on cultural studies: "We can no longer conceive of 'the individual' in terms of a whole, centered, stable and completed Ego or autonomous, rational 'self'. The 'self' is conceptualized as more fragmented, incomplete, composed of multiple 'selves' or identities in relation to the different social worlds we inhabit, something with a history, 'produced' in process. The 'subject' is differently placed or *positioned* by different discourses and practices" (1997a, 226).

A similar disruption occurred when cultural studies was challenged in the 1970s to grapple with the critical questions of race, ethnicities and politics. This institutional focus at the Birmingham Centre for Cultural Studies emerged in wake of concern with street crimes committed by black youth. Its scholars engaged the manner in which this fed into a new hegemonic construction of British nationalism under Margaret Thatcher, predicated on the scapegoating and othering of new immigrants from south Asia and the West Indies as social threats to British society (Hall 1996). Structuralist, semiotic and poststructuralist theoretical revolutions of the 1960s and 1970s challenged cultural studies scholars to take on board yet another range of issues including "the crucial importance of language and of the linguistic metaphor to any study of culture; the expansion of the notion of the text and textuality, both as a source of meaning, and as that which escapes and postpones meaning; the recognition of heterogeneity . . . the acknowledgement of textuality and cultural power, of representation itself as a site of power and regulation; of the symbolic as a source of identity" (Hall [1996] 1997, 105). As a result, contemporary cultural studies must grapple with the interface between the indeterminacies of the text and the politics of representation as they interface with real-life institutions, genders, classes, offices, agencies, nations and races. A case in point is the use of forensic linguistics to interrogate judicial statements which demonstrate the impact of gender prejudice in judgments handed down in domestic violence cases (see Morgan and Youssef 2006).

It is in the cultural studies trajectory within the American academy that the study of popular culture has come into greatest focus. Traditionally dissociated from serious intellectual enquiry and underrepresented in its theorization, popular mass culture has migrated from the margins of the academy, although it has not quite managed to arrive at the centre. In the wake of the proliferation of sprawling modern cities, new media, mass production, the ubiquitous global flow of musical forms, images, entertainment, celebrity culture and fashion cycles – the common person's valorization as consumer and appropriation of means of cultural production has demolished the barrier between the cultured and the popular. Contemporary consumer culture has made nonsense of canons of arts, architecture and good taste and nullified the gatekeepers of high culture. The Marxist masses of early cultural studies have now been transformed into historically situated and invariably consuming subjects. From the 1970s onwards, notions of postmodern culture defined a shift. According to Iain Chambers, "The shift which is certainly not unified can nevertheless be traced in critical, historical, political and aesthetic terms. It is marked by a movement away from an idealized, theoretical production that reveals the 'real relations' and political agendas of a culture and world rendered transparent by critique" (1997, 206). As practised in a cross-section of American institutions, cultural studies has been critiqued for too strong a focus on popular culture with minimal emphasis on scholarship which has the potential for transformative impact in relation to social issues.

In the Caribbean, notions of culture and cultural studies have from their inception been engaged with political hegemonic associations among colonization, culture and civilization. The focus has been on social issues closely associated with the anti-imperialist project and the quest of Caribbean people for what cultural critic Rex Nettleford terms "cultural certitude" (1978, 140). Nettleford argues in the wake of centuries of cultural denigration as a basis for political and social ascendency, notions of cultural affirmation for formerly oppressed groups have been pivotal to the process of shaping a viable mode of being in the New World. He argues, "The two pronged phenomenon of decolonization and creolization (or indigenization) represent that awesome process actualized in simultaneous acts of negating and affirming, demolishing and constructing, rejecting and reshaping" (p. 140). This is manifested in the ongoing concern with highly contested and politicized issues including Eurocentrism, Afrocentricism, Indocentrism, multiculturalism, migrations, creolization, indigenization and cultural marginality. Culture's key markers within multiethnic, historically diverse, multilingual, Caribbean island, ancestral and migrant communities are equally diverse, complex and subject to contestation. In relation to language as a pivotal cultural marker, for example, contestation emerges in the relative value given to the oral and scribal; official tongue, mother tongue, standard English, Creoles, nation languages; ancestral languages; bilingualism; multilingualism. A similar proliferation of issues abounds in relation to religion, music, dance and literary expression, and countless other cultural practices.

For Caribbean cultural critic George Lamming, culture and culture studies has retained its Marxist connections with labour and labour relations. Lamming, in his essay "Language and the Politics of Ethnicity", insists on an acknowledgement not only of the material base of all culture but its grounding in labour and its relations:

> I believe that labor and the relations experienced in the process of labor constitute the foundation of all culture. It is through work that men and women make nature a part of their own history. The way we see, the way we hear, our nurtured sense of touch and smell – the whole complex of feelings which we call sensibility – are influenced by the particular features of the landscape which has been humanized by our work. (2009, 30)

For cultural critic Gordon Rohlehr, significant engagements for Caribbean cultural studies include the valorization of the people's bards and poets – the calypsonians and the spoken-word practitioners – and the development of methodologies and modalities for the preservation and analysis of their work. He explores the submerged though ubiquitous African presence with which Caribbean societies must grapple if they are to escape the duppies of history and persistent cycles of social unrest. Rohlehr enquires into the bad seeds sown in the violent and cataclysmic origins of the contemporary social order, with a focus on the impact of its unresolved traumas on a generation of youth – casualties of societal and familial neglect who have been seduced by mass-mediated badmanism and the ready availability of guns and gangs into criminality and what he terms a "culture of terminality" (2010b).

Cultural studies is a diverse field which travels in innovative ways. It brings to the table literary scholars, historians, media theorists, sociologists, anthropologists, cultural critics and even social activists. Apart from a certain transdisciplinarity, cultural studies is constantly guarding against the establishment of new hierarchies and hegemonies in knowledge creation. It remains suspicious of itself, and hence it tends to be self-reflexive. It seeks to give voice to all while privileging the expression of the dispossessed, the underprivileged and the marginalized. This multivalency is matched by its quest to explore its target through multiple lenses – as it is represented through myriad discourses and through lived experience and as it is shaped by its various local, communal and global contexts. It is subversive and rooted in the local, the common and the everyday; it is simultaneously global and transnational in orientation. Within this field of study, any- and everything becomes a text. This accounts for the iconic status of James's *Beyond a Boundary*, which explores cricket as theatre, as exemplary of power relations in the broader social order, as ground of contestation over the construction of masculinity, as indicative of the capacity for governance, long before it was fashionable to think in these terms.

Cultural Criticism: Approaching the Literary Text through Cultural Studies

I have indicated that cultural studies is concerned with the forms and practices of culture and how they interface with and reflect power relations among diverse social practitioners and performers. The field retains a particular emphasis on foregrounding voices and subaltern cultures and unmasking the interface among culture, hegemonic ideologies and power relations. It is also concerned with popular and mass-mediated culture and the social practices and symbology of everyday life. In applying a cultural studies approach to a literary text, we must bear in mind how this field of study has posed a challenge to disciplinary structures within tertiary academies.

From the 1940s through the 1960s, *New Criticism* dominated literary study with its focus on the primacy of the text rather than on socio-historical contexts, authors or readers. The literary work as an object of study by trained readers was treated as an organic system of relationships possessing inherent thematic and structural coherence. In pursuit of unravelling this organic system, the skilled critical reader would do a close reading of the text with attention to thematic parallels, paradox, irony, diction, connotative and denotative meanings, symbols, images, point of view and tone. Most significant was how all of these elements interrelated to produce a single, coherent argument. Literature was seen as a distinctive, rarefied form of discourse, whose creators were situated above the mundane and were empowered by sensitivity and towering intellects to educate the masses. Language was perceived as possessing the power to confidently convey reality, and the text was seen as possessing an objective existence and a clear, compelling message.

Cultural criticism constitutes a radical departure from this notion. This analytical approach insists that literature, with its fluid and diverse ways of apprehending and knowing, must not be interpreted as universal and transcendent. Its thinkers argue that practices of writing and reading – representational and interpretive frameworks – are not simply innocent, universal and true. In "The Sovereignty of the Imagination" Lamming states, "Knowledge is never passive. It is always intended to be put in the service of some specific intention. It may serve to protect and stabilize the dominant values of a particular context of social relations, or it may serve to subvert or transcend those values. . . . Knowledge is therefore social in character" (2004, 350). One branch of cultural criticism emerged in the wake of the global decolonization movement which wrested control of two-thirds of the then known world out of the hands of Europe's geopolitical empire. Its thinkers embraced the imperative to deconstruct the master's house using his tools – language in particular – to undermine the enduring and destructive legacies of cultural imperialism.

These include some who live and work out of North American academies and identify as postcolonial critics, notably Edward Said and Homi K. Bhabha and a considerable cross-section of Caribbean-born creative writers and thinkers who embrace postcolonial concerns but not the label. These include C.L.R. James, Frantz Fanon, George Lamming, Gordon Rohlehr, Wilson Harris and Derek Walcott. Charles Bressler, in *Literary Criticism: An Introduction to Theory and Practice*, places postcolonial criticism under the broad heading of cultural studies and identifies a gap between "the theory and practice of those trained and living in the West and those third world, subaltern writers living and writing in non-Western cultures" (2002, 202). Despite their differences, these thinkers agree that the "universality" of classical canonized European literary texts and the civility/civilization which they modelled were deeply politicized weapons in the imperial arsenal deployed to justify geopolitical subjugation with cultural denigration. Their collective body of work demonstrates how literature can be deeply implicated in unjust transnational power relations and in ideological attempts to redress such injustices.

Yet another branch of contemporary cultural critics take as their point of departure the manner in which globalized forces of late capitalism have shaped writing, reading and interpretive communities. Far from embracing literary works as classical examples of high culture produced by visionaries of enlightened sensibility that deserve to be exalted above the mundane, the commercial and other manifestations of the griminess of everyday life, these thinkers see literary works as cultural products which are just as socially situated, mass produced, mass disseminated, mass consumed, and mass mediated as corn flakes and artificial Christmas trees.

The most immediate consequence of both of these approaches is to destabilize the concept of the Western literary canon from its pride of place above other discourses. Predictably this process also dethrones the creative writer from pride of place above other producers of representation and discourse. A cultural studies approach to literature – which many traditionalists decry as debasing the value of literary works – includes among its emphases the exploration of how aesthetic value is constituted, how literariness is constructed and how intricate can be the artistry of common daily practices. For this breed of critic, the flair of a pannist engaged in a passionate performance is every bit as worthy of careful scholarly scrutiny as a minutely crafted dramatic presentation; spoken-word poetry is as valid a target of intellectual enquiry as a meticulously wrought poem by any eighteenth-century British master or Shakespearean drama.

Cultural critics go further to interrogate the factors which construct the authority of literary classics. They expose the underlying assumptions by which a given literary work is identified as the "greatest" of its kind. Indeed they unmask and interrogate the processes by which canons are made and dismantled. They pose questions such as

- What factors undergird such aesthetic judgments?
- What constitutes good taste in any given cultural and geopolitical context?
- Why are certain creative and cultural products valued more than others?
- How do texts and other works of art which originally emerge as popular expressions wend their ways into classical canons?
- How do notions of good taste undergird and promote cultural discrimination?
- To what extent can we relate these judgment calls to the nationality, class, gender and ethnicity of the writer and the reader? And, further afield, what does this complex indicate about how human societies are organized?
- Why do societies mask the ideologies and power relations which establish and maintain literary and other canons?

This invites the question of how cultural critics actually engage texts. If one dispenses with the notion of a literary *canon* – a body of work which has stood the test of time, executed by widely recognized literary masters on transcendent universal themes – what then is the text? Any creative, cultural and material product becomes a text. Rohlehr's painstaking, grounded research, including his collaboration on the volume, *Voiceprint* (Brown, Morris and Rohlehr 1989), has resulted in many a calypso finding its way into secondary-school classrooms and examination syllabi. Today they are given scholarly scrutiny equal to any nineteenth-century British classic; hence, we have learned to treat calypsos as complex, layered, socially situated and deserving of close textual analysis. Note though that this is not to imply that cultural critics want to contest the statement that Shakespeare is the world's greatest dramatist by asserting that Mutabaruka is the world's greatest spoken-word poet. Instead they challenge the notion of canon formation in the interest of replacing the practice of ranking with the practice of situating cultural expressions and products.

Other critical concerns include but are not limited to the deployment of standard English, Creole/nation language and ancestral languages; the suppression and emergence of voice (who is allowed to speak and on whose behalf); the politics of representation in relation to race and ethnicity, nation, and gender; the hegemonic and counterhegemonic values, cultural contestations, and world views represented and endorsed within the text; the historicity of the text and the textuality of its histories; and the textual emphases, silences, erasures and gaps.

How, then, does one place a given project or target of enquiry into a cultural studies theoretical and methodological framework? Cultural studies is inclusive insofar as it draws from the full range of existing theoretical approaches and their related methodologies to produce the knowledge required for a particular project. Its focus is variously on lived experiences, discursive formations and real-life social contexts. And these research emphases may be applied individually or in combination. The questions posed are, How effectively does research capture lived realities? How effectively does the research unravel problematic social discourses that mediate how we perceive lived realities and people? How effectively does the research capture the relevant sociocultural and geopolitical contexts?

While cultural studies is multivocal, it retains a focus on subordinated knowledge or research on submerged groups. It seeks ways of knowing and research methodologies truer to the ontologies of the subordinated group. Cultural studies values a prismatic approach which applies a range of theoretical and methodological lenses and causes them to interrogate each other. Paula Saukko argues in favour of prismatic research, using the metaphor of crystallization. These are research approaches which reflect externalities as well as refract themselves from within. They support the contention that reality is fluid and the researcher is not seeking absolute truth but is engaged in a process which socially constructs the reality under exploration (Saukko 2003).

In practice, this form of critical reading challenges notions of culture as a static, fixed and coherent whole in the interest of grasping after cultural contexts, practices, and subject constructions and formations which are constantly in flux, morphing in unexpected and challenging ways. Cultural critics situate literary texts within their sociocultural contexts. They relate them to economic conditions and to a wider range of social discourses. Let us consider finally how this works in practice.

A New Critical approach would arguably read Emily Brontë's Heathcliff (*Wuthering Heights* [1847] 1985), for example, as a dark brooding hero within a romantic or gothic tradition. A cultural studies approach would arguably read Heathcliff as the swarthy, fatherless, ambiguously raced spawn of the Liverpool docks which are so famously implicated in the transatlantic trade in enslaved Africans. The reading would begin by citing a range of documents on the social conditions which obtained in Liverpool because of the impact of the triangular trade. It would ferret out submerged biographical evidence of Brontë's insight into this social scenario and follow through by minutely picking over the text for traces of discourses on the resultant social issues, incorporating references to relevant media issues, popular songs and political statements. The cultural critic might then scrutinize *Wuthering Heights* in search of salacious details to support a nontraditional reading of this text which revolves around a dark, highly sexualized hero who disrupts class hierarchy, lineage and rights of inheritance and even threatens the sanctity of the grave.

How would the eclectic interplay of a range of critical perspectives con-ceivably shape a reading of a literary text such as Jean Rhys's *Wide Sargasso Sea* (1966)? Such a reading would arguably engage the text from a feminist perspective which positions white Creole women in a disadvantageous position relative to the dictates of patriarchal society. It would simultaneously apply a postcolonial perspective with its focus on race and power relations to shed light on the Creole women's complicities in the colonial domination systems. Its sus-picions of the processes which feed into the establishment of new hierarchies

A study of literary representations of race in the Caribbean could readily lead to exploration of Phantom cartoons, which were common daily newspaper fare for decades; personal narratives on how students perceive themselves in relation to common race classification; films about the impact of racism; media constructions of discourse on race relations; and court judgments whose outcomes were prejudiced by racial ideologies. The reading would then yoke the insights and analytical strategies of historians, linguists, sociologists, economists and psychologists to the critical task at hand. The literary text becomes one discourse which is juxtaposed to a range of other discourses with the intention of setting up a framework for understanding and applying a range of ways of knowing to a social phenomenon which shapes everyday life. Structure, coherence and organization of this form of reading can be challenging.

would yield a critique of Rhys's subtle incorporation of tropes of enslavement to convey the location of her protagonist – a placement which erases the specificities of the experience of enslavement for black women and men and its impact on the material conditions of their lives. The cultural studies approach would read the character's individual social location and everyday experience as reflective of historical traumas which are related to transnational power inequities and flows of ideologies and finances. It would explore the fictional evocation of the problematic relationship between the white Creole protagonist and the black child Tia against evidence of lived realities governing interracial relationships at that time. The semiotic engagement would question how key terms in the text come to mean – What is a *whitey cockroach*?

A cultural studies approach would also turn its attention to *Wide Sargasso Sea* as an object which is marketed to and consumed by diverse audiences differently over time. It would read the market forces which undergirded the decision to change the illustration on the book covers from a distant and delicate Caucasian beauty to a pair of husky, earthy, black girls when African Caribbean women writers and protagonists gained symbolic and material currency. It would explore the availability or lack thereof of this text in the Caribbean. It would examine the politics surrounding its placement on school and examination syllabi. Additionally it would argue that the literary text is not to be privileged over historical records or legislative documents on life and social customs of that period. It would read *Wide Sargasso Sea* against visual representations of similar forms of life in that historical period and media reports about the customs, mores, diet and other cultural practices of the time.

In summary, a cultural studies approach to literary study locates literary texts within cultural production and interpretative frameworks; discursive frameworks; representational and ideological frameworks based on gender, ethnicity, class and nation; and social and institutional processes and power relations. It focuses on submerged knowledge, discourses and histories. Caribbean thinkers, theorists and creative writers have systematically engaged such issues and perspectives from the inception of modern Caribbean thought. Their works have been instrumental in the establishment of cultural studies within global tertiary academies.

Chapter 3

Culturometrics
An Integrated Research Approach to Cultural Studies

Béatrice Boufoy-Bastick

Culturometrics is concerned with who we are and how we change. To this end, it offers measures of cultural identity that enable such changes to be identified and quantified so that associated causes and influences may be researched. By focusing on the flux and flow of cultural identity, culturometrics shares the agenda of cultural studies but emphasizes the language of process rather than the language of object – as in its definition of "cultural identity" being "values in context". This approach can be used in cultural studies research to deal with a greater variety of groups and nuanced issues (Alasuutari 1995, 36–37).

Culturometrics is an empowering humanistic philosophy based on personal choice of cultural identity. Quantification of the philosophy enables continuing development of objective methodologies for researching the dynamics of changing cultural identities. Many works on Caribbean cultures evidence perspectives which are meaningful from the standpoint of a single cultural group and therefore work towards authentically "iconicalizing" a cultural identity for the group. Typical examples are *place-novels* with details of cultural code and Creole inserts that can authenticate the cultural identity of diasporic readers as Afro-Trinidadian, Jamaican and the like or more generally as Caribbean. This is one important purpose for products of Caribbean cultural studies, and culturometrics supports this purpose with research methodologies for objectively identifying persons who exemplify a group's cultural identity and then ethnographically elucidating a verifiable authentic description of their cultural identity. However, elucidating Caribbean cultural identities from an emic perspective is not the only purpose of culturometrics. It was Rudyard Kipling who once asked, "What should they know of England who only England know?" (Kipling 1892). What is special about a culture can most readily be appreciated in comparison to other cultures. Thus, for example, French diasporic pseudoemic Haitian writers can, by comparison with their French European culture, more readily identify and iconicalize what is special about Haitian culture. Current authentic cross-cultural evaluations are made from the single cultural perspective of the mulatto, the blasian, the mixed race Afro-Indo-Trinidadian and so on. The relevance of culturometrics to Caribbean cultural studies is that, to better understand what is special about Caribbean cultures, it gives objective comparisons of any group cultural identity from the perspective of external cultural groups and from the perspectives of different internal component cultural subgroups. For example, culturometrics can measure Jamaicanness from a male Jamaican perspective or from an American perspective, or it can measure differences in younger and older female Jamaican perspectives of male Jamaicanness, and so on (Boufoy-Bastick 2010).

In this section the philosophy in question is outlined. How it may be applied to give objective measurement of intrasubjectivities such as cultural identity is also described. We explain how the cultural identity of groups, relevant to group membership/exclusion and social distance/proximity, is negotiated via consensus of individual cultural identities of the group members and measured by culturometrics.

The Culturometric Framework

Culturometrics is also a constructionist philosophy within a framework that focuses on the flux and flow of cultural identities. The central concept is cultural identity and its measurement – simply "who we are", which is evidenced by demonstrations of our values in a given context. This can be used to extend cultural studies and add objective research techniques consistent with its agenda.

A quick three-step thought experiment illustrates the definition of *cultural identity* as "the demonstration of values in context":

- Imagine a person or a group which displays a strong cultural identity.
- Write down three attributes which will identify them.
- Note that you have described three demonstrations of their values in context.

Cultural Identity

Our cultural identity changes in strength and content with the changing contexts in which we find ourselves in time, in place, in knowledge and in emotion (Edwards 2009, 20; Fong 2004, 19–20). For example, we are likely to display different values in formal contexts than we do in informal contexts. Yet, overall, we may retain an overarching set of values that tends to determine our behaviour. So, for instance, although we might display the values of a parent in one context and the values of a spouse or a lover in a different context, overall we display to different extents the values influenced by our sex, class, religion and nationality. The level of generality or specificity with which the researcher finds it useful to consider cultural identity semantically parallels the generality and specificity of the contexts encompassed by his or her research. If our researcher were interested in gender or generational differences in cultural identity, then values of men would be compared with those of women and values of the young would be compared with those of the older generation. The researcher might even explore how cultural identity in the context of wealth – the cultural identity of the wealthy – might be instrumentally different from cultural identity in the context of poverty – the cultural identity of the poor – for male or female, for young or old. Thus, culturometrics sees demographic/organismic categories, which often become our independent variables, as redefinable contexts in which we display our values. Our cultural identity can change in different contexts because our values can change when we are in differently defined contexts.

It can be seen that a more generalized cultural identity, like being Trinidadian, will comprise component cultural identities such as those observed mostly by displays of Indian values, African values and Anglo-American values (Boufoy-Bastick 2009a, 2009b). These composite cultural identities come to the fore and recede into the background as they become relevant to the current context. For example, Trinidadians who self-identify as mixed race based on their inherited stereotypic body types, commonly identify more as Indo-Trinidadian or as Afro-Trinidadian at election time. This is also an example of how our changeable values are better predictors of our behaviour in that context than are the immutable categories of ethnicity, age or gender.

Changing Cultural Identities

The defining concern of culturometrics is the freedom to change who we are rather than to be forever contained by neoliberal options (Gilbert 2012) or other sociocultural stereotypes by whomever and for whatever purposes these socio-cultural stereotypes exist. It is at this point of identity fluidity (Chuang 2004, 51–52) and flux that culturometrics' concerns are also those of cultural studies.

An illustration of how culturometrics is defined by concern for individual freedom to change and modify cultural identity will also illustrate how culturometrics extends cultural studies beyond its traditional group categories and issues of conflict and power relations. In particular, culturometrics' concern for the dynamics of cultural identity determines its own typology of cultural groups. Culturometrics classifies cultural groups according to the freedom group members have to change their group cultural identity, that is according to the rigidity/flexibility of group determination – how open to change are their criteria for group membership – along the continuum from the most immutably fixed to the most flexibly self-determined. Three generic types of cultural groups are the following:

1. Groups that are to some significant extent physically determined ; for example, ethnic, racial, gender and age groups, and groups with congenital and developmental illnesses. It is very difficult indeed for these group members to change their group cultural identity because of structural determination of membership.

2. Socially determined groups; for example, unmarried mothers, the poor/wealthy and employment groups (e.g., students, teachers, nurses). It is

difficult for these group members to change their group cultural identity because of sociocultural enforcements of group determination.

3. Self-selected groups; for example, gangs, clubs, loyalty groups (e.g., brand customers, fans). Although often challenging, it is the least difficult for these group members to change their group cultural identity because such group determinations can be unlearned.

The Culturometric Perspective: Linguistic Reframing Construct as Identity

The very partial enumeration of each of the three generic types of cultural groups illustrates a far greater range than is typified by traditional issues addressed by cultural studies. What extends this definition to a much larger range of cultural groups is the reversal of a linguistic trend, particularly in English. This linguistic trend limits how we think about research methods, causation and relationships. It does so by nominalizing process, often for the emotional security of increasing our perceived control. For example, education is a complex individual process of change in behaviour, cognition and resulting relationships. When it is nominalized, we think of it as an object that is more within our control. For example, "He couldn't afford to get a Harvard education so he got his education from MSU." In this fashionable parlance the meanings of education have been circumscribed to that of an object, an object that might be bought at a particular locality – or even online. Thinking in nominalizations can reduce the humanity of our research. For example, research on objects privileges control, as is more pertinent to the sciences, whereas research on process privileges relationships, as is more pertinent to the humanities. In this respect, a research project with the nominalized title "Effects of Depression in Female Authors" promises to be very different from a research project with the equivalent process title "Writings of Women Who Are Depressed". Culturo-metrics reverses this linguistic trend by perceiving the usually nominalized researched construct as a contextualized role expressed as a person's cultural identity. Thus, *education in a person* is reconceptualized as an *identity/role of an educated person*, a role that we know by observing demonstrations *in situ* of that person's educated values. Similarly, *depression in a female author* is reconceptualized as an *identity/role of a depressed woman writer* that we know by observing demonstrations of her depressed values – her values in her context of depression. So, each of the multifarious constructs to be researched is construed through the culturometric lens as perceived values in context. Cultural identities can be observed through demonstrations of people's values in the contexts of how they define the construct. Hence, subjective cultural identity can be objectively measured to the extent that these demonstrations of values can be objectively measured. We next address possible confusions that seem to arise when researchers contemplate the objective measurement of intrasubjectivities such as shared cultural identities.

Objective Research Process versus Subjective Research Content

Culturometrics brings the rigour of scientific or objective research methodology to subject areas, such as literary theory (Eagleton 1996, 106) and cultural studies (Baldwin et al. 2004, 41), so profoundly epitomized by their inextricably rich and indefinable intrasubjectivities.

Objectivity is basically what can be confirmed, for example, by the agreement of observers who experience the same thing; whereas *subjectivity* cannot be so confirmed, usually because the same subjectivity cannot be sufficiently experienced by many observers. An example of objective fact is an individual's weight. This measurement can be confirmed by other observers who see the same reading as the person on the scale. An example of subjectivity is how one feels about what one weighs. We cannot tell whether the observers watching someone on the scale can experience exactly what that other person feels inside and so be in a position to confirm that feeling. It is most probable that no one can exactly know another's inner pains and pleasures.

It is interesting that there are limitations to the value of objective situations for significant research. This is because we all can know about them relatively easily by simple observation. The research on objective situations is usually a faithful counting or recording of observations. In contrast, subjective situations do make for significant research although we do not have the research tools to completely unveil their mysteries. As Probyn observes in the 2007 Working Papers of the Centre for Contemporary Cultural Studies, however, "we have yet to rebuild a method of research that effectively grasps networks of human inter- and intra-subjectivity" (p. 432). We can never completely know the emic subjectivity of another, for we are not them. Research communications, however, endeavour to evince our professional understandings through veracious experience adduced by various interpretations of symbolic representations of these subjectivities (Bottero, 2010). Culturometrics is only a facilitator of applied research to uncover our intrasubjectivities. It objectively identifies and measures subjectivities that cannot be completely known so that, having identified them, researchers can enquire further into their meanings, their causes and how they change. Examples of these mixed-methods approaches – qualitative and quantitative – are described in other chapters. In this chapter, we note only that it is a misconception that one must understand a construct before one can measure it – as noted by Campbell, Converse and Rodgers (1976), who remarked that the insertion of subjective indicators draws criticism from some observers because they are "soft" measures and "we do not know what they mean" (p. 475). In fact, one need only be able to recognise a construct in order to measure it.

Empowering Our Research Subjects: Getting from the "Who I Am" to "Who We Are"

Thus far, we have considered the cultural identity of individuals and the cultural identity of groups. Here we simply explain the most parsimonious system dynamics of group membership/exclusion and associated objective measures of social distance/proximity.

In culturometrics the unit of analysis is the cultural identity of the individual person. Hence, unlike traditional research methods that focus on the properties of measurement instruments (R-methods), culturometric research methods always retain information on an individual's values in context (Q-methods). We can see from practical examples in the culturometric literature how this plays out in the design and development of particular research enquiries, for example, how we can understand the cultural identity of groups as a negotiated consensus of group members' individual cultural identities (Boufoy-Bastick 2009b, 369–71). Thus, group change is effected through commensurate changes in cultural identities of individual members. From this postmodernist perspective of culturometrics, group cultural identity is a *social constructivist* construct and individual cultural identity is a *radical constructivist* construct. More explicitly, cultural identity is "an aggregate of individual, group and ethnic identity development, construction and negotiation . . . shaped by complex inter-related sociocultural influences" (Boufoy-Bastick 2007, 369–71). We might note in passing that the positivist/constructivist schism is but an unsubstantiated denial that positivism is just another socially constructed construct. Thus, culturometrics defines and measures cultural identity relative to self-expectation (self-normed) and is grounded in group values. However, to measure changes in group membership and exclusion, for example, to compare in-group and out-group perspectives, we can choose to ground identity in the values of the member group or in the values of another group. A joint significance of this applied philosophy to the shared aims of culturometrics and cultural studies is the resulting cultural empowerment of our research subjects in defining and authenticating their own identities – they own the truth of who they are.

Dynamics of Cultural Change

The central agenda of culturometrics is facilitating self-determined change in cultural identity. Its methods of measuring cultural identity – profile differences and changes in primary identity components – can validate that specific factors constrain or drive the dynamics of cultural change. If our research is to make this difference, then we had best target change agents of enculturation and bricolage. In particular, whereas *enculturation* drives the ontogeny of individual cultural identity (Geertz and Jensen 2011) from a socio-anthropological perspective, it is *bricolage* that best describes the most usual processes of contact-driven cultural identity change for individuals in multicultural societies. In multiethnic diasporic societies like Trinidad, cultural identity is changed by interethnic mixing and cultural borrowing of selected behaviours and their associated values, which make the traditional nominal categories of ethnicity unreliable indicators of cultural identity and poor predictors of preferred behaviours (Boufoy-Bastick 2002a, 2002b).

Artistic and therapeutic practice-based research of any significant kind acts, as do education and experimental treatment, to engage participants as bricoleurs in a research experience that attempts to change who they are, their temporary and perhaps permanent cultural identities. (See, for example, Reiss 2002, chs. 7–11.) Consider Finn, Jacobson and Campana's example: "The practice of popular theater is, in effect, a practice of bricolage. Participants literally sculpt their vision of existing realities and possible alternatives. Drawing from the collective wisdom of the group, they reframe problems and possibilities and create new meanings from the resources at hand" (2004, 339). Culturometrics then directly validates the success of this practice-based research experience by measuring pre–post changes in the targeted components of participants' cultural identities – changes in their values wrought by the experience engineered by the practice-based researcher. Walcott poetically describes the power of bricolage to affect our values in context, as discussed by David Lowenthal:

> The West Indian Nobel laureate Derek Walcott lauds the process of bricolage that commingled Caribbean legacies once derided as broken. "Break a vase, and the love that reassembles the fragments is stronger than that love which took its symmetry for granted when it was whole. It is such a love that reassembles our African and Asiatic fragments, the cracked heirloom whose restoration shows its white scars. This shipwreck of fragments, these echoes, these shards of a huge tribal vocabulary, these partially remembered customs" are living traditions in polyglot Afro-Indo-Euro-American cities like Port of Spain [Walcott 1993, 69]. Exclusivity is crucial to identity – and to cherished difference. We must cosset our own heritage, or we cease to be ourselves. But we can never keep ourselves to ourselves, hold the outside world at bay. No heritage was ever purely native or wholly endemic; today's are utterly scrambled. Purity is a chimera; we are all Creoles. Heritage health lies in accepting the medley as a creative advance over what purists would uphold. (2000, 21–22)

The Historical Imperatives:
Why We Need Culturometrics Now

We have inherited two main problems with the use of traditional instrument-based research methods, particularly with multicultural groups. One is that different people use their different expectations to interpret and reply to questions, which gives us subjective data that we cannot correctly use to make comparisons. The second, related problem is that in modern culturally diverse societies we cannot objectively know the meaning of our results because we have no norm group with which to authentically compare them.

An example will illustrate the problem of cultural bias: In health research, a most notoriously misleading research question is to ask people to judge how healthy they are on a five-point Likert scale which ranges from very unhealthy to very healthy. When their subjective judgements are checked against objective medical measures, we find that people's subjective judgements tend to be unreliable. That is, the most healthy people rate themselves as very unhealthy and those who are unhealthy tend to rate themselves as healthy. This is because healthy people tend to have higher expectations for their own health than do less healthy people. Consequently, these more stringent values depress their subjective responses, whereas the reverse is the case with less healthy people (Salomon, Tandon and Murray 2004). The most common expectation biases are culturally situated; that is, group members make subjective judgements using the shared cultural values of their group. So, for example, representative subjective judgements of acuity of vision are higher in China than in Finland, although objective optical examinations show that the reverse is true. Similarly, subjective evaluations of political freedom are higher in China than in Mexico, whereas government restrictions point to the reverse. The lack of specificity in these subjective judgements, as Gary King argues, "provides an insufficiently precise means of understanding" (1993, 400). However, these expectation biases disappear if we interview only people who have the same expectations or if we use culturometrics to allow for these biases. Then we would get the expected result validated by objective measures.

To illustrate the norm group problem, if we wanted to objectively identify men who have long arms, we would traditionally measure the length of their arms and use norm tables to see how far above or below the mean male arm length these measurements fall. We would conclude that a man has long arms if his arm length were more than some defined cut-off point above the norm group mean. This was fine before increased globalization brought recognition of enhanced cultural diversity. Now, we are no longer so culturally homogeneous that we can blithely assume a person is represented by a published norm group. This traditional process tells us only whether his arms are long compared to the published norm group. If the norm group were Pygmies – Pygmy men average 137 centimetres (4 feet 6 inches) in height – we might conclude that he had long arms. If the norm group were Tutsi – men average about 183 centimetres (six feet) in height – then perhaps we would conclude that he had short arms. In contrast, culturometrics refers to the person as his or her own norm. So we might use the arm length in relation to another body length such as height. Because the same growth process is responsible for both lengths, the ratio tells us about that individual's growth process. If the ratio is large, then the person has long arms. If the ratio is small, then the person has short arms. This culturometric notion of self-norming is characterized by the icon of da Vinci's *Vitruvian Man*, as shown in figure 3.1, and is common to all the family of culturometric methods and techniques shown in figure 3.2, which are applied by culturometrics to the objective measurement of intrasubjectivities such as cultural identity.

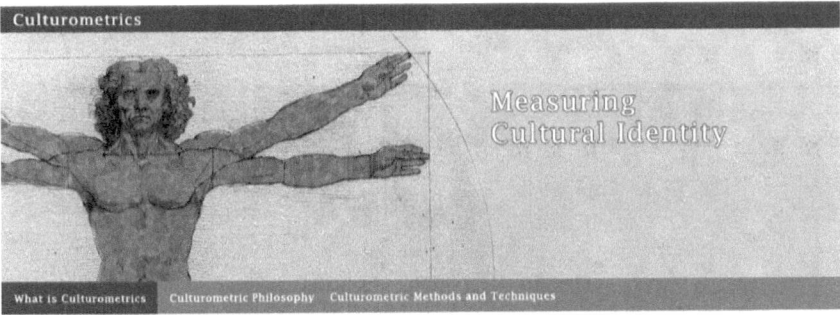

Figure 3.1 Representation of culturometric self-norming – Leonardo da Vinci's *Vitruvian Man*
Source: Adapted from the culturometric website, http://www.culturometrics.org.

Today, after more than half a century of exponentially increasing cultural mixing, nearly all regional urban population groups and most regional rural population groups exhibit very different cultural values. These cultural expectations are now so heterogeneous that we can no longer ignore them and invalidly continue to use instrument-based analysis to compare respondents' subjective judgements or use "foreign" norm groups to qualify and position individuals. This is particularly so in the field of cultural studies, which seeks to understand the very cultural differences that invalidate traditional research methods.

The Culturometric Family of Research Methods and Techniques

A major contribution culturometrics brings to the appreciation and enhancement of sociocultural diversity is an ever-growing family of empowering and objective methods and techniques facilitating cultural research. These methods regulate personal expectancies so that rich subjective information can be validly compared within and across cultural groups.

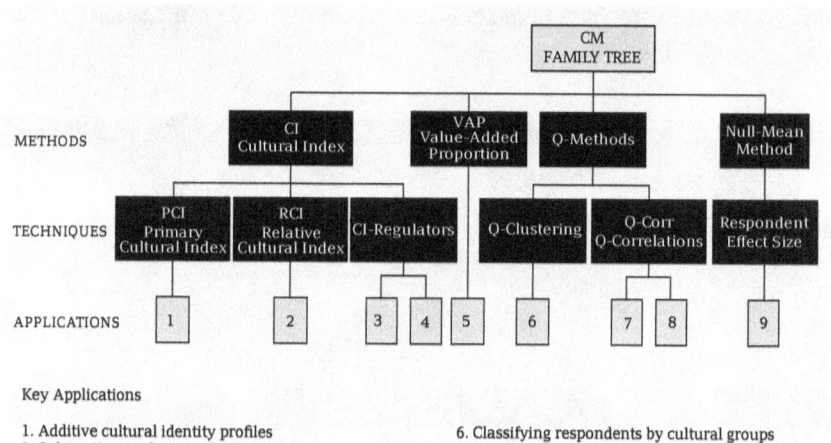

Key Applications

1. Additive cultural identity profiles
2. Subtractive prediction of cultural behaviours
3. Data cleaning – identifying consistent value respondents
4. Defining, norming and screening cultural identity
5. Questionnaire fatigue
6. Classifying respondents by cultural groups
7. State/trait proportions
8. Data cleaning – identifying reliable respondents
9. Respondent stress effect size

Figure 3.2 The culturometric family of research methods and techniques

The common key to this growing family of methods is that, rather than being based on classical response theory and instrument psychometrics to standardize a person to some foreign norm, each person is compared to his or her own personal standards, which are then grounded in the consensus values of their cultural group.

Culturometrics continues to develop this family of intuitively acceptable humanistic methods and techniques based on individual cultural identity – the demonstration of values in context.

Chapter 4

Discourse and Caribbean Criticism

Barbara Lalla and Valerie Youssef

Language analysis is crucial to the interpretation of literary and other discourse, but it is especially important in the Caribbean, where writing and speech are especially marked by regional linguistic characteristics. These are still in the process of being adequately described and validated, and the intermixing of language varieties in individual and societal codes is ordered even in the extent of its diversity (e.g., Youssef, 1996).

Literary and nonliterary discourses differ in their social, cultural and linguistic dimensions. *Social* and *cultural dimensions* encompass value systems and ways of knowing that form the context in which speakers and listeners or writers and readers interact, while *linguistic dimensions* express those value systems and ways of knowing and may be selected for their ideological implicature. In analysing literary discourse for structure, theme, genre and so forth, linguistic information must usually be complemented by contextual information to derive meaning and arrive at interpretation. The voice represented as speaking in a variety of Caribbean Creoles may be more effective than the voice represented as speaking standard English, since in the Caribbean context this Creole voice (readily perceived as the authentic voice of the man in the street) lends itself to undermining the status quo.

Caribbean literature should be informed by an understanding of Caribbean language and read in the framework of the Caribbean language situation. So, for example, Karen Sanderson-Cole pays close attention to lexical semantics in examining the Caribbean popular romance (2003) as she discusses ideological implications of expression in dialogue and narrative. Also, Caribbean criticism of other literature has been informed by Caribbean experience and values, by our "way of knowing". Thus Michelle Harricharan's study "Culture Collision and Hybridity in Selected Works of J.R.R. Tolkien" (2008) is informed by Caribbean experience and scholarship on cultural contact, on linguistic encounter and on resistance to imperial oppression.

Similarly, in the field of media and political discourse, we cannot merely expect norms established in Western metropolitan countries to resurface in the Caribbean but must assess them carefully to establish whether they fit the postcolonial Caribbean experience. Recently a graduate student examined media representation of the first female prime minister of Trinidad and Tobago for significant differences from representations of First World female politicians. Another is focusing his research on newspaper editorials concerning a political feud between the former prime minister of Trinidad and Tobago, Patrick Manning, and his rival, Dr Keith Rowley. How far can the depiction of this feud find common ground with such debates in much longer-established nation states? Are the stakes not different, the ideological underpinnings of democracy more or less sullied by time?

Text and Discourse

In the examples above, then, the term *discourse* covers different genres. Distinctions between the use of the terms *text* and *discourse* vary widely, often with a loose association of *text* with writing and of *discourse* with speech. The term *discourse* is usually applied to the broad range of media, professional, political and everyday language which is sometimes delivered in speech and sometimes in writing but which is most often analysed in writing. The phrase *textual analysis* is widely used in referring to the examination of literary works specifically. There are, however, other ways of distinguishing text from discourse.

Text and discourse (considered free of the labels *written* and *spoken* respectively), each constitute a linguistic unit larger than a sentence. A *text* is often defined as having its own integrity and definable significance, a unit that can be decoded in order to derive meaning. Ultimately, however, the text gathers meaning if placed in a particular linguistic context. When a text is contextualized in this way it becomes a discourse. Alternatively, any discourse might produce a text that is observable as an independent unit of expression. Within the field of discourse analysis, however, a subfield called conversational analysis is similarly constrained to textual analysis: it claims that all the meaning to be derived from the conversation can be obtained from its immediate form with no reference to external information.

Thus the concept of the text may nowadays be extended to shared social realms seen as artefacts with their own integrity. However, because most real-world discourse is conceived of as involving contextual influence, as a unit of language subject to external shaping and capable of multiple influence, the application of the concept *discourse* to social situations is somewhat different from the application of the concept *text* – more malleable, more inclusive. It is possible to speak of legal discourse as a discourse type defined by a domain, of children's literature as a genre defined by its audience and of patriarchal discourse as a mode defined by power distribution. Thus, intertextuality, the complex way in which one text interacts with and is informed by other texts, is important to discursive analysis, as any discourse depends for its effect on the receivers being able to recognize and respond to intertextual referencing. Derek Walcott's *Pantomime* (1980), for example, responds to Daniel Defoe's *Robinson Crusoe* ([1719] 1983).

Because discourse is language in use by real human beings for actual purposes, its strict analysis must go beyond linguistic analysis that disregards context and function, so linguists regard the production of discourse as a social act and recognize that written discourse scribally represents this act.

In one approach to analysing the literary text as autonomous, meaning is considered to reside in the words, syntactic arrangements and idioms that appear in the text, but it is impossible to mark off idioms from their cultural context. Another approach lies in the assumption that words can be related to relatively few fixed meanings (as defined in a dictionary), but dictionary compilation and updating is so time consuming as to render full representation of word meaning in actual use impracticable and almost impossible. Each word has an individual experiential meaning for each reader. In the Caribbean, where words may differ in meaning from their English sense (e.g., the word *ignorant*, meaning "angry") or even differ in meaning from one territory to another, the differences (English and Caribbean) may be played on in ways difficult to isolate and separate from contextual information.

The interactions between the text and circumstances beyond it or the interactions between writer and speaker or between reader and listener with each other or with circumstances surrounding the text or with aspects of the text itself – reconfigure that *text* to a discourse resting critically on intertextual and interdiscursive understandings. Inevitably, as noted above, reader involvement in construction of the discourse requires an inferencing beyond direct decoding of the text.

Literary texts are self-sufficient in contrast with nonliterary texts, which are located in real-world circumstances, in social situations from which these nonliterary texts cannot be isolated. Literary texts carry all these circumstances within themselves, explicitly or implicitly. At the same time, literary texts – however vividly they contain their created realities that constitute social contexts for their invented participants – themselves are products of external realities. The biographical details of their writers and the sociocultural phenomena that frame their creations constitute the *contexts* that transform the creative texts to discourses.

In interpreting the literary text, the reader infers significance of a *discourse*, entering into a dynamic connection with the material. In this sense a graduate researcher might interact with J.R.R. Tolkien's discourse in bringing to his texts a postmodern and postcolonial experience of cultural interface (Harricharan 2008). *Discourse* as language in use, associated with *parole* rather than *langue*, is in many ways a more productive concept for the literary work than *text*. As discourse, literature can be viewed (in keeping with current trends in literary theory) as unstable, revisionary, transactional and communicative. Literature can be viewed as socially transformative.

Approaches to Analysis of Discourse

Stylistics investigates text through analysis of language and of how language functions in the text, but it also looks beyond the text to see how the language functions in relation to extralinguistic features, a context-sensitive approach. *Literary linguistics* focuses on texts that adhere to recognizable forms associated with a literary genre. Some literary linguistics functions yet more specifically as *linguistic criticism*, analysing the language of literature for the purpose of critical interpretation using linguistic analysis as a tool.

Applying linguistic analysis to literary interpretation involves give and take on both sides. The text must be examined not only as an object of (literary) study but as a unit within a (linguistic) system. The text may be selected not only from an existing (literary) canon but from any source deemed likely to provide reliable (linguistic) data and has to be evaluated not only by applying traditional literary criteria but empirically, as the data prompts. Linguistic data draws on utterances in the real world or, in the case of literary discourse, draws on utterances framed in invented worlds.

Linguistic rules are generalized theoretically on the basis of an ideal speaker producing language as an abstract system devoid of context, but sociolinguistics is crucially concerned with contexts of production. Hymes (1972) makes an unmatchable case for the importance of communicative rather than linguistic competence, the capacity to shift one's speech style according to contextual features of the situation at hand. Similarly, creative authors select styles according to contextual factors for narrator, characters or personae. The critic who applies linguistic or discourse analysis to the literary work must be prepared to satisfy the requirements of both disciplines. Current research on the language of Samuel Selvon's fiction, for example, must integrate discourse analysis and sociolinguistic theory with postcolonial criticism (see Mah-Chamberlain in progress).

So analysis should address all levels of description (phonological, morphological, syntactic, lexical, semantic and pragmatic) in seeking verifiable conclusions. Yet interpretation may not be fixed but open to shifting, alternating, multiple and even contradictory conclusions. The analysis should demonstrate how the language of the text operates in its (stated) context to facilitate such ambiguity or contradiction.

Bringing together more closely linguistic and socio-political theories, critical discourse analysis (CDA) focuses especially on how power is enacted through discourse, how ideology is represented and how social variables (e.g., gender or ethnicity) are constructed for the reader from the ideological perspective of the writer. CDA treats discourse (language that is in use in a text under definable circumstances) as social practice and analyses it as such. It works largely with political and media speeches, but it can usefully be applied to literature. Power, as defined by Foucault, is a "net-like organization which weaves itself discursively through social organizations, meanings, relations and the construction of speakers' subjectivities or identities. . . . Individuals are always . . . simultaneously undergoing and exercising this power" (1980, 98). Because CDA deals with the ways in which power, dominance, abuse and even manipulation are enacted through discourse, its primary domains are media and politics, and it has been used extensively by researchers such as Norman Fairclough (e.g., 1989, 1992, 1995) and Teun van Dijk (e.g., 2000a, 2000b) to interrogate these domains of European discourse.

However, the possibilities of CDA are manifold. It analyses language to reveal ideologies represented in the discourse and opinions presented as if they are fact or authoritative when they are mere viewpoints. Writers of fiction presenting their own perspective on the world or representing those of others are also products of their times and political systems and may be similarly interrogated. Postcolonial readings of colonial fiction apply CDA in the sense that they unmask the colonialist imperative implicit in the discourse of such writers as E.M. Forster or Daniel Defoe, whose works came to compose a canon through which cultural supremacy could be entrenched. Because CDA has been applied to real-world politics primarily, the term has so far not been much used in literature, but its techniques have been applied and the field is wide open for such studies. It assumes, however, that power resides most saliently with government and the empowered, and it does not deal with the way in which the oppressed may assert themselves through discursive means also.

Poststructuralist discourse analysis (PSDA) establishes this and thus has much to contribute to literary study as well as to the fields of education and management, where it has most recently been applied (Baxter 2003). PSDA challenges the binary thinking implicit in CDA and is concerned with the multiple voices that may be raised within any discursive context. The "them" and "us" of van Dijk's ideological square (1998) is not fixed but may be redefined by the traditionally oppressed, who may themselves emerge as empowered. Baxter argues that it differs from CDA in that it is a "more complex perception of the ambiguities and unevenness of power" (2003, 55); taking a specifically feminist stance, she argues that, while CDA might "polarize males as villains and females as victims", feminist PSDA would argue that females are multiply located. Women, like other less-enfranchised groups, have the potential to overturn their traditionally perceived roles as victims. It has been possible to interrogate Haitian women's narratives of their experience using this per-spective, for example, to show that, in the very act of describing the extreme oppression to which they have been subjected, these women also describe their diverse ways of overcoming this oppression through mutual support, through creative acts of different kinds and through their belief systems (Morgan and Youssef 2006, 101–27). This approach can be applied to fiction as well as to nonfiction.

Oral and Scribal Discourse

Despite the frequent association of text with writing and discourse with speech, then, texts may exist in a variety of media while discourse (as language in use and as text in context) may be spoken or written.

Caribbean linguistics has given us an approach to linguistic description which respects the integrity of oral Creole language in its own right. It has established incontrovertibly that Creoles are linguistically rule-governed systems and so must be analysed as seriously as other languages. Further, linguistics recognizes that oral discourse is primal and that writing systems are merely based on speech and in that sense are representational to begin with. Code shifts between Creoles and standards and varieties in between reflect significant shifts in perspective, and code-switching can be analysed for its ideological implications in both oral and written discourse. In addition to depicting and describing Caribbean Creoles as integral to Caribbean literary discourse, Caribbean linguists and writers have paid considerable attention to code-switching as defining speakers (e.g., Youssef, 1996) and fictional charac-ters respectively (e.g., Lalla 1998b).

Oral discourse remains in many ways focused on the exterior circum-stances of which it is a part, rather than interiorized to the same degree as scribal discourse. So the oral performance is communal, and may even be sacral; it engages and prompts interactivity. This openness contrasts with the closure and relative autonomy of scribal discourse. Oral discourse must carry along its audience and so adopts mnemonic devices, like repetition or formulaic expression, and employs sound effects, such as rhythm, alliteration and so forth.

Because oral discourse addresses its audience directly, it is often framed in the vernacular. Performance poets and storytellers like Louise Bennett and Paul Keens-Douglas deliver their verse and prose in Caribbean Creole varieties and represent this oral voice in writing. Indeed writing usually precedes the oral performance, and there is much movement between varieties of English and Creole. Jean D'Costa's (1984) study of variation in the expression of Miss Lou (Bennett's speaking persona) applies linguistic analysis to the written version of her oral performance. On the other hand, scribal discourse is not so limited to a particular time or location and is expected to be more widely and permanently applicable. Access to it also depends on some level of education, so scribal discourse is often expected to be in an official and widely known form of the language, the form associated with education. In the Caribbean, English was, therefore, traditionally the expected code for written discourse.

The official form of a language is not, however, the only form expected in literature. Dialogue in nonstandard varieties of language is common, often for characterization and setting. In Shakespeare's *Henry V*, Emily Brontë's *Wuthering Heights*, Charles Dickens's *A Tale of Two Cities* and J.R.R. Tolkien's *The Hobbit*, nonstandard English is drawn on for the voices of particular characters. In Caribbean literature, representation of the vernacular offers a particular challenge, the vernacular being a Creole that is linguistically distinct from English. This Creole, however, contributes to the branding of the literature as Caribbean. Growing interest in the work of Nalo Hopkinson, for example, in *Midnight Robber* (2000), must thus take into account her representation of Caribbeanness through an amalgamation of not only cultural but linguistic attributes of different territories.

A literature is defined in many ways, one criterion being a sense of an "authentic" voice of a people. In contemplating authenticity in so complex a situation, one may not only link regional or national discourse with identity but associate "authenticity" in the Caribbean voice with a dissonance that reflects multiple and even conflictual identities (cf. Hall and du Gay 1992, 277). Maureen Warner-Lewis's analysis of social and situational language variation in Selvon's fiction ([1984] 2003) demonstrates the crucial part played by linguistic representation in conveying such complex and fluid identity (see also Le Page and Tabouret-Keller 1985).

The use of Creole today in literary texts has grown beyond an early impulse to convey the exotic and subsequent inclinations to realism, gathering force through a disobedience to traditional rules (see Lalla 2005). Though it still presents challenges, the representation of the Creole voice in fiction has now been well crafted by its own speakers, such as Samuel Selvon and Merle Collins, and has achieved a marked level of authenticity despite the challenges of appealing and being legible to metropolitan markets. Barbara Lalla's study of narrative attitude in Hopkinson examines a new departure in linguistic disobedience – the revision of the Caribbean voice through construction of a pan-Caribbean Creole as distinct from a representation of speech in a specific territory and through a silencing of the non-Caribbean voice (Lalla, forthcoming). At the same time, as writers represent the Creole to signal the Caribbean voice as closely as they can (though, often, not closely at all) without impairing comprehension, ambivalence arises as to code selection. Such choices of representation are therefore politically fraught.

The various types of analysis alluded to in this section should, overall, give the researcher a solid basis from which to begin to establish a frame for text and discourse analysis. Ultimately the choice of a particular approach depends on the kind of data to be analysed as well as the ideological perspective which frames it.

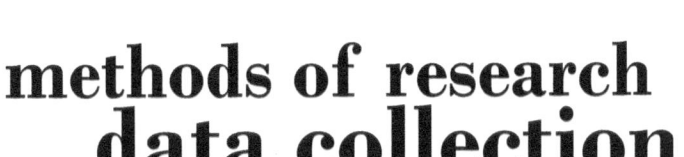

methods of research
data collection

Chapter 5

Fieldwork and Data Collection

Valerie Youssef, Paula Morgan and Barbara Lalla

Fieldwork

Valerie Youssef

Fieldwork – gathering information in the real world – is the essence of most good research, even that which superficially might not appear to require it. It is equivalent to "getting the hands dirty" in disciplines like engineering and agriculture for it is the practical real-world encounter in humanities research without which an individual's research may seem conceived in an ivory tower, irrelevant to real-world contexts. In the humanities, fieldwork means collecting data from others rather than relying on one's own intuitions. It is of critical importance to the Caribbean because in the past so much was recorded from the perspective of the colonizer, with the native Caribbean person having no voice or one that was so distorted as to be made ludicrous. The ascription of voice and the inclination to let that voice speak for itself are all the more imperative today.

Because it can be time consuming, necessitating repetition and recalibration of interviews, recordings and the like, fieldwork is often avoided. Researchers may prevail upon assistants to do the fieldwork to relieve themselves of it, when it is only that first-hand experience which can bring reality to the research project as a whole. We have come to a time when interviews in the field are more often video recorded than merely audio recorded, but still a researcher's absence is not advisable, since any questions that may arise for the informant(s) or the primary researcher may remain unanswered and – even more important – the researcher will not experience the interviewee's real-world context personally.

Fieldwork in the humanities may be secondary or primary to the research aims of the investigator. If interview data or live recordings of interactive situations are being collected for discourse analysis purposes, then obviously it is the crux of the research. If a researcher is building a profile of an individual with profound cultural influence in the Caribbean region, then interviews are equally important, both of the individual and of those close to him or her. If one is examining a process, say the development of steel pan, interviews of practitioners and instrument makers are also extremely important.

It may be only in the field of literary studies, whether textual or film, that the need for fieldwork or data collection beyond the text(s) to be studied may come into question. A student beginning research may even opt for literature in the hope that research may be carried out in an armchair by reading texts with the help of prior critiques, without any interface with the real world. Everything is there in the book or the film or in criticisms thereof. Why do more? But most literary and film studies benefit from individual interventions in the field, whether these involve interviewing the writers or producers thereof, interviewing those around them or even verifying the background situations that the texts speak to by visiting the areas identified and examining the reality out of which the text was constructed.

A study of diasporic women's writing is substantially enhanced by interviewing its authors with regard to their motives and experiences in writing the Caribbean from outside the region, as well as with regard to their definitions of Caribbeanness. A graduate researcher, for example, might interview Marlene NourbeSe-Philip for insight into the perspective of the diasporic writer (Moise, in progress). NourbeSe-Philip herself engaged in extensive data collection to produce *Zong!* (2008) not only through archival research into the legal case surrounding the Zong massacre but through forensic anthropology, through Internet research and through a journey to Ghana in 2006. Both critic and artist benefit from serious fieldwork.

Field methods may be as invaluable to creative writers as to discourse analysts. This is immediately apparent in the case of travel writing, that of V.S. Naipaul being an obvious example (as in [1981] 1998, 2010). Less obviously, accurate field observation underlies most creative writing informally and, perhaps, unconsciously. But such observation is often consciously applied. In her novels of the maturing girl in the developing nation, Merle Hodge (1993) based her portrayal of primary school education on actual experience. In building characters and setting in *Arch of Fire*, Barbara Lalla (1998) visited a mental hospital, consulted a member of a field expedition in Jamaica's Cockpit Country, interviewed and analysed records of interviews with elderly Jamaicans who had experienced the Kingston earthquake in 1907, worked with an elderly informant to observe characteristics of Chinese Jamaican speech and revisited parts of the island for close observation. For research in which texts or files are historical, some archival work may be necessary to build up as realistically as possible the factual circumstances surrounding the text under study. Verification of detail can be particularly important.

Again, in order to write on the intense social–psychological problems engendered by the ways in which diverse societies and institutions are dealing with the HIV/AIDS epidemic, the researcher may gather material to produce a novel such as Jamaica Kincaid's *My Brother* (1997) or Lawrence Scott's *Aelred's Sin* (1998) or, alternatively, may set up a focus group consisting of persons who have lost a family member to the disease and have them discuss what it has been like to deal with their loved one's suffering and loss within a culture of silence, taboo and shame. Talking with persons who are currently coping with the condition as well will doubly enrich the study (cf. Skeete 2007).

Fieldwork has a variety of constraints upon it, both ethical and practical, particularly when it involves recording. It has long been considered morally wrong to record individuals or groups without their knowledge and consent. However, when the interviewee is aware of recording, a researcher is confronted with what Labov (1966) describes as the *observer's paradox*: that an individual's most normative or natural speech is the object of investigation, but the very process of recording militates against achieving naturalness, for, once a recording device is introduced, the informant becomes inhibited. Researchers have tried to overcome this problem in a variety of ways, including making surreptitious recordings and only subsequently informing the persons recorded and requesting their permission. This may succeed or may be met with anger. For a study of participant observation in minor gambling activity, specifically playing fruit machines, it was felt that the gamblers in question would be hostile to interviewing since their activity was not regarded as socially acceptable and might even have breached their concerns for privacy.

Consequently, the researchers positioned themselves in a gambling arcade, as participant gamblers or members of staff with whom regular gamblers became familiar. In this way, they could carry out the research effectively "under cover". This was not ethically acceptable, though it might have yielded useful information. The research infringed the real-world privacy of persons observed in a covert and hence dishonest way. It is essential to find a balance. The simple answer is to get permission beforehand for any observation or interview and to consider beginning the recording some way into the observed activity when those present are comfortable with the situation.

From a practical perspective, it is important to make some working plan for an interview, and this is essential if the main researcher is not planning to be present for the event. It is useless to come away from an extended period of talking with someone, only to discover that the questions which needed answering were perhaps asked but never answered. A clear focus, some pre-pared questions and the moral and logical sensibilities to find ways of soliciting information without breaching privacy boundaries is much needed. This is discussed in detail in the section of this chapter on the literary interview.

With regard to ethical considerations, should there be any potentially pri-vate information divulged, the interviewer should share the manuscript with the informant before publishing it and obtain permission to do so. The use of a clear and explicit consent form signed before an interview or recording takes place is most useful. It is important in the case of disempowered subgroups in society to consider advocacy on behalf of the group. Studies which describe the rules of a nonstandard language variety, for example, have been used in courts of law to establish educational discrimination practices (Labov 1980). Taking this a step further, researchers may actively involve interviewees, allowing them to speak for themselves and indeed create their own research questions. It may be possible to play recordings back for interviewees and ask for their commentary on what they hear and experience as they listen. All these considerations can only enrich the data set.

Much research in the social sciences and in linguistics is undertaken in a broadly ethnographic framework, and a most popular current means of data collection is participant observation, being introduced to a societal grouping by some "friend of a friend" mechanism, to better ease one's naturalistic absorption into the group. In Jenny Cheshire's (1982) study of youth language in Reading in the United Kingdom, she became a part of the group, buying a motorbike and joining them for three months before saying that she needed to collect their language. William Labov's (1972) research on the vernacular of young African American speakers benefited tremendously from his using an interviewer who was a member of that community.

Ethnography is the source of most anthropological investigation (Boas and Stocking 1974); in its fullest sense, it entails investigating whole cultures by immersing oneself within them for extended periods of time and describing societies in their own terms and according to their own value systems. It was recognized in the early twentieth century that individuals with a Western or "First World" view initially impose their own view and values on what they observe in a very different and materially less-developed society and that such bias is undesirable. By immersion in the culture for an extended period of time, and, if possible, taking up a role within the community, individuals learn to see as the society under investigation sees and their external biases are diminished.

This issue of sight is worth considering further. Just as there are many ways of knowing, so there are many ways of seeing reality. In a postmodern frame there is no real objective reality but different ways of seeing the world. As mentioned earlier, the great value of ethnography is to give the outsider the eyes of the native. If one views a marriage ceremony in a foreign culture, for example, it is useful to observe it in terms of the value system which it represents, and one must ask what the purpose of marriage is within the culture under study, what is the stance of husband toward wife and vice versa, what are the norms for interpretation of particular statements and nonverbal communication. Dell Hymes's (1974) SPEAKING mnemonic is particularly useful in this regard. For any given speech event, he found it important to record setting and scene, participants, ends, acts sequence, key, instrumentalities, norms, and genre in order to be able to understand the event fully in its own cultural terms.

Needless to say, the objective of value-free observation is rarely achieved. One may view a society positively or negatively, depending on the quality of one's subjective experience, but one cannot entirely obliterate one's value system, however long one remains. To know this and reckon with it is an advantage to researchers, who can then do their best to achieve as objective a stance as possible. A balance between insider and outsider perspectives on a community must be attained, and it is important to pay attention to selecting one's informant. Two phases of data collection are useful: a first, which may be exploratory, and a second, when the data needed is gathered systematically. While it is common to associate the descriptor *empirical* with scientific research, the reality is that the word means simply "based on observation". If one can achieve effective neutral observation and interview techniques in carrying out humanities-based research, then the quality of one's work will be better assured.

Ethnography is being used today in fields like medicine which traditionally worked only within the quantitative paradigm. This is because it can illuminate the situation of patients and medical staff in ways that quantitative data cannot. What is the lived experience of terminally ill patients or their caregivers or doctors? These are realities that cannot be quantified and which have been associated specifically with the work of Erving Goffman, who maintained the internal consistency of his work, its depth and attention to detail as very significant factors. Perhaps his most famous work, worth the reader dipping into, is *Asylums*, first published in 1961.

Today good ethnography does not attempt to be nonsubjective but underlines its subjectivity, details what the perspective of the investigator will add to the study. It is common for ethnographers to write on their own environment or one in which they grew up. What is important becomes not whether they achieve objectivity but whether, from within their subjective positioning, they can accurately record the positioning of members of the community under study.

Data Collection: Discourse

Valerie Youssef

Discourse analysis is a methodology employed in collecting naturalistic data on a range of text types including narratives, media communication, political speeches and the like, and each genre makes different demands as to what should be collected and how the data should be analysed. Interviews are also analysed, for example, medical or legal interviews or others in professional settings. Some debate surrounds the issue of whether a researcher in discourse analysis can carry out an interview him- or herself and then analyse it discursively since it is not naturalistic but designed and administered as a research tool from the outset. While the vote is still out, interviews are so much the stuff of everyday life, beginning when the two-year-old is "interviewed" for preschool, that, even if set up for analytical purposes, it is not an unusual or daunting experience to most individuals in Western societies.

Discourse analysis in linguistics is about *how* something is said rather than merely *what* is said, and this concern goes across all of its subtypes. Within the qualitative paradigm, many interviews in the social sciences are subjected to content analysis, which deals in the information content of an interview. This is not our focus here but rather the linguistic analysis of discourse, which provides insight into meaning by careful consideration of the lexicon used, the particulars of grammatical structure (e.g., active versus passive verb forms), strategic use of nominalization and so on and also entails study of conversational features such as openings or closings. The *how* may also entail study of discourse structure or narrative structure in the case of storytelling. The way a person says something, or writes an article in the newspaper, can display that person's set towards the addressee, as well as ideology and attitude to a condition or situation beyond the words. This is its tremendous value. In the previous section, ethical issues in interviewing and specifically in recording data were discussed. It is worth reiterating that it is very important to gain permission to record material from one's informants and that the use of consent forms is advisable. Often difficulty can be overcome if the informant may gain from the interview, and individuals are often willing to participate in cases where there is some benefit in publicizing their situation.

While the extent of engagement with critical theory differs from one subtype of discourse analysis to another, the field is broadly concerned with asymmetries of power and the ways in which they are worked out in discourse. This is most evident in the field known as critical discourse analysis (CDA), to which different approaches may be found in different parts of the world. (See, e.g., Norman Fairclough [1995] for the United Kingdom; Teun van Dijk [2000a, 2000b] and Ruth Wodak [1996] for Europe; and James Gee [1999] for the United States.) The student of literature may analyse conversations within texts for what they demonstrate about power relations by using this approach. An interesting application to such criticism may be possible in considering the conversations in Lawrence Scott's (1998) *Aelred's Sin*, in which a young novice tries to work out his monastic relationships with older monks in diverse positions superior to his own, who shroud reality in circumspect taboos and half-truths.

Five major genres explored through discourse analysis may usefully be considered:

1. Professional/institutional encounters
2. Newspaper writing
3. Political speeches
4. Specific case study interviews (e.g., interviewing victims of violent encounters or marital abuse, investigating group interactions, storytelling)
5. Naturally occurring discourse which typifies a particular setting, society or both.

There are other categories beyond these, and categories do overlap, but these five should provide a basis and some guidelines for decision making that may be applied to other kinds of discourse.

Professional/Institutional Encounters

Data collection of professional/institutional encounters entails recording interviews in the professional setting under investigation and is often carried out to support the professionals involved and to enable them to negotiate their encounters more effectively and humanely, rather than merely for information gathering.

Some twenty years ago this author volunteered to transcribe a set of interviews between HIV/AIDS counsellors and their clients. At the time counselling for HIV/AIDS in Trinidad and Tobago was relatively new, and the professionals involved had no experience to guide them in this delicate arena of sexual areas which are taboo in public talk and the handling of life-threatening disease.

Professor David Silverman, the primary researcher, was not only using it for academic purposes but as the basis for a series of workshops to support professionals in this burgeoning new field. Counsellors were involved in pre– and post–HIV-test counselling, in the first gathering biodata and information on clients' lifestyles and sexual preferences, and in the second discussing with the clients the possibility of their being found to be HIV positive. Ultimately a series of papers arose out of those interviews and some follow-up work with the National AIDS Hotline (Youssef and Silverman 1992; Youssef 1993; Youssef and Russell-Brown 2001). Broadly, the research analysed which interactional strategies succeeded in these interviews and which did not, and this produced numerous pointers which could guard and guide counsellors' interactions. The most salient point is that what clients considered appropriate to an interview was key, that if counsellors stepped outside their expected role, even to bridge a perceived communication gap, it never worked. This applied in broad interaction types as well as in the use of a specific lexicon.

When an interviewer attempted to ask questions rather than merely provide information, clients might react against what they perceived as normative. Although the textbook would advise the counsellor to ask questions rather than to supply information in order to engage the client, the reality was that this technique often provoked the following response type: "Why are you asking me all these questions? You are the doctor. You are supposed to tell me."

In a case involving a single vocabulary item, a counsellor attempted to use slang for taboo sexual activities to bridge a professional gap in a nonemotive way. He asked a client whether he "bulled" people or was "bulled by them". The client, whose accent indicated that he was fairly educated, immediately asked, "Why are you asking me the question in that way?" sounding quite offended. The slang continued, however, and the answer to the question never surfaced. Again, this entails the issue of propriety, where the medical term for the encounter would have been considered more suitable by the client.

Informative as this interview set was, it involved much data gathering since a large number of interviews need to be conducted to establish general and specific trends. This was, of course, in the context of professional interviews, which one cannot control. In such cases, it may help to set up a stratified sample of interviews, deciding what features of the interview situation may make for substantial differences, and then interviewing as many as one can of each subtype. One may select clients and counsellors on a gender basis, for example, or even on an ethnic basis, or one might consider it important to compare private with public health facilities. Having worked out the significant variables, one might opt for a total of twenty interviews with an equal number of males and females and an equal number in public and private health-care professionals. To do more would be time consuming, since transcription and analysis are extremely painstaking in this kind of encounter.

Often discourse analysts run foul of quantitatively oriented researchers who accuse them of subjectivity because of their limited sample, but the reality of this field is that richness and density of the data is its strength. This is generally accepted and the information which accrues is manifold. It is currently being used in postgraduate research to investigate the support systems for clients in the Legal Aid system of Trinidad and Tobago, as it has been used to investigate workplace relationships of a number of different kinds (see, e.g., Heritage and Drew 1993). Work that is going on in the area of forensic linguistics is also critical. Mindie Lazarus-Black (2007) has done extensive work on domestic violence and its treatment in the law courts, and Sandra Evans (2010) is examining interactions in this same context between patois-speaking witnesses and court personnel in St Lucia.

Newspaper Writing

Journalistic writing is another rich source of data, widely used in consideration of the kinds of information which are put across to the public and their effect. Newspapers have undergone an immense tabloidization in the last twenty years, so that front pages have been transformed by an overwhelming focus on visual impact. One of the current issues in the Caribbean, most specifically in Jamaica and Trinidad and Tobago, is the apparent obsession with different kinds of violence in newspapers. It has been argued that the rate of crime is not demonstratively higher than in a number of other states, but media coverage makes it appear so, keeps the tourist at bay, and harms the psyche of both developing children and the adults who are exposed to this kind of coverage daily.

It is useful then to find effective ways of selecting and analysing newspaper articles of different kinds to allow a society to examine itself, become more self-conscious and ultimately open the possibility for improvement. As noted earlier, critical discourse analysts hold that our minds are controlled by the power brokers who use media to promote prejudiced and manipulating perspectives. They present the world in a particular way, and we receive it thus without realizing that we are being duped. A more optimistic view seems reasonable, that our Caribbean press is not always aware of the harm it may do. Sensitive analysis of articles might be used to run workshops for media personnel, who have themselves been duped to produce sensationalism which will sell. Front-page news reports following a particular crime have proven useful for analysis in this way and have demonstrated the prejudice in the media against some categories of women (Youssef 2009a) as well as the sensationalist and misleading depiction of crimes against minors (Youssef 2009b).

When considering how the opinions of government and the opposition is presented to us, we may need to interrogate editorials and feature articles, and in this arena it will be useful to compare and contrast across, rather than within, the daily newspapers. A particular theme may be pursued over a period of weeks or months in the main dailies. However, here again one can run foul of having too much data, for a full editorial analysis may run to fifty pages. These kinds of issues have arisen in the graduate study described in chapter 4 concerning the conflict between the former prime minister of Trinidad and Tobago and his arch rival within the People's National Movement (Shepherd 2010).

Political Speeches

This type of analysis has always been popular perhaps because the world's major speech makers have been so eloquent and their most renowned speeches tantamount to poetry. How well we remember Martin Luther King Jr's "I Have a Dream" speech and John F. Kennedy's "ask not what your country can do for you but what you can do for your country". Barack Obama has already made numerous memorable speeches, and it will be history itself which will select the best from this new era of inclusion in American politics.

Within the Caribbean, we forge our own traditions and perhaps should spend more time than we do sifting the significant speeches of our leaders as measures of an era, its ideology and what it represents. Despite a considerable body of policy analysis, there has been much less analysis of what politicians actually say so as to divine how much has real substance. Questions to be asked include whether elections are still won under a postcolonial mantle which barely masks a neocolonialism of dominance and exploitation. Only careful attention to how these speeches are put together can unmask the rhetoric and lay bare what is beneath. Very often the future actions of political leaders can be read in how they frame their speeches. Such predictive power suggests that governments could usefully employ a team of discourses analysts to better equip them to predict the actions of other states.

Specific Case Study Interviews

This type of interview may be easier to work with because the researcher directly controls the encounter in question and targets a specific individual. It is critically important though that the researcher carry out the interviews personally or train and know the research assistant carrying out the interviews. It is also advisable, even in the context of a relatively open interview, to specify certain question types or broad areas of concern to be covered. Without this attention to detail, an entire interview can be inappropriate and a waste of time. It is important to make interviews as natural as possible. As long as informants feel "interviewed", the information that they share remains stultified; making the informant feel comfortable means working out an encounter that is more satisfactory for all concerned, but this does have to be genuine and nonexploitative.

A challenge with this interview type, depending on its subject, may be in finding persons willing to talk about their experiences. In collecting data for *Writing Rage* (Morgan and Youssef 2006), a text on the discourse of abuse, it proved impossible to obtain any data from spousal abusers. A zealous young research assistant thought she would have no problems carrying out interviews of this kind in a rum shop in her native village, but the exercise proved abortive. It may have been necessary to interview in the prisons where the criminal act had already been proven and where confession may have supported the prisoner in the rehabilitation process, but to date it has not proven possible to explore that avenue of research.

Where interviews are possible with the victims of abuse, they can be extremely rich – not only in what they reveal about the state of mind of the interviewee but also because they demonstrate the way in which the individual reckons with and reconciles to the experience through the very retelling and rationalization entailed. Interviews may be diverse and clearly not all will be so sensitive, but even on such subjects as working out gender identity in using a foreign language, in an interview set collected quite recently at the University of the West Indies, St Augustine, information presentation by the interviewees and their self-reflection dovetailed very effectively (Youssef 2009c).

Another possibility is to set up group scenarios, as, for example, in asking a group of students to discuss a particular subject. These can be used not only to get their views on a subject but, more important, to assess how they interrelate.

This can be done by varying the composition of the group in significant ways to assess how an individual renegotiates identity according to group composition. We know well that identity is fluid and always in remaking, but to be able to demonstrate this from conversational data is an exciting discovery. In this kind of situation, transcription of data can be challenging, for everyone tends to talk at once and it can be difficult to disambiguate not only what is said but who is doing the talking.

It is also possible to construct focus groups which are moderated encounters in which the researcher ensures that certain questions are asked and issues raised while remaining as unobtrusive as possible. One graduate researcher profitably used this technique in eliciting emergent adults' perspectives on gender identity as a cause of interpersonal communication conflict (Barratt, in progress).

Another kind of interview type is concerned with the collection of narratives. Such data may be concerned with the incident described or with how individuals structure their storytelling. The possibilities are numerous, but in every case there needs to be careful planning, and some aborted recordings are inevitable along the way.

Discourse Which Typifies a Particular Setting

Throughout this book we recognize the significance of specific Caribbean studies and the absolute need to register forms of practice which may differ from those in other parts of the world. For too long we accepted studies carried out mainly in the United States and United Kingdom as typical, without realizing that even within English-speaking territories there are marked differences of culture and, by extension, interaction. Discourse modes are a particular area of concern in this regard. Kathryn Shields-Brodber (e.g., 2001a, 2001b) has undertaken discourse studies including interactions on a Jamaican radio talk show and language use on the performance floor, and her work must be recognized for the insights it has provided.

The range of foci discussed above all fall within discourse analysis, demonstrating that it is a most useful interpretive frame through which to approach scribal or oral discourse within the Caribbean.

Data Collection: The Literary Interview

Paula Morgan

In a literary interview the researcher engages in a conversation with a writer, motivated by a desire to meet the creator behind the literary scenario and its slate of characters. The interviewer seeks to ferret out the connections between the implied author – that shadowy presence created anew with every text – and the persona of the writer. The interviewee offers a conversation which is an act of artistic self-representation for public consumption. The interviewer acts as a conduit to the public with whom the writer is conversing. The literary interview has evolved out of traditions of journalism, portraiture and polemic. Researchers also conduct interviews with critics, publishers, readers and others about literary critique, production, history and readership.

In *Performing the Literary Interview*, John Rodden's definition centres on the portraiture:

> The interview is co-production via the materials of verbal discourse, typically a written transcript of an oral performance that shares similarities with dialogue in novels and plays. It gives the readers the sense that we are encountering the live human being who breathed life into the art. . . . Ultimately, the interview as docudrama is a complex combination of numerous literary genres and forms: melodrama, comedy, dialogue, dramatic monologue, and others. (2001, 16–17)

Based on his extensive experience of conducting literary interviews, Rodden identifies three types of authors/interviewees – traditionalists, raconteurs and advertisers. The *traditionalist* foregrounds the literary work and its socio-cultural context. This type of interviewer proceeds in an objective, factual, businesslike and self-effacing manner (p. 7). The *raconteur*, or storyteller, relies heavily on anecdotes to foreground him- or herself and casts the interviewer in a supporting role as a "side-kick" and "minor co-creator" (p. 9). The *advertiser* uses the interview as an opportunity for undisguised self-promotion and experiments with the persona being constructed for public display.

Rodden also identifies three types of interviewers – stagehands, supporters and usurpers. The self-effacing *stagehand* guides the process with an invisible hand and functions as a respectful listener. The *supporter* establishes full dialogue with the author and may even challenge claims and point to gaps in self-fashioning but nevertheless remains focused on the portraiture. This is not the impulse of the *usurper*, who shows off his or her understanding of the subject. Each interview is a coproduction generated by the dynamic interplay of these various personalities, agendas and styles. The interplay also demonstrates intricate and diverse power relations. Hence it is important for the interviewer to think through the power dynamic which would most effectively facilitate the objective of the research.

Predictably, readers and literary scholars in particular hold a range of perspectives on the role and significance of literary interviews. At one extreme, some regard interviews as serious sources of primary information which can serve as an invaluable key to unlocking the biographical underpinnings and the sociocultural contexts of a literary work. At the other end of the continuum, some regard the literary interview as a public relations ploy which blurs the boundaries between celebrity "low popular" culture and academic "highbrow" literary culture and is geared to sell books and to feed mass audiences' lust for infotainment.

The Interview Process

A literary interview is an extension of our natural sense of curiosity and a need for understanding, insight and connection. The crucial issue is movement from the free-floating give and take of conversation to the formal interview. Several elements required for good conversation and basic human interaction are incorporated into the literary interview, beginning with the need to make interviewees comfortable and to demonstrate a focused interest in them and their responses. The stages of the literary interview include topic selection, identification of the appropriate interview type, choice of interviewee and conduct of the interview.

Topic Selection

Both the topic and the style selected for the interview depend on the broad framework for research, the purpose for the interview and the disclosures one is seeking to elicit. There will always be a diverse range of topics from which to choose. The study may benefit from a biographical focus. This would include an exploration of the life and times of the writer – social contexts, family life, early formative literary and cultural influences, impact of reading community and the publication industry, reception of the work, and the writer's evolving literary career. These topics can be explored in relation to an individual writer or a group that emerges out of a particular national, geographical, historical, ethnic or social context. For example, interviews are a useful strategy to explore the social forces which impelled the first wave of Caribbean authors to write against deeply entrenched frameworks of oppression or to determine the factors which accounted for the emergence of Indo-Caribbean women writers in the 1980s. Interviews can also usefully explore a given issue through shared or divergent perspectives; for example, At what stage do authors self-represent as creative writers? Why do they opt to leave or stay in the Caribbean? Does self-definition change based on gender, ethnicity, publication record or public recognition?

Identification of Interview Type

The interview may be formal or informal, structured or semistructured, individual or group, author focused or arranged as an exchange between peers. The selection of the type of interview depends on its purpose and is also affected by setting. It may be challenging, for example, to conduct a formal interview during a wordfest at a beach venue. The researcher establishes a number of guidelines in advance, such as the intention, the extent of the interviewer's control and the conversational structure most appropriate to the research interest. Whether the interviewer is an established scholar or a student will determine, in the context of Caribbean social norms, the appropriate stance of the interviewer to the author or critic.

Finally, the form of the interview selected will also be mediated by the ideological approach to knowledge and meaning formation. For example, if one is invested in the New Critical approach, which views the author as imbued with superior gifts and transcendent perspectives which can illuminate the common man, one would be inclined to conduct the interview in a monologic fashion and erase or minimize the presence of the interviewer. If one is invested in the cultural studies approach which sees the author as determinant of the process of making meaning out of the text, one would be more inclined to use a dialogic interview and to pay attention to how broader socio-historical and contemporary temporal relations and contexts impact on the meaning-making process. The objective of this approach would not be to ferret out a defini-tive authorial intent but to provide a framework for the interplay of diverse elements of meaning construction, with a focus on those elements which go against received interpretations. This approach is particularly useful for an interview which is not concerned with predetermined agendas. All of this is to highlight the inherent connections among the theoretical, empirical and analytical frameworks of the interview process.

The choice of interview is also connected to its mode of distribution. A dense and complex thirty-five-page interview with a major writer or critic would be best suited to publication in a scholarly journal. A podcast interview for web publication should have crossover appeal to scholars as well as to educated laypeople. A case in point is the podcast series *Spaces between Words: Conversations with Writers* (www2.sta.uwi.edu/podcasts/spaces, edited by Giselle Rampaul and Ryan Durgasingh) emanating from the Department of Literary, Cultural and Communications Studies at the University of the West Indies, which takes advantage of the simple production procedure, swiftness, and wide reach of open access web publications, to make available a substantial range of literary interviews on Caribbean writers and scholars. These offerings are calibrated to be insightful enough to support significant scholarly activities, brief and interesting enough to keep the listener's attention, and wide-ranging enough to appeal to the educated layperson.

The selection of the appropriate interviewee relates to the purpose of the interview. The researcher ensures in advance that the strategy selected will elicit all the information required. The structured interview assumes that the interviewees will speak a truth which will illuminate a specific area of enquiry. For the most part, the structured interview targets a specific subset of persons who can be expected to possess information on the topic. There is generally a set introduction, and questions are asked in the same order and manner, often with closed response. This approach would be ideally suited, for example, to reader response analysis: Who is your favourite author? At what age did you first encounter said writer? Do you consider X to be either a popular or a serious writer or both? Janice Radway's (1981) groundbreaking research on readers of romance novels used this strategy effectively.

The group interview is suited for sweeping questions on a shared sociocultural context or experience. For example, one could conduct a group interview on the early Caribbean writers' wave of migration to metropolitan countries, the emerging sense of Caribbeanness which drew young writers together on alien soil or the Caribbean Artist Movement in London which was a seedbed for nurturing young writers in the late 1960s.

The semistructured interview is more flexible and allows for the greater interplay of the various dynamics identified by Rodden. The interviewer has greater freedom to allow the interview to take its own direction and remains open to and prepared to probe the unexpected.

Conduct of the Interview

Because managing an interview requires deftness, sensitivity and tact, researchers may usefully conduct a pilot interview to identify gaps and limitations in interview design. Logistical decisions are made in relation to initial contact, setting, modality (whether face to face, telephone, email or other Internet mediated), and means of recording (script, audio or video) – all of which impact the dynamics of the interview. For example, even when permission is freely given to record an interview, respondents are likely to produce a far more relaxed flow of conversation when the recording device is turned off. Although confidentiality disallows disclosure of material gathered "off the record", this intelligence can still inform the overall analysis of the topic. Generally persons are more comfortable and settled in their own homes and offices. Even a casual informal interview requires advance preparation and promptness to safeguard the interviewee's time and personal boundaries.

In setting up the group interview, the researcher closely observes the composition of the group and manages potential for conflict. The larger the group and the more inflammatory the topic, the greater the skill required to manage the interview. All voices must be heard, even those of shy, withdrawn interviewees. In-depth interviews require sensitivity, attention to detail, and social and listening skills. The challenge is to find the appropriate balance between allowing the interview to flow smoothly and maintaining its focus.

To encourage persons to speak freely, the researcher selects appropriate levels of formality. It is crucial to be sensitive to the ways in which one can potentially offend. Within a Caribbean social framework, the researcher does not assume first-name familiarity, especially with older persons. Nor does one transgress the interviewee's sense of personal space, especially when interviewing persons of the opposite sex. Familiarity can be offensive, but stiffness impedes the flow of conversation. In a cross-cultural scenario, the requirements become increasingly complex and delicate. Consider the implications of the following scenario outlined by cultural critic George Lamming:

> I must take you back to a visit I made to Kenya in the middle 1970s. I had spent a day in the village in Limuru, at the home of the very distinguished novelist Ngugi Wa Thiong'o. There was a big family and much jubilation all around. In a very relaxed way I asked him, "How many children do you have?"
>
> He asked me in turn whether I would like to have another drink. I said, "Yes, of course," accepted the drink and repeated my question: "How many children . . . ?" And he said, "As we were saying before. . . ." This abrupt detour made it clear that there was not going to be an answer to my question. A day later I was talking to a mutual friend and reported the episode and was told, "Oh, but no, no, no, no, that question wouldn't be answered. Among the Kikuyu, you never count offspring; to do so is to invite calamity." And now decades later, it makes me think how extraordinary are the multiple frontiers of behaviour we have to explore and negotiate, to find ways of entering with courtesy into each other's world. (2009, 18–19)

If we accept the notion of literature as giving readers access to pleasures in language and narrative structures, creating mimetic and paradigmatic models of human interaction, laying bare sociocultural structures and formations, then the literary interview must be conducted in a manner that facilitates these functions. The interview must therefore be fluid and expressive enough to allow the reader to sense the author's use of language and idiom. It must be flexible enough to convey the interviewee's ideological stance, positionality and mode of interaction. Moreover, it must convey something of the interviewee's social context and its impact on self-fashioning and making meaning out of life's experiences.

Analysing the Material

The analysis must consider the interviewee, the story, the audience and the interviewer – or prompter. All of these elements are situated socially, historically and relationally and are constantly shifting in complex interplay. The speaker can occupy a range of speaking positions in relation to the experience. We understand this quite readily when analysing fictional narratives. Consider for example the difference it would make if *A House for Mr Biswas* ([1961] 1966) were related from the vantage point of Mrs Tulsi. Similarly consider the impact of its author V.S. Naipaul being interviewed by an Islamic fundamentalist on the text *Among the Believers: An Islamic Journey* ([1981] 1998) or by an avid Caribbean nationalist on the evocation of the Caribbean in *The Middle Passage* ([1962] 1978).

To enhance the objectivity of the research, the interviewer can engage in a process of self-questioning, the response to which may inform the research design and analysis:

- What role is the interviewer/researcher undertaking – prompter, questioner, interpreter, reporter or author of final outcome?
- How have the social circumstances of the interview shaped the interviewer's self-construction?
- Which ideological frameworks were embraced or challenged?
- What methods were embraced or rejected in the research process?
- What is the correlation between the initial research design and the final product?
- How did the writing process and publication requirements influence the finished process?
- How should the interviewer respond when the narratives spills over the carefully structured questions?
- How would the researcher analyse stories structured teleologically to highlight the inevitability of a predetermined end?

A crucial consideration in processing material derived from the interview is whether the interview comprises personal narratives and life stories whose integrity and commitment to truth telling are to be respected at all cost. Sensitivity demands that the analysis takes the interviewee's self-fashioning in good faith; nevertheless, this respect does not mean taking the interview at face value. Any analysis should probe beneath the surface for paradoxes, contractions, gaps and omissions. Similarly self-reflexivity requires researchers to treat their analyses as interpretive acts filtered through their own values, assumptions and motivations. An interview can become an epistemological tool which leads interviewer, interviewee and audience into new processes of knowing. The analysis may highlight the points at which the interview has become an act of discovery, an occasion for arriving at and articulating notions and reasonings never before considered and articulated. The analytical task is to emphasize this process. In other words, an interview – as an act of self-representation or a recounting of perspectives on a range of issues – can also provide insight into how and why a narrative can be constructed and related.

Data Collection: Rare or Archival Material

Barbara Lalla

A researcher on the culture of an earlier age, its beliefs, behaviours, forms of expression or actual historical circumstances may not find all that is needed in published writing or even through oral testimony. In addition to relevant publications in libraries, there may be noncurrent, unpublished and unique material in other repositories. These may offer direct, individual observations of matters under investigation, or published material may survive in rare and scattered copies. To verify circumstances in a novel, including earlier forms of discourse, researchers may need to trace such elusive data. This type of information contextualizes a literary work, substantiates valid critique and documents sources; or it provides a socio-historical base for creative writing, discourse analysis or literary history.

What comprises archival material of likely value to literary and discourse culture, and where is it likely to be found? Some documents are put together by individuals, families, firms or institutions out of a specific interest. A collection around a particular topic may comprise a range of media: written documents, old reel-to-reel tape recordings, maps, memorabilia, sketches, architectural drawings, ships' logs and so forth. The literary documents may include notes, letters, unpublished manuscripts and clippings from magazines now rare and out of print. To find information on Jamaica Kincaid, one might search a library catalogue for her books and for critical or historical commentaries but also seek a university's unpublished citation on Kincaid as an honorary graduand in campus records of citations or through contact with the campus orator.

The search begins in official repositories, where material pertaining to different subjects is kept separate. The Thomas Fisher Rare Book Library, for example, maintains a collection devoted to Lorna Goodison. Nevertheless, one needs a sense of how collections are organized. Much archival material is arranged according to provenance; the order in which records are arranged by an organization tends to be preserved when that material becomes archival. However, if a family has passed material to some repository in the order in which they encountered it, this material may be organized in the same order. So some knowledge about the organization of the material is crucial. In an official repository, accessing archival and rare material depends on finding aids: various types of lists like indexes, inventories, deeds of gift or resource guides.

Another guiding question is, where may collections of this kind be found? Such material exists in university libraries and rare book collections, national libraries, museums and archives in individual territories, as well as institutions in countries historically connected with the Caribbean, like the British Library. Centres for Caribbean studies are to be found at Emory University, London Metropolitan University, New York University, Ryerson University, University of Connecticut, University of South Florida, York University and Warwick University. Moreover, affluent institutions abroad are quick to acquire important Caribbean collections. So the papers of C.L.R. James can be found in the Rare Book and Manuscript Library of Columbia University; Derek Walcott's literary papers and the Lorna Goodison collection in the Thomas Fisher Rare Books Library, New College, University of Toronto; Jean Rhys's collected papers and ephemera as well as the V.S. Naipaul archive at the McFarlin Library, University of Tulsa. Researchers must go far afield beyond the Caribbean to find Caribbean material. Further, Caribbean research is distinguished not only on the basis of topic but of approach, so a Caribbean approach to a writer from beyond the region requires access to material in foreign repositories (as in Lalla 2008 and Harricharan 2008). At the same time, official centres like university libraries are not the only repositories of archival material; private homes may preserve a wealth of material. Uncovering such informal collections is itself a challenge. Some are accessible only through interview of elderly informants who may have family papers, collected notes, unpublished papers or newspaper clippings regarding some special interest.

Accessing archival and rare material requires planning and arrangements in advance of visiting the repository. To avoid wasting time, the researcher first defines what is being sought and its precise relevance to the research question; the time frame to which the archival material must belong and places, persons or topics to which it may pertain; and a hypothesis regarding sources of such material, places where it may have been generated, a means by which it could have been transmitted and hands through which it may have passed.

Important preparation involves secondary material in readily accessible libraries, searched by date, name, topic, and keyword, and through databases, indexes of periodicals, newspapers, government records and online catalogues. Subheadings (like diaries, correspondence, personal narratives and interviews) can be useful. Bibliographies, foot- or endnotes, and encyclopaedias may supplement information that is better found before time-consuming and expensive visits to archives and rare book rooms.

Indeed, one first establishes whether it is necessary to go or whether there is an alternative route to the data. Unique material that existed only in archival form for a century or two may come to be published as years pass. For example, a file with fragments of the first-known novel by a resident of Jamaica, *Busha's Mistress, or Catherine the Fugitive* by Cyrus Perkins (2003), studied up to the late 1990s as fragile and scattered remnants of a serial publication, was published in 2003. Researchers following a reference to *Busha's Mistress* in Barbara Lalla's *Defining Jamaican Fiction* (1996) may well travel to the National Library of Jamaica, but a search of secondary sources would save the airfare. Early texts like E.L. Joseph's *Walter Arundell* ([1838] 2000), Frieda Cassin's *With Silent Tread* ([1890] 2002) and others have become available through publication since 2000. There are often less expensive and time-consuming avenues than travel.

Sometimes, specific information like a date on a death certificate may be requested by mail through direct correspondence with an archivist. Occasionally some rare though not precisely archival material can be viewed through interlibrary loan; some reduplicated as microfiche, microfilm or photocopy; some scanned, digitized and emailed. One considers the condition of the material. Because photocopying is impossible in the case of fragile material, arrangements for copying may take extensive time, and two to three months should be allocated. A single copy of a diary kept by George Ross (1800), who accompanied Jamaican Maroons being transported through Nova Scotia to Sierra Leone, existed in a library in Sierra Leone until the National Library of Jamaica requested a copy for two researchers in language history, who included an excerpt in their collection (see D'Costa and Lalla 1989). Meanwhile, the whole diary was transcribed by hand and, later, published by historian Mavis Campbell (1989).

Obstacles may include routines associated with the destination; dropping in may not be an option. Before visiting either an official repository or a private collection, the wise researcher arranges the date and time of access and is flexible about appointments with individuals. Collectors are often elderly, and one may encounter them just as they are recovering after an illness or the loss of a loved one. The time allocated must be adequate for the researcher to listen to the informant's account of the circumstances under which the material of interest was assembled. Indeed, in such circumstances one must allow time for talk on a range of other subjects before viewing the material. Usually, notes must be taken on-site, as the private collector may view the material as too precious to be taken from the premises. It is essential to be respectful regarding reticence on sensitive topics or an inclination to hold back some of the papers.

Advance arrangements are best for formal as well as informal collections. Some official repositories close for repairs or to move location. (The British Library moved over an extended period!) Some are closed on certain days of the week or have different opening hours on different days. To visit without checking availability is to run the risk of finding that collections, or crucial items in a collection, are unavailable – perhaps withdrawn for preservation or repair.

Even when the researcher is sure of admission, a practical time frame is essential for completion within the period available for the visit. It may not be possible to return. On actually achieving access to the archival or rare material in a repository, the researcher requires time for sifting through what may be a vast collection of material containing perhaps two well-hidden but invaluable bits of data. Such time is best allocated in advance, bearing in mind that a collection may exist in a wide range of media, from travellers' letters to inscriptions on artefacts. In the chapter that follows, Glenroy Taitt examines yet more elusive material, ephemera, and gives valuable guidance on accessing and applying it.

The researcher may well encounter some unfamiliar regulations and must accept their terms. Rare and archival material may be fragile, and, normally, nothing is to be taken in that can damage what is irreplaceable or that may be a mechanism for smuggling it out. The researcher goes prepared to leave bags outside and to read in a restricted, controlled area, taking in only pencils and a laptop (its battery wisely charged in advance). Material entrusted for study is not to be reordered, mixed or marked in any way. A paper place mark is the only proper means of keeping one's position in papers of this kind.

Photocopying is out of the question for material too delicate to be handled, pressed or subjected to intense light, and digital photography may not be allowed. Note taking demands rigorous documentation, as it is often impossible to return to a repository. So quotations must be noted exactly – to the last comma – and notes require a record of the full citation (the personal owner or the institution that owns the material and the address, as well as cataloguing information on the collection and on any individual item used). In case it does become necessary and possible to return, it is helpful to keep a note on how the material was found. Careful records regarding ownership of the material also facilitate requests for permission to publish, should these be required. Because the original owner may well be deceased, the issue of ownership may take time to determine, so it is best to have all information in hand so as to begin the process of requesting permission early.

Before leaving, the researcher notes any further information regarding the schedule or procedures for accessing this collection in case there is reason and opportunity to return. Seasoned researchers build a network of acquaintances in a range of repositories; expressing appreciation to the archivist or assistants is both a fundamental courtesy and basic good sense.

Search for Archival and Rare Material: One Case

The following account illustrates archival research in a project involving literary, linguistic and cultural material.

Approximately twenty-five years ago, Jean D'Costa and Barbara Lalla undertook to locate evidence of early representation of the Caribbean voice in scribal and, especially, literary discourse. What they sought had to be clearly defined. First, they established chronological boundaries: material would come from the seventeenth century to the end of the nineteenth. Next, this time frame being wide, they defined narrow geographical limits. Jamaica was selected as the single territory for the study. Then they further narrowed the topic to focus on linguistic reconstruction of early Jamaican Creole as represented in written texts. They were looking for written seventeenth-to-nineteenth-century texts that represented Jamaican Creole speech.

They identified places in which these might be found. Preliminary library work included consultation of published collections of folk material – proverbs, folktales and songs (as in Jekyll 1907), historical dictionaries, encyclopaedias and catalogues of libraries likely to contain relevant material (from the National Library of Jamaica to the British Library). Further direction to the evidence came from indexes, abstracts and lists of dissertations, and guides to scholarship locating the study in relation to other relevant research. Guides to critical works on Caribbean material, literary histories, folk collections and biographical sources supplied references to early writing from or about Jamaica.

Gradually the researchers moved to rarer material. Journals and travellers' accounts and letters provided anecdotes, records and notes on Jamaican Creole speakers. Some were in rare and fragile printed copies. To make sense of the data, they consulted historical background material, including church history and social history, finding further clues to useful material.

Meanwhile, the researchers tested their hypotheses regarding the location of source material but also consulted curators, archivists and historians regarding private collectors and informants. Essential questions took form for bringing this submerged voice to the surface: Who would have recorded black speakers of the time or tried to represent what they had to say? Who would have thought they had anything to say? Who might actually have paused to listen?

Answers emerged in reconstructing the society of the time, its writers, their topics and language choices. Perhaps there were curious travellers with an ear for the unfamiliar, perhaps missionaries who insisted that the speakers had souls, perhaps residents sending away descriptions of their surroundings, perhaps a bored official or sea captain enlarging on his regular records by jotting down observations of his charges or cargo.

So useful genres to target might be early fiction set in Jamaica by a visitor or, better, a resident; well-researched historical novels; anecdotes in letters containing quotations, interspersed in sociohistorical accounts and domestic manners; biographies and autobiographies of residents or visitors; travel writing; missionary records and correspondence with transcribed prayers or sermons by local speakers; descriptions of local language; literary histories and British novels that referred to Caribbean discourse; and collections by experts in local culture like Olive Lewin, who recorded old songs with obsolete words and with pronunciations trapped by rhyme and rhythm. Libraries produced some material, like the journal of Captain Hugh Crow, master of a slave ship; private collectors like H.P. Jacobs provided unpublished manuscripts, files and note boxes. And the material came to light. Sometimes a single item recurred in varying forms, often in fragments. A song, "Quaco Sam" (Lalla 1981), was reassembled from an old newspaper clipping, H.P. Jacobs's notes from elderly informants in Trelawny, excerpts printed on pottery and a musical score with words recorded by Olive Lewin.

On the basis of such material, a wealth of analysis evolved. The researchers made accessible early songs, prayers, tales, speeches and dialogues in Jamaican Creole and developed linguistic reconstructions of the early history of a Caribbean Creole. They drew inferences about the development of a literary discourse and critiqued elements of the early literature. They and others using the material developed arguments about Creole history, and the material went on to inform discussion of the significance of Creole representation to the "Caribbeanness" of the regional literature and to offer a basis of comparison with evolving vernacular discourses in other places and other times.

The decision to transcend limits takes the researcher to new information, sometimes from very old sources. The first essential step is to define clearly what is being sought. The next is to conceive of areas in which it may be found that have not been tapped before and to work out the obstacles that have prevented them being tapped and the paths around these. D'Costa and Lalla questioned themselves and others, along the following lines:

"How might a Jamaican slave in the late eighteenth century have spoken?"
"You'll never find that out."
"Why?"
"Who would write down what a slave said?"
Who indeed.

Conclusion

This chapter has emphasized that there is much data collection to be done both in the critiquing of existing discourse, literary and mediatized, and in the creative writing process. In cases where one is analysing media, poiltical or other real-world data, the selection of the sample for analysis is critical as it must be in some sense representative or typical of its kind. In addition, the mode of analysis selected must be suited to the rigours of the specific task at hand. Further, any contextual information one can gather as background to the piece in terms of the larger context or the ideological postioning of the author is particularly useful. The same need for background information is true for the critique of the literary work and must be sought from archival resources or through interviews with relavant persons, who may incude authors themselves. Finally, in putting together a creative piece a rigorous researching of the history, geography and social circumstances of the context of the work should accompany the writing process to assure its authenticity.

Chapter 6

Unlocking the Potential for Research
West Indiana
Glenroy Taitt

A vast diversity of source material lurks in university libraries, which can usefully be illustrated by focusing on a single repository and on one particularly inconspicuous type of material: ephemera in the University of the West Indies Library at St Augustine, Trinidad and Tobago. Despite prior undergraduate experience, graduates are often unaware of the profound richness of the Main Library's West Indiana and Special Collections Division. This division, the library's premier research section, houses a comprehensive collection of published and unpublished material on the anglophone Caribbean. While it is well known for its extensive collection of books, it also possesses a rich stock of nontraditional material; in fact, its uniqueness lies particularly in these holdings. This chapter therefore has three objectives: to promote the use of nontraditional sources, to encourage the exploitation of a wider range of traditional material in such repositories and to sensitize prospective researchers in Caribbean cultural studies to the immense value of such repositories.

Over the years, librarians at St Augustine have observed an underutilization of the division's stock. While no scientific study has focused exclusively on the West Indiana and Special Collections Division to gauge the pattern of use, staff have noticed that the most heavily used items are, in order of frequency, books, theses and newspapers. Before proceeding further, a glance at the wider context would suggest that St Augustine students are not necessarily atypical. While the information-seeking habits of mature scholars in the humanities are well known, few studies have focused on the behaviour of graduate students.

Andy Barret, however, found that graduate students in the humanities at the University of Western Ontario relied largely on primary sources: contemporary journals, recordings, individual recollections, museum artefacts, original manuscripts and books (2005, 327). B.T. Fidzani identified journals, library books, textbooks, lecture notes and handouts as the main sources used by graduate students at the University of Botswana (1998, 336). He also claimed that lack of awareness by students at that institution was a major barrier to greater exploitation of the library's resources (1998, 337).

While researchers at the University of the West Indies, St Augustine, draw heavily on the books in the West Indiana and Special Collections Division, many appear to overlook bibliographies, though these are a valuable tool for novice researchers, providing a useful shortcut to pertinent sources on a given topic. Like the bibliography at the end of an essay, research paper or thesis, these bibliographies offer a listing of relevant writings. It is therefore helpful in preparing a literature review, though its usefulness goes beyond this stage of the research process.

Bibliographies vary in scope and coverage, as the following examples from the division indicate. Arthur Dayfoot and Roscoe Pierson's *Bibliography of West Indian Church History* (2004) is a list of books and other printed materials relating to the history of Christian denominations in the English-speaking Caribbean (including Bermuda). It has annotations for most entries. Interestingly, it states the repository where each item is located. Linda De Four's *Gimme Room to Sing* (1993) is a bibliography of music, properly known as a discography, covering calypsos by the Mighty Sparrow recorded between 1958 and 1993. Apart from giving the title of each calypso and a short description of the song itself, she also identifies the arranger, year recorded, record label, orchestra, musicians, background vocalists and chorus groups. *Paradoxes of French Caribbean Theatre: An Annotated Checklist of Dramatic Works, Guadeloupe, Guyane, Martinique from 1900* by Bridget Jones and Sita Littlewood (1997) covers theatrical works since 1900 from France's three overseas departments in the Caribbean. Information supplied includes the author, director, theatrical company, the year when the work was first produced or published along with the country where it was first performed, the language, whether French or Creole, as well as a brief description of the work itself. Emily Williams's *Anglophone Caribbean Poetry* (2002) is an annotated bibliography which includes anthologies, poets' individual collections, recorded works both audio and audiovisual, interviews and critical works. The period covered is 1970–2001. Enid Brown's *Martinique, Guadeloupe and French Guiana (Guyane) in English* (2001) is a partially annotated bibliography which covers all types of publications in English on the three territories, though she indicates that many tourist brochures have been omitted. Date of publication was not a criterion for inclusion. This bibliography is unpublished, but the library holds a manuscript copy.

Although, as noted, researchers draw heavily on newspapers, they are limited in their range of use, by and large sticking to the local daily newspapers. Unfortunately, since newspapers do not appear in the library's online catalogue, it is difficult for researchers to know the breadth of the collection. It contains newspapers mainly from Trinidad and Tobago; while there are several from other Caribbean territories, most of these are not current. Apart from the *Trinidad Guardian, Express* and *Newsday*, the three currently daily newspapers, the division has a wide range of local newspapers from the nineteenth century to the present. These have been put out by religious organizations, corporate bodies, community groups and political parties. The oldest newspaper in the collection is the *Port of Spain Gazette* (1825–1956). Among the more recent titles are the *Anglican Review* (1959–1972) published by the Anglican diocese of Trinidad and Tobago; the *Catholic News* (1892 to the present), *Hindu Mahasabha* (1940–1941), produced by the Trinidad Maha Sabha Organization; *Moko* (1968–1973), produced by the Trinidad and Tobago–based United National Independence Party; *TATEC News* (1968–1975), produced by the Trinidad and Tobago Electricity Commission; *Texaco Star* (1959–1984), produced by Texaco Trinidad Incorporated; and *Vanguard* (1965–1994), produced by the Oilfield Workers' Trade Union. The latest acquisition is the *T and T Chinese Weekly*, launched in 2010 and published in Chinese.

One collection which is infrequently mined is the library's bank of oral interviews. Since 1981, the West Indiana and Special Collections Division has had an oral history programme, the Oral and Pictorial Records Project (OPReP). Under the aegis of OPReP, the library has been collecting data on a wide variety of subjects relating to life in Trinidad and Tobago: politics, religion, culture, education and language are just a few. Some of those interviewed are persons who created history, as it were, but others are ordinary citizens who have given rich eyewitness accounts of events. To date approximately 140 interviews have been conducted. Researchers have access to edited transcripts of these interviews. There is a guide to the OPReP collection called *Spoken History*.

Before looking at specific types of nontraditional material in the division, it would be useful to discuss some issues pertaining to their use, since this type of material presents unique challenges. Nontraditional sources, in particular ephemera, offer immense possibilities for research on the Caribbean but, sadly, are often overlooked. The word *ephemera* suggests that such material offers little potential contribution to the research process – an entirely erroneous view. Issues that arise from the scholarly use of ephemera will also be discussed and some examples of such (held at the libraries at the St Augustine and Mona campuses of the University of the West Indies) are featured at the end of the chapter.

Ephemera are generally seen as documents intended to be short-lived: "documents that have relevance only for a short time, normally day or days of the event or situation they relate to" (Twyman 2008, 19). However, they have also been described more broadly as "anything that is printed and isn't bound in a traditional book format" (Young 2003, 12). In the discussion that follows, therefore, an ephemeral document is one which is meant to survive for a short period or is too lightweight to remain upright on a shelf.

Printed ephemera – the present digital age having created electronic ephemera – include posters, flyers, handbills, concert or other event programmes, postcards, wedding invitations, first day covers, calendars, tracts, restaurant menu cards, catalogues of art exhibitions and more. The genre even encompasses funeral programmes which "many people in the English-speaking Caribbean believe that it is unlucky to hoard" but which "have much to tell about social life" (Higman 1999, 41).

Information on everyday life at all social levels can be gleaned from ephemera. They bear witness to how people enjoy themselves, mourn, observe the various rites of passage (often at home) and conduct their social and political struggles. Moreover, ephemera convey a vitality which is absent from sober official documents. The evidence that is embedded in ephemera is revealed through both text and images, for ephemera can be excellent visual sources. Issues of identity, gender and class, for example, can be discerned from an in-depth study of the pictorial first day covers issued in any Caribbean territory, from Belize City to Bridgetown and from Port of Spain to Port-au-Prince. Emerging Caribbean researchers will find that ephemera are excellent sources of information on popular culture and social history.

Scholars have been slow to recognize ephemera as valuable pieces of the jigsaw puzzle, notwithstanding their advantages. Nurtured for so long on hard sources such as biographies, journals, newspapers, diaries, letters, minutes, speeches and official reports from government and corporate bodies, academics have been sceptical of soft materials like ephemera because of their short-lived and even fugitive nature. Fortunately, though, researchers have slowly begun to recognize the worth of ephemeral materials. In a recent study on British concert history, tickets, handbills, programmes, posters and the like have been described as "a source of almost unimaginable richness" (Bashford 2008, 460).

Assessing the intellectual content of ephemeral material can be challenging. Missing or incomplete information often threatens to disorient the researcher. Frustratingly, postcards, unless postmarked, often lack dates, so the student has to seek other evidence to situate them in time. Posters, handbills and invitations, too, are sometimes short of details such as date or place: while the day and month are prominently displayed, the year may be absent; or the venue is advertised without sufficient data to identify the place. Contemporaries do not generally view these gaps as an issue; problems only arise when the documents, living beyond their expected shelf life, fall into the hands of the hapless researcher years later.

The accuracy of the item in hand is another consideration for the scholar. Invitations and programmes do not necessarily confirm that an event occurred as advertised. The event may have been rescheduled or even cancelled; perhaps an actress identified in the poster was replaced on short notice. Patrons attending an extended run of a play may have received the original programme which failed to reflect subsequent changes of date, venue and even cast. Postevent coverage, such as a newspaper report, should be consulted for verification. Visual records, too, can also be misleading. Postcards are notorious for presenting stereotypical portrayals of Caribbean society. The presumably everyday attire of an Indo-Trinidadian woman in a nineteenth century postcard may be anything but that, as the subject may have been dressed up for the photograph or she herself may have chosen to enhance her daily appearance or may have presented herself to suit the expectation of the photographer, a problem which anthropologists recognize as feedback.

Bias, whether intentional or unintentional, is another issue with ephemeral material. The researcher trawling through a collection of press releases from the People's Revolutionary Government in Grenada may naturally be alert to possible prejudice, but that same researcher may fail to perceive that seemingly innocuous restaurant menu cards may subtly – and sometimes not so subtly – leak issues of ethnicity, class, and health and wellness. These concerns of missing data, accuracy or bias should not discourage researchers from making use of ephemera. Rather, they demonstrate the need for critical assessment, in-depth analysis and confirmation with other sources.

Locating printed ephemera within a library collection poses its own challenges. Libraries, for their part, are guilty of downplaying ephemera. They are reluctant to accept ephemera because of their flimsy nature, irregular size and – to the cataloguers' dismay – confusing absence of conventional descriptive information such as author, title, publisher and International Standard Book Number (ISBN). In short, ephemera are difficult to treat. As a result, those libraries which have accepted them have often neglected to create sufficiently helpful pathways for the users. Of late, however, information professionals have become more receptive to these troublesome bits of documentation, appreciating their research potential and heritage value. As Beverley Wood and Barbara Chase, librarians at the University of the West Indies, Cave Hill, explain: "When we consider that often the only means by which information is communicated is by a pamphlet or flyer, that the resources to produce even these items are so limited, and that many of these items are virtually the only 'official' communications from and by Caribbean people, we cannot ignore the need to collect whatever resources we encounter" (2007, 82). In the West Indiana and Special Collections Division, ephemeral material is to be found in (several of) the special collections, the vertical file and even in the rare books collection. The special collections are "a separate category of materials within the West Indiana Collection. They are generally unpublished source materials – personal papers, archival materials, manuscripts" (Rouse-Jones 2003, 1). The library currently has seventy-six such collections. A list of these along with short descriptions is available on the library's website, and its online catalogue also contains a record for each collection. However, since this record generally gives an overview of the respective collection, specific details on ephemeral content are usually scant. Nevertheless, printed finding aids and supplementary electronic databases often provide deeper folder-level descriptions of these collections and permit retrieval where ephemera are buried within a collection.

Libraries use their vertical file to store odd items that are not processed individually. In the West Indiana and Special Collections Division's vertical file, items are grouped together in folders by subject with minimum descriptive information provided. Each subject file has a title and corresponding call number, with a printed index serving as a finding aid. The index provides the enquirer with a list of subjects along with matching call numbers but without any indication of the contents of the files. At present, the library's online catalogue does not provide access to the vertical file, but this is expected to change soon. Despite its relatively inaccessible nature, the vertical file contains extremely valuable items, as we shall see later.

Taken together, the special collections, vertical file and rare books collection constitute an impressive repository of Caribbean-related ephemera. Because of how they are processed, it is impossible to state the total quantity held in the library. The following examples, selected from among the lesser-known collections, show their scope and potential. One example is drawn from the West Indies Collection at the University of the West Indies, Mona, to awaken the researcher to the extensive pool of Caribbean-related ephemera available in the university-wide library system.

Burials and Funeral Services

This small collection in the vertical file consists mainly of funeral programmes. Among the contents is a brochure highlighting Daisy Voisin, who at the time of her death in 1991 was considered Trinidad's queen of Parang – the island's traditional Christmas music sung in Spanish. The brochure includes a photograph and biographical sketch of Voisin along with a brief history of her band, La Divina Pastora Serenaders. Also to be found in the file is an extremely informative eulogy delivered at the funeral in 1981 of Isabel Teshea, social worker, politician and diplomat. A founding member of Trinidad and Tobago's oldest political party, the People's National Movement, Teshea became the first female minister of government in Trinidad and Tobago in 1963. After she left office in 1970, she served as ambassador to Ethiopia and then high commissioner to Guyana.

The Calendar Collection

One of the special collections, the Calendar Collection contains, to date, approximately 150 calendars, mainly from Trinidad and Tobago. The earliest dates from 1969. Most of the calendars were produced by large corporate bodies, particularly those in the insurance and energy industries, as well as by the Caribbean Community (CARICOM) Secretariat in Barbados. The calendars depict diverse themes, including architecture, visual arts, flora, calypso and religion, just to mention a few. Among the religious calendars are a Hindu calendar for 1987 (number not yet assigned), a Spiritual Baptist sacred solar calendar for 2007 (calendar number 125) and a Muslim almanac for 2008 (number not yet assigned). The Benedictine monks in Trinidad produced a calendar in 1979 (calendar number 107), but theirs is not overtly religious, as it presents various sketches of the abbey at Mt St Benedict along with an introductory message by the abbot. Costumes and Festivals of the Caribbean is a calendar produced by the Colonial Life Insurance Company Limited for 1997 (calendar number 18). This contains sketches by the well-known artist Carlisle Chang, depicting festivals and costumes such as Koo Koo, Mavis Band, Speech Band, Pierrot Grenade, Javanese Dancer, Stickfight, Pique, Zouave, Ramleela and Junkanoo with explanatory notes. Decidedly different is the 1995 calendar produced by the Princess Elizabeth Centre for Physically Handicapped Children in Trinidad and Tobago (calendar number 26). It is unpublished, being in the form of a scrapbook, and so is undoubtedly unique. This simple calendar contains sketches of flowers which the artist Ferdinand Romilly donated to the centre in 1988. The calendars in this collection have been arranged in numerical order rather than in chronological sequence, with an electronic database providing detailed access.

Cover Album: Official First Day Cover Album

Housed among the rare books is this fine three-volume collection of first day covers issued mainly by the postal authority in Trinidad and Tobago. The period covered is 1958 to the present. Regional integration is a major theme, with covers depicting its various manifestations over the years: the West Indies Federation, the Caribbean Free Trade Association, CARICOM and the Caribbean Single Market and Economy. Included are first day covers issued on 22 April 1958 by nine of its ten member countries to mark the inauguration of the West Indies Federation. Other dominant themes are sport, beauty pageants and Christmas. Tobago is reflected in two covers depicting the Tobago Heritage Festival and Tobago's stamp centenary, 1879–1979. First day covers were also issued to celebrate the bicentenary of Chinese arrival in Trinidad in 2006, religions of Trinidad and Tobago (Bahá'í Faith, Christianity, Hinduism and Islam) in 1992 and the fiftieth anniversary of the Art Society in 1995. Parang was the subject of a cover issued in 1984. Interestingly, the researcher can draw on both this latter first day cover and the vertical file for information on Parang. The cover album can be accessed through the online catalogue.

392nd Medical Malaria Control Detachment, Trinidad, B.W.I.: Historical Report United States: Army, 194-?

Inserted in the voluminous report held in the rare books collection is an attractively designed brochure published by the United States War Department in 1943. The miniature item was a vital weapon in its antimalaria campaign in Trinidad and Tobago during the Second World War. Issued to the American forces stationed locally, the brochure recommended safeguards against the dreadful anopheles mosquito. It was provocatively entitled *This Is Ann: She's Dying to Meet You*. The booklet is an example of the communication strategies used in public health campaigns in the Caribbean. The historical report can be found in the online catalogue.

Tanzilo Collection (University of the West Indies, Mona)

The librarian Frances Salmon described the Tanzilo Collection, named after the donor, Robert Tanzilo, an American musician, journalist and reggae enthusiast, as a collection of ephemera mainly from the United States relating to Jamaican reggae artists (personal communication, e-mail, 19, 24 and 26 February 2009). The collection also includes information on recording studios, record producers and concert promoters, all involved in reggae music. It contains flyers, press releases, advertisements, posters, biographical information and reviews covering the 1980s and 1990s. The collection, which has not yet been catalogued, contains approximately one hundred and eighty vertical files with an alphabetical listing.

Caribbean-related ephemera offer immense possibilities for researchers. Funeral programmes, first day covers, wedding invitations, posters, flyers and the like can actually contribute greatly to scholarly investigations. The five collections highlighted here give an indication of the wide range of ephemeral materials held at the libraries at the University of the West Indies, also suggesting possible avenues of enquiry. Lurking in the West Indiana and Special Collections Division are the untapped raw materials – the creative methodology – for many a research project. Hopefully, this short discussion will spark interest in the resources in the division and so assist in strengthening the capacity for innovative research.

Chapter 7

Process and Method in Creative Writing

Elizabeth Walcott-Hackshaw and Barbara Lalla

Despite the perception of many readers and perhaps aspiring creative writers that artistic creation is entirely inspired, it is, at its best, the result of diligent preparation and application of describable processes, methods of discovery and analysis. This chapter addresses the creative writing process and those research methods that can be applied to artistic creation.

Research Process in Creative Writing

Elizabeth Walcott-Hackshaw

Every writer has a process for creating fictional work; there is no one perfect plan. As each idea, image or line begins to take shape in the writer's mind, this process begins to emerge. Seasoned writers know how they work best; some let the ideas simmer and then sit for extended sessions to write what has lived in the mind for a period; others need to keep their hand in by writing every day, inspired or not. Some ideas expand slowly, while others flow freely. The process of transference from idea to word may also depend on the genre of the creative work. Writers developing short fictions may have the luxury of these extended sessions, creating a piece from beginning to end; those working on novels do not have a similar time frame and as such may rely on regular sessions to sustain a voice(s), delineate characters and be "in touch" with the novel's world. In every case, short story, novella or novel writers need to develop a process that will ensure that the work will actually be completed.

An idea may activate the mind but it is only the beginning. A simple but effective suggestion is to record all thoughts or images that come to mind. In a sentence, a phrase or even an image, try to move it from idea to ink. Similar to any other researcher, the creative writer should keep track of the process. Some writers use journals, while others record their ideas orally; either way is useful, although oral recordings will eventually have to be transcribed and as such the written record may ultimately be more effective. The method of recording should be systematic: note the date of the entry, and make image, voice, character description or location as detailed as possible. Time is essential to this process; there are many occasions when a writer will encounter something that could be useful to the work but not remember to write it down and may forget the treasure. Hence the need for timely entries. It is also good practice to review entries weekly and integrate them into the piece quickly, lest they stay forever a journal entry rather than entering the fictional world. Most novelists rely heavily on this note taking, mapping the many characters, scenes, and evolving shapes of the work. Without these notes it would be very difficult to keep track of the entire world being created.

The following are examples of journal entries; they vary in length and try to capture different "real-life" moments of landscapes and light (examples 1 and 2). Example 3 is an idea for possible expansion of a novel's narrative.

1. *5:30 am – dark, full moon over the valley, blue grey sky, sun emerging soon, hills like shadows*
2. *March morning, rain falling through the sunshine, glistening on leaves. Pouring, sweet rain like white sugar, fronds, light on each leaf, birds, and blessings*
3. *There would be one crime and then the rumours would spread, for example if a young sixteen-year-old schoolgirl was kidnapped, shoved into a car, blindfolded and taken into a warehouse where she heard male voices around her, the newspapers might just say sixteen-year-old schoolgirl missing, last seen leaving home . . . but we would know the truth: there was always more.*

The Writer as Reader

In creative writing classes it is always interesting and often enlightening to note what writers read. But there are times when the question, what have you been reading recently? may be met with silence. As obvious as it may seem, it needs to be emphasized again that writers must read, and read a great deal. Those collections of a writer's favourite books and the personal reading experience of writers are essential to the development of the craft. This personal anthology may change over time as the writer's interests expand or become more concentrated with maturity. Writers may be attracted to certain genres, styles or historical periods that influence their work. The influence of other writers may not always be obvious; nevertheless, it is important that writers at least be aware of works to which they are drawn. Part of the creative writing process is being part of these literary worlds. Relying too heavily on experience, or even a fertile imagination, cannot replace the act of reading a text as a writer. The attention to the way in which another book is crafted, recognizing its strengths and weaknesses, is important to any writer's growth. This process of appreciating and critiquing is a skill that the writer can only refine through the act of reading others. There has always been a tradition of apprenticeship: young artists learned from the masters, and so too should writers sharpen their skills by studying the works of those recognized for their outstanding skill. The selections in a writer's personal anthology should be expansive, including great works from around the globe and from the Caribbean region. This apprenticeship is particularly important in the early stages of a writer's career, but throughout a writer's life there is a never-ending desire to keep chiselling away at the work. Many writers emphasize the significance of reading: William Faulkner, for example, recommends that writers "read, read, read! Read everything – trash, classics, good and bad; see how they do it. When a carpenter learns his trade, he does so by observing. Read! You'll absorb it. Write. If it is good, you'll find out. If it's not, throw it out the window" (1951, 68). The popular author of contemporary horror and fantasy fiction Stephen King offers this advice: "If you want to be a writer, you must do two things above all others: read a lot and write a lot. There's no way around these two things that I am aware of, no shortcut" (2000, 145).

Perspicacious reading can also be a creative, dialectical process which may lead to intertextuality and counterdiscursive practices. There are several examples of Caribbean works of this nature, including Maryse Condé's *Windward Heights* (*La migration des coeurs*) ([1995] 1998), inspired by Emily Brontë's English literary classic *Wuthering Heights*, first published in 1847. Condé's work examines similar thematic constructs of the original (love, prejudice, oppression) within a Caribbean context. Another example is Aimé Césaire's *Une tempête*, an adaptation of Shakespeare's *The Tempest*; Césaire uses the play as a site to explore the problematics of Western imperialism and racial conflict through the ideological lens of Négritude.

First Readers

The act of revision is another point where writers must create their own process. Writers often have readers for their work; in formal situations, creative writing programmes structure the process around these sessions where a writer's work is critiqued by the group. For those writers who are not in formal programmes, the critiquing process is an important step towards the completion of any project. What must be considered, however, is at what point the writer allows the work to be critiqued. Again there is no one magic point; some novelists prefer that the manuscript be completed before having it critiqued, while some short-story writers with a different time frame prefer that each story be critiqued rather than awaiting completion of the entire manuscript. Most first readings lead to revisions of one nature or another, and a writer must in the end make the final editorial choices. Any writer needs a good editor, as the critiquing and editing is an integral part of the process. Betsy Lerner's book *The Forest for the Trees: An Editor's Advice to Writers* (2001) gives an in-depth account of the publishing process from the moment the manuscript is sent out for review to its publication. The book also looks at writers as their own editors. *Becoming a Writer*, Dorothea Brande's 1934 classic, draws from Freudian psychoanalysis the notion of the child artist and the adult critic; the child artist writes early in the morning in a free, uninhibited manner closest to the dream state but returns to the work in the evening with a critical, adult eye. However, both are integral to the creative and editorial process.

Explorations in Genre

Any writer attempting to write in a particular genre be it short story, novel, poetry, play or screen writing should become fluent in that particular genre, even (perhaps, especially) if they go on to reconstitute the genre as, say, Nalo Hopkinson does by inserting folk characters in science fiction. The electronic system that supports her high-tech world of *Midnight Robber* (2000) is a Nancy web (tricky like Annancy) and presided over by Nanny, vigilant as her namesake, the revered female Maroon warrior. Fluency in this context is attained when the writer is able to move beyond literary language and delve into the language of others; a Caribbean writer should certainly be aware of other short-story writers from the region but should also explore the form in a wider context. This will allow engagement in comparative analysis and, more importantly, discovery. In his book *The Art of the Novel*, Milan Kundera talks of the novel as having "a spirit of complexity. Every novel says to the reader: 'Things are not as simple as you think.' That is the novel's eternal truth" (1988, 18). Kundera's book is an example of this fluency, where genre, in this case the novel, is placed within its literary historical context. Several Caribbean writers have developed and enriched Western genres like the bildungsroman. Merle Hodge's *Crick Crack, Monkey* (1970) gives a perspective of a young girl growing up in the Caribbean; similarly, Jamaica Kincaid's *Annie John* (1997) creates a young protagonist whose personal education mirrors that of her young island nation of Antigua. Novelists cannot know all of what has come before, but fluency should be attempted through discovery, allowing the writer to gain perspective, location and context.

An Overview of the Creative Writing Process

A writer's creative method or process may be as unique as the work itself, but there are some considerations worth noting:

- Many writers set production goals, in which case there should be a daily and five-day quota.
- The quota should be a realistic number of words or pages. This is preferable to setting a time, since a good halfhour could be spent seeking divine intervention as opposed to getting words down on a page. If the daily quota

is not met, then the writer tries to be disciplined enough to complete these pages on the weekend.

- If meeting the quota proves difficult, then it should be readjusted, taking into consideration the real time available for the craft when the demands of everyday life, a particular event or crisis are factored in.
- If possible the writer commits to regular times for writing; these depend on personal schedules and time challenges, but maintaining regularity drives the process and creates momentum.
- Any writing is better than nothing at all. Every writer has good writing days and days when the entire manuscript seems to demand tossing! But ultimately writers must produce work to be revised and read.
- On a final note it must be said that writing every day is the best way to get to the end of the manuscript.

Research Methods in Creative Writing

Barbara Lalla

The concepts of creative writing and scholarly research may seem contradictory to the uninitiated: one requiring inspiration and deriving from a "gift"; the other flowing from conscious and prolonged effort. However, what Wordsworth termed "the spontaneous overflow of powerful feelings" (in his preface to *Lyrical Ballads*, 1800) has to be forged into a communicable message, beaten into words, crafted into a unique style. Moreover, substantial research may be involved, especially for lengthy and complex productions such as a novel, full-length play or epic poem, although the extent of each writer's research will depend on personal work style and on the nature of the undertaking.

First, the writing itself (as described above) is a discovery procedure. The manipulation of form, the development of character, the analysis of thought demanded by regular and committed writing carry one to increasingly profound understandings of experience and ways to express such experience. The concept of creative writing as a research method is explored by John Cook (2005), while Denise Riley (2000) discusses the degree to which this particular method of study is vested in operations of language.

There are other resources for the creative writer. Archival research is often needed for historical background to literary essays, fiction, verse or drama set in a bygone age, and serious reading on social organization and culture is important for contemporary settings in a country other than that of the writer. The Caribbean preoccupation with its past and its multiplicity of cultures makes archival and other library search methods indispensable. V.S. Naipaul engaged in extensive historical research to produce *The Loss of El Dorado*, and a map precedes his text. Without such grounding a creative work may be superficial. The setting, vaguely or erroneously drawn, may not convince. The characters may fail through culturally inappropriate behaviour, dress, eating habits, motivation or speech.

The need to apply suitable methods of research is not limited to the writer whose subject is framed in a different age or geographical space. No writer enjoys unlimited experience of any society. Well-grounded descriptions or character study may demand a field trip to inaccessible terrain (like Jamaica's Cockpit Country) or a tour of some restricted area (like a Trinidad oilfield) – apart from more easily achieved exposure, to, say, morning market, a hospital waiting room or a street corner rum shop. Absolute authenticity can never be achieved because some characteristics must be selected from many and because the writer's sensibility remains distinct from the consciousness being evoked, yet a level of authenticity may be reached – enough to convince the informed reader anyway. Even local writers may require assistance from reference texts, guides and maps, or persons with specialist knowledge (from botanists on the nearest university campus to fishermen in seaside villages).

This need to identify adequate and accurate information is, of course, even more urgent and challenging for the writer from beyond the Caribbean. In such cases local contacts are invaluable, but researchers should be aware of information available from scholarly sources. There are dictionaries in print, like F.G. Cassidy and R.B. LePage ([1967] 1980), Richard Allsopp (1996), Paul Crosbie (2001) and Lise Winer (2009), and there are works on place names (Inez Sibley 1978) and on food (Higman 2008; and Allsopp 2003) and of course on the art of both the region and individual territories.

Actual production of a creative written work calls for intense application to integrate information seamlessly or to allow the data to inform the construction of a fictional world. Other forms of work besides writing may be involved.

Walcott's plays come into being by many routes taken simultaneously, including storyboards through which, as a painter himself, he gives visual form to characters who begin as mental constructs. Similarly, house plans, local area maps or timelines may be essential in clarifying the dimensions of crucial spaces or periods in which the action is set and in providing a record for the writer to maintain a consistent setting over the full term of production.

In writing *Cascade: A Novel*, for example, this author needed to plot the events of the story line against a timeline of Jamaica's history, Trinidad's history (Tobago was not involved) and world history. The development of characters not only took place within this composite framework (which was only rarely explicit) but had to be planned in stages of ageing, taking into account the development and course of illnesses and the growth of a child. The child's speech, for example, had to be convincing with regard to his age. Indeed it proved helpful to have a table showing the relative ages of the main characters at the time of major events. This provided a guide when questions arose, for example relating to the physical capabilities of an elderly man with Parkinson's disease or the degree of exposure to the Internet that one might expect of a child at a given date in the past. To refine the treatment of setting, it was necessary to draw house plans and roughly sketch the layout and distribution of land around one of the houses.

In planning the fictional space, the usage of crucial terms may need to be established. Terms like *porch* and *cupboard* differ somewhat in meaning between Caribbean and, say, Canadian speakers. This is important because a character leaping from a porch in the Caribbean (where the porch may be upstairs) may have a longer way to fall than one doing so in Canada (where a porch is found downstairs). *Gallery* (for an upstairs porch) is specifically Trinidadian and is also a verb, meaning "to show off". Specific usages may need to be contextualized enough for maximum comprehension, and research in comparative use of such terms may be required to ensure sharp mental pictures for diverse readers.

Character construction involves producing a convincing voice, and some writers may find a working knowledge of the appropriate language variety invaluable in shaping sentences, selecting vocabulary and choosing register. Descriptions by Caribbean linguists will be useful to some writers but not of particular interest to others. It is advisable, however, to know what relevant information exists.

As travel to, from and within the region has increased over the past decades, Caribbean writing has increasingly crossed territories, bringing together characters who are speakers of different varieties of anglophone Creoles. There may be need to verify usage in the less-familiar variety. Even a familiar territory may demonstrate ethnic variation in terms for food or for family relationships, differences between progressive urban and conservative rural speech, and distinctions in usage by old and young. In these circumstances it is useful to consult speakers in different groups, and sometimes a description by an expert on Caribbean language may sensitize a writer effectively; a historical character may be rendered more vivid by a phrase appropriate to the period or rendered unconvincing by a glaring modernism.

The writer who creates a wide range of characters interacting over generations may need to construct a family tree to ensure realistic connections between the passage of time and the experiences and interrelations among characters. Such a genealogy needs to be related to a detailed time frame of births, marriages, deaths and other major events of the work alongside a chronology of crucial socio-historical or natural events that take place within the timeframe – like World War II, the Abu Bakr coup in Trinidad, Hurricane Ivan in Grenada, Mandela's release, revolution in Cuba and the Haitian earthquake in 2010.

A wide variety of resources are available to supplement personal experience, invention and memory, but these inner resources are significant. Ann Gray (2003) discusses issues involved in recounting experience (associated with constructions of self), in describing different modes of storytelling like autobiography and testimony and in mining memory. Information on setting, events and writers themselves is immediately and widely available on the Internet (from Antiguan carnival to Tarun J. Tejpal's conversations with V.S. Naipaul on YouTube [2011]).

Finally, the publisher's readers and editors constitute a valuable resource. Here is an example of a useful comment by a sound reader:

> The novel is dialogue and thought driven, and, as can happen with that sort of focus, here there's sometimes a lack of orientation regarding characters within a scene. For example, inside a house what room are they in? . . . A related issue is that I had trouble visualizing the layout of [the] house (floors, doorways, stairs, gates).

> I think this is in part because of lack of description, and perhaps in part because I'm not familiar with norms in [Caribbean] homes.

Every writer wishes for unqualified praise, but inevitably there are aspects of a work that draw criticism. Most of the time such comments, however intrusive or inconvenient they may seem at first glance, uncover real areas of weakness or potential lack of clarity. Some suggestions offered by readers turn out to be impracticable, yet even these may trigger alternative ideas that improve the work, and editors operate from a wealth of experience that makes their views worthy of serious consideration.

Supplementing the range of resources described above, scholarly procedures for searching, recording, documentation and review are crucial operations in creative writing, even though many creative writers gather and process data informally and even unconsciously.

None of these research processes or methods can replace a fertile creative imagination, but they can support and complement it in invaluable ways. Lengthy productions, such as a novel or epic poem, demand methodical planning and execution and sound time management. The data for such a large project has to be categorized and may require careful record keeping, and it has to come from somewhere. For example, the development of convincing dialogue may be enhanced by transcriptions of the speech of informants or of real-life persons whom the writer selects. Creative writing, like scholarly exposition, is built on rigorous observation and analysis of data which the artist may arrive at through such methods as interviewing, visiting important sites or archival search.

methods of research
application
and analysis

Chapter 8

Oral Tradition and Calypso Research

Louis Regis

Preindustrial societies honoured their storytellers, who also functioned as oral historians and guardians of ancestral memory.
In the Mediterranean world and the successor states of western
Europe, the primacy of the bard was threatened by the development of
writing, which was simultaneously the cause and effect of the sophisti-
cation of society. Writing introduced over time a formalization of rules,
devices and conceits, a process which led inevitably to the declaration
of a canon. In the West the city, the locus of civilization, privileged
the canon of literature, the written word, at the expense of the verbal
repositories of orature, the spoken word. Orature and the oral traditions
were largely relegated to the realm of the primitive but conveniently
appropriated by literate poets in their search for vigorous form as well
as for what romantics see as "the soul of the nation".

Reading the Oral Tradition

The clash of cultures in the Caribbean from the sixteenth century
onwards exaggerated the dichotomy between orature and literature.
Europeans controlled the stage of the encounter and arrogated to themselves the moral and intellectual authority to determine validity and
quality of artistic and other endeavours. This resulted in a ubiquitous
and insidious two-tiered system corresponding in large degree to the

basic social divisions of the plantation system. As far as creative endeavour was concerned, literature, the Caribbean extension of the great European tradition, was deemed infinitely superior to the non-European oral traditions which, with their practitioners, were written off as inferior and unworthy of serious consideration. They were relegated to the domain of folklore, the collection of quaint practices which entertained or frightened the illiterate and semiliterate masses. Contemporary interest in and validation of the oral tradition derives from the coincidence of several related academic, artistic and social movements which have their genesis in the late nineteenth century. Inquiry into the African past and investigation into the African contribution to Western civilization informed ethnomusicological interest in neo-African musics in the New World. Contemporaneously, a new academic interest emerged in social history and in narrative inquiry as a major source of history that decentres the metanarrative told from the perspective of the victor. Oral history is now acknowledged as being as important as plantation literature in the development of West Indian social historiography and literary tradition. It is fitting that the West Indian initiative was spearheaded by regional scholars.

In the early 1940s, the calypso, Trinidad's unique song–dance art form, which achieved pan-Antillean popularity in the 1930s, generated a fierce public debate which involved literary personalities, folklorists, social scientists, aficionados and calypsonians. These individuals debated the origins and aesthetics of the calypso, enthusiastically elaborating theories based on their own subjectivity. J.D. Elder's doctoral dissertation, "The Evolution of the Traditional Calypso: A Socio Historical Analysis of Song Change" (1966), effectively brought temporary closure to the debate. The true value of Elder's magnum opus lies in its scientific evaluation of the constituents of the calypso. At the same time, it periodized the chronology of the traditional calypso, providing descriptions of and explanations for each period.

By a remarkable coincidence, the following year at a session of the Caribbean Artists Movement which was discussing the aesthetics of the newly emergent West Indian literature, Gordon Rohlehr, a young scholar then completing his doctoral studies in England, proposed to read the calypso along with the novels and short stories of Samuel Selvon and V.S. Naipaul to determine whether these creative oeuvres established a characteristically Caribbean sensibility. His presentation, "Sparrow and the Language of the Calypso", met rapturous reception. Anne Walmsley, who was present, assesses the presentation: "Rohlehr's paper was a landmark in West Indian literary criticism. By applying the same criteria to the sung lyrics of a popular calypsonian as to the poems of literary writers, he attempted for the first time to break down the separation between the oral and written traditions. By looking at Sparrow's attitudes to society, he drew attention to expression of the experience of the 'masses' by their own spokesman" (1992, 70). Rohlehr himself writes of his process:

> I began to recognize the importance of using the music to understand the society. So two things were necessary. One needed to have some broad concept of the society and, at the same time, one needed to bring a particular focus to bear on what the society produces artistically before one could begin the discourse: one had to adopt a two-way approach – the society through the creations, the creations through the society and to somehow try to keep the balance. (In Aiyejina 2003, 251)

For the next forty years he refined his approach, and his numerous publications have been in the vanguard of the new movement towards legitimizing the calypso as an artistic form and an anthropological artefact.

Towards a Methodology for Calypso Research

The classic calypso "What Is Calypso" (1968), composed and performed by the Mighty Duke (Kevin Pope), explains that Trinidad and Tobago's unique performance song–dance complex is

> a feeling that comes from deep within
> A tale of joy or of suffering
> It is an editorial in song of the life we undergo.

Duke's lines distil in simple, unambiguous language the complex essences of Trinidad's most celebrated musical artefact. Duke foregrounds the metaphysical dimension of the calypso ("a feeling that comes from deep within"), captures its range of theme and human interest ("A tale of joy or of suffering") and pronounces on its sociological relevance ("It is an editorial in song of the life we undergo"). This last implies a transmission of opinion on a common or familiar reality, and, while consistent with the romantic perception of the calypso as "the poor man's newspaper", it expands the scope of mass media

activity beyond the mere reportage to which the calypso has been traditionally – and inaccurately – reduced.

Duke assumes a national calypso-listening, perhaps calypso-loving, community. Many individuals, including calypsonians, have perceived the calypso
to be an artistic representation of a sensibility which has come to characterize
the nation as a whole. Ideologues, propagandists and calypsonians serving
those roles have romanticized the calypso as "the voice of the people", a con-
testable generalization given the notorious difficulties of defining "the people"
of Trinidad and Tobago.

Emerging in the last decade of nineteenth-century Port of Spain, the calypso
is the product of cross-fertilizations of several kindred West African musics
and neo-African hybrids creolized by the experience of plantation slavery in
the Caribbean. The resultant form later incorporated melodies and rhythms
from the European, Caribbean and Asiatic musics which shared or came to
share the Trinidad space. It is at best a popular seasonal voice in a multivoiced
society. More accurately, it is a chorus of voices which admits difference and
dissensus and is in itself a dialogue of viewpoints among the commonality. It
is a form of discourse which the national community has grown accustomed
to and looks forward to hearing because it is to a large extent Trinidadians
and Tobagonians speaking in a language readily understandable – though not
necessarily agreeable – to all.

Researchers attempt to impose academic discipline on the chaotic experience of the calypso. Their work is predicated upon the fundamental truth of
ethnomusicology that music is "a creative aspect of culture [which] can lead to
understanding of basic human problems of creative life as well as the values,
goals and meanings of the culture in which it functions. We can trace the problems of cultural stability, individual variations in performance, the reworking
of old values in new situations and most particularly the general processes
of culture change" (Merriam 1951, 2). Caribbean thinkers have arrived independently at similar conclusions about regional musics. Rex Nettleford opines
that "the presence of artists in the region and their examination by way of
artistic articulation of the phenomena of race, culture and class separately and
their shifting relationships need to be considered as legitimate representation
of Caribbean reality" (1984, ix). V.S. Naipaul, a self-confessed Trinidadphobe,
writes that "it is only in the Calypso that the Trinidadian touches reality"
([1962] 1978, 75). This is a truth which most Trinidadians endorse – except

when the reality endorsed by the calypso exposes or threatens their private ideology. The logical corollary to the Naipaul thesis is that it is through the calypso that Trinidadians best express their perceptions of reality.

The calypso's major achievement of the twentieth century has been to elevate itself from its status as an urban African underclass music, deprecatingly accorded semiofficial recognition in the French Creole–owned *Port of Spain Gazette* of 20 January 1900, to that of a semiofficial national music with regional and international credibility. In the twentieth century the calypso established beyond a reasonable doubt that it is a form of popular oral literature legitimized by its practitioners' intuitive and conscious control of sophisticated literary technique. It also established its bona fides as a vitally alive model, metaphor and wellspring for West Indian literature. The twentieth century has witnessed the plethora of nonentertainment uses (anthropological, artistic, educational, ideological, nationalistic and political) to which the calypso can be put. But it has also witnessed marginalization, manipulation, misinterpretation and misrepresentation. Latterly, interethnic contestation, increasingly centred on the calypso as culture, has become politicized, and politics "culturized". Articulating a proper methodology for calypso research will pre-empt epistemologically bizarre revisionisms of past calypsos, neutralize most of the engineered antagonism of the present and preclude implausible interpretations in the future.

In his 1991 essay "Researching Calypso", Rohlehr stresses that the calypso is a form of discourse originating in the underclass and still representing underclass opinions. He cautions that the calypso is a form of poetry and song which is subject to conscious shaping, selection and editing of information so that the "facts" presented cannot be interpreted simplistically as reflections of reality. He cautions, "We may be dealing with a wide range of literary and dramatic devices; and these may be of greater importance than the actual sociological content of the song" (p. 15).

Rohlehr's own numerous writings are the practice of a methodology which has evolved from his preoccupation as literary critic with poetic form, structure and shaping of theme; this preoccupation is married to a social scientist's concern with the phenomenal world inhabited and discussed by the artiste. This methodology requires researchers to familiarize themselves with the techniques of literary criticism; the history, meaning and development of the art form, including its patterns of performance; the biography of the practitioners; the political and social history of the country; and relevant information about the particular subject of the calypsos under examination. Noting the continuities in calypso tradition, Rohlehr identifies "moments" in time and clusters of calypsos generated by said moments. He then subjects selected texts to a close reading, again in light of documented reality as well as performers' career record and the song (sung) view of their peers. This multidisciplinary approach originates in a perception of the calypso as a complex multifaceted whole, the true value of which can only be apprehended within the social and literary contexts which it seeks to elucidate. Rohlehr's *Calypso and Society in Pre-Independence Trinidad* (1990) demonstrates that the calypso provides valuable maps of meaning to Trinidad society before – and after – 1962 and is in effect a valid social history of modern Trinidad.

Of late there has been welcome progression in social and political anthropology from simplistic use of the calypso as illustration to the calypso as invaluable resource material. Gender studies has long acknowledged the sociological importance of the calypso. In 1975 Frances Henry and Pamela Wilson concluded, "Some of the themes which show the dualisms [of male–female relationships] are better described in calypso than in the anthropological literature which has not devised ways and means of researching the essential relationships between the sexes" (p. 165).

In considering the practice itself, it is useful to bear in mind that literary analysis of the calypso conforms to the principles and practices of sensible literary criticism in stressing a common-sense interpretation of the text. The calypso text, however, needs to be "read" in terms of several interrelated social and sociological contexts which impart meanings implied in or absent from the text itself. In "What Is Calypso" Duke observes, "The words and phrases that we rhyme and sing / Are only half the thing". In this way he draws attention to the musical, rhythmic and also performative dimensions of the calypso. Optimally calypsos need to be experienced in performance because they are also shaped by criteria and contexts of actualization, which add to the overall meanings of the individual songs. Gesture, mime and the range of body language either assist the audience in interpreting content, or they can convey meanings other than those suggested by the lyrics. Further, contexts of performance may dictate or encourage changes to the song text which can be adjusted to suit the composition of the live audience or can be modified by factors arising between the time of song composition and performance. Folk wisdom / folk folly combines with imprecise notions of what is acceptable or desirable in and expected of the calypso to influence composition and performance: the composer and performer must be aware of the inner and outer limits of audience tolerance, and this is especially crucial when dealing with a subject as explosive as ethnicity. Calypsos on ethnicity, for example, pose the additional difficulty of being coded or masked messages which have to be deconstructed according to social context.

Building on Rohlehr's methodological base, I have considered the cross-sectional and longitudinal views; that is, the treatment of the same subject or incident by different calypsonians in the same calypso year (cross-sectional) and the treatment of a particular theme or particular themes by the same singer over time (longitudinal). At the intersection of the longitudinal and cross-sectional approaches, one may find the explanation for many a calypso, although in some cases the calypsonians themselves may be unable to account for a particular choice on their part.

At the intersection of these approaches, too, one can find an answer for those academic critics who allege the strictures of the art form are limitations to its potential for exploration of complex issues. Subconsciously many academics, well intentioned though they may be, are not intellectually prepared to accept the calypso as truly insightful commentary on society. Selwyn Ryan, defending Gypsy against mainly academic attacks on the selectiveness and inaccuracy of his "Little Black Boy", writes, "But Gypsy was singing a calypso, and could not be expected to deal with all the facets of a complex issue" (1999, 147). Similarly Kenneth Ramchand (1997) tries to exculpate Brother Marvin from the mischief of the lines of his "Jahaaji Bhai" (1996) which invite those of African descent who are "playing ignorant / Talking 'bout true African descendant" to

> Take a trip back to yuh roots
> and somewhere on that journey
> You go see a man in a *dhoti*
> Saying he prayers in front a *jhandi*.

Ramchand writes that "it is possible that in the short space of the calypso and given the demands of the form, Marvin was bound to put things in a way that could give offence" (1997, 9). I find it impossible to agree with this comment. Marvin's discography reveals that he protested Hulsie Bhaggan's anti-African hysteria in the name of "We Africans" ("Miss Bhaggan", 1994). In 1996, given the ascension to office of the United National Congress, a party with its centre of gravity in the Indian communities, he chose first to foreground his *dougla* identity which he then subsumes in his Indian ancestry. Then without explanation he launches into an attack on African nationalists. The researcher who is aware of Marvin's background, including the fact that he is an excellent composer, will not excuse him as readily as Ramchand does.

The objection to Ryan is that his comment devalues those numerous classic calypsos which have presented in a single song, if not all, certainly the salient facets of complex issues. Sparrow's "Get to Hell Out" (1965) presents in three stanza-choruses the towering arrogance of Dr Eric Williams as well as Sparrow's subtle rejection of the politician he once idolized. My objection to what Ramchand calls the "short space of the calypso" (p. 9) is that the four-stanza format is simply a convention which singers adopted for recording purposes. Maestro's "Mr Trinidadian" (1974), recorded live at a session of the Calypso Revue, features seven stanzas, as does Crazy's "Shoes" (2000), also recorded live at a tent session. In any event, there is nothing to debar a calypsonian from presenting two songs on the same issue. Explainer's "Absolutely Free" and "Caribbean Change", both on his 1984 album *The Awakening*, discuss the fall of the Maurice Bishop regime in Grenada. Also there is nothing to prevent a singer from presenting two songs with the same name, as Rudder has done with "The Ganges and the Nile" (1999). On his 1990 album *1990*, Rudder wrote nine songs, each reflecting a different aspect of the apartheid system then alive in South Africa. One song could not do justice to multiple aspects of a complex situation, and so Rudder, who challenges conventional limits to the calypso art form, composed nine.

The Interview

It is, above all, the interview that immediately suggests itself as an indispensable instrument for implementing the above-mentioned approach. The circumstances of calypsonians' lives inform their values and shape the views they project in song. Their familiar world may condition their themes, their moods and their style; it may even affect their decision to compose, record, perform or compete. Knowledge of the circumstances and currents of their existence therefore may explain change or ambivalence in their attitudes or expression.

Conversations with calypsonians can be stimulating and enlightening, for they provide meaningful insights into the minds and lives of creative artists; one is ushered into the magical private world of creativity and into the robust public world of performance. One sees what happens when the private calypso bubble is let down into the maelstrom of tent politics and the entertainment industry; how tensions, anxieties and jealousies buffet it one way or another, fulfilling great expectations or delivering hard times. One sees as well how entertainers adjust to circumstances in calypsodom and in the larger society.

One important feature about the interview is that it assists in identifying the ubiquitous *I-narrator* whose indiscriminate employment in calypso fictions, fantasies, commentaries and testimonies creates problems for those who cannot differentiate between person and persona and between the many masks assumed by calypsonians in their several traditional roles. The stylistic use of *I*, one of the three aesthetic tropes of performance in the British West Indies (Abrahams 1967, 456), allows calypsonians to (1) voice their own opinions or those which they think accord with the views of their audiences and (2) create fictions and situations in which they either aspire towards verisimilitude, (3) seek the temporary ego-gains of wish-fulfilment, or (4) present themselves as persons in the know. While the calypsonian is under no pressure to differentiate the *I* of fiction from the *I* of confession or declaration, the critic must essay this or run the risk of flawed interpretation, as happens with the Ryan discussion of Gypsy's "Little Black Boy" and the Ramchand comment on Marvin's "Jahaaji Bhai".

On Carnival Sunday night, 5 March 2000, the viewing public was given an excellent demonstration of the difficulties of disengaging public from private personae. Shadow won the national calypso monarchy, and, while he was driving out of the Queen's Park Savannah in the automobile he had just won singing "What's Wrong with Me?" (2000), he was asked by a young reporter, "What's wrong with you?" To this Shadow replied calmly, "Nothing". This enigmatic answer invites us to dissociate Winston Bailey, the person, from Shadow, the persona/performer. Further we are invited to attempt the more complex task of separating the person from the I-persona of what seemed a confessional song. One way of reconciling these tasks in light of the context of Shadow's answer is to agree that nothing was wrong with him anymore, because after thirty-odd years of professional calypso singing he had finally won the coveted calypso crown.

Each song has its story, and many times the story behind the song contributes to our understanding of the song or of its performance. Experience has taught, however, that information gleaned through interviews must be rationalized. Calypsonians are understandably reticent about work done before they developed a desirable public image; like other public personalities, they present their best profile to public view. Experience has also taught that calypsonians are sometimes genuinely unable to explain subject choice and treatment and sometimes performance style; like other creative artists, their work is, as Rohlehr theorizes, a combination of intelligence, temperament and sensibility, experience personal or vicarious, and imagination; the whole subject to a shaping by processes conscious and unconscious (1992, 1). To do them justice, then, one needs to examine their creative output treating the individual songs as products of particular contexts.

One other difficulty about the interview is that some calypsonians are averse to answering questions about their work. Shadow, for example, refers questioners to the work itself and refrains from commenting further. The business of cultivating an artist's trust can be very time consuming and may require the aid of another person with whom the artist is intimate. When interviewing Kitchener in 1985, this author was advised to make sure that Pretender was present, and the time advised was a Sunday afternoon when the two greats were taking their leisure. Pretender's presence contributed immeasurably because, in addition to jogging Kitchener's memory, for most of the session he was the one to whom Kitchener spoke directly, rather than to the researcher posing the question.

The Calypso as Commodity

The researcher not only gathers data but evaluates ethical issues that such data reveal. Serious investigation must take into account the circumstances of production, which require the researcher to factor the profit motive into the calypso-performing equation. Commercialization has long mediated the communication between calypsonian and community, and it is no secret that the invisible hands of ghostwriters have propelled many singers into successful orbit and have arrested the free fall of many burned-out stars. Looking briefly at the phenomenon of the "ghost" even in the pre-Sparrow era – that is, before 1956 – Rohlehr concludes that "collaboration, borrowing, adaptation and downright plagiarism have all been part of the Calypso tradition" (1990, 531). The inexorable pressure of having to please or appease voracious audiences every year with new songs makes collaboration with ghosts understandable. Traditionalists, however, find total dependence intolerable and in violation of the ethos. Most will agree with separation of the industry into two types: *true-true kaisonians*, who compose and perform their own work, and "quacks and invalids" who depend on ghost writers. Pretender's "True-true Calypsonian" (1987) reserves the noble appellation *true-true calypsonian* for the composer/performer, while Chalkdust's "Quacks and Invalids" (1986) deplores the unwelcome (to him) presence of the pretenders who preen themselves in borrowed plumage. Valentino's "Who Is Who" (2002), condemning the existence of a "calypso factory" as a violation of his tradition, proposes separate competitions for true-true calypsonians and non-writers. What provokes the ire of traditionalists like Pretender, Chalkdust and Valentino is the fact that the performers are competing successfully at the National Calypso Monarch Competition, thus providing the true-true kaisonians of their just rewards. While I sympathize deeply with the traditionalists, I appreciate the complexity of the industry and of the market forces which have birthed the pure calypso performers (voices). I also note, however, that in the same year some kaisonians like Explainer write songs for themselves and for "voices" but they also perform and record songs written by others. As said before the situation is quite complex and resists simplistic description.

Accusations that the "quacks and invalids" are actuated by profit do not ipso facto acquit kaisonians of the charge that they too may well be motivated by monetary considerations as much as inspired by ideological ones; their intent in composing particular songs or in presenting particular lines of argument through the years may also be weighted by gross considerations. What the presence of the ghosts and voices does is to introduce a new range of factors which impact upon methodology. The storied career of the Mighty Sparrow is an excellent illustration of this conundrum. Sparrow has recorded more than five hundred songs in a career from 1954 to the present, and this roughly works out to ten songs per year; in the mid-1960s he actually produced two albums of ten songs each per year. Sparrow (Francisco) has reluctantly admitted to collaboration with Reginald Joseph up to the mid-1960s (Rohlehr 1990, 529), and it is popularly rumoured that he has employed other ghosts, among them Maestro, Merchant and "superghost" Winsford Devine, who replaced

Joseph as Sparrow's greatest collaborator and composer between 1971 and 1991 (Ogunlade 2006, 8, 17–20). The Francisco–Devine authorship credited on album sleeves to a mere six songs greatly undersells the seventy-one Devine claims to have written for Sparrow (p. 2). The point to all this is that, given the number of ghosts with whom he is reported to have been associated, it is well-nigh impossible to appraise Sparrow as composer. While this is not necessarily cause for anxiety, one wonders how far multiple composers have contributed to the contradictory positions adopted by Sparrow in his 150-odd narratives, fictions and commentaries on the male–female question. The dramatic contradictions in the Sparrow's opus fit tidily into traditional patterns of calypso in which singers subscribe enthusiastically and energetically to the ancestral macho archetype in their fictions and commentaries but confess male anxiety and inadequacy in the face of female sexuality. But Sparrow's 150 songs embrace a wider range of contradiction consistent with the explorations by several minds of the limitless possibilities, fictional and otherwise, suggested by the universal male–female debate.

Interestingly, except for Lady Iere's "Saga Boys in Town" (c. 1940s) and Rose's several affirmations of women as liberated sexual beings, the hugely popular calypso statements on women's liberation were all composed by men. Singing Francine's "Woman's World" (1975) was composed by Maestro; Singing Sandra's "Sexy Employers" (1987), popularly called "Die with My Dignity", was written by Tobago Crusoe; Denyse Plummer's anthem "Woman Is Boss" (1988) was written by Reynold Howard and Len Boogsie Sharp; Sandra's "The Equalizer" (1998) and "Voices from the Ghetto" (1999) were composed by Cristophe Grant, and the list goes on. This was before women like Nadia Batson finally entered their own voice, although many divas like Sanelle Dempster of "The River" fame still depend upon male composers.

All of this raises issues which are worthy of consideration. The first of these has to do with the nature of the composer–performer interface: Whose position does the song reflect? What is the composer's stake in the song: Does he or she merely anticipate audience response and cater for it? What is the performer's stake in the song performed: Does he or she merely buy a song, does he or she buy one in keeping with a designed stage image, or does he or she commission one to reflect feelings which he or she may not have the talent to voice? What is the performer's involvement in the song: Does he or she contribute melody, lyric, beat? Does the performer alter the song significantly? Can a man capture the interior reality of women sufficiently to write a song that truly reflects how women feel?

The ultimate question is, whose song is it? Singers generally take credit for performances, while composers shoulder responsibility when controversy arises. GB, the composer of "Shat Vision" (1998), found himself defending his controversial prize-winning composition while Prowler, the performer, remained silent. It may be useful to point out here that GB's several interviews profile Anansi-type opportunism on his part. At first he admitted that the calypso "deals with the ugliness of racism", explaining that he meant no disrespect to the Indian community, with whom he has familial ties, but that he was trying to reply to the inflammatory statements made by Satnaryan Maharaj, secretary general of the Sanatan Dharma Maha Sabha. In the same interview, however, GB confessed that his discussion of racism could have been deeper but that the Dimanche Gras audience "is not as literate as people like to think and they fall for a certain kind of commentary" (Gajar 1998, 15). Sometime after this he publicly called for an end to *mauvais langue* on the calypso (Hassanali 1998, 3), and still later he confessed that he had known that the couplet "Children will be having fun / Shooting gramozone in they watergun" was "ridiculous" but retained it because it was drawing six encores nightly at the tent (1998, 85). GB then read audience hunger and catered to it cynically. This experience teaches that honesty in calypso, then, is not to be presumed.

In response to the wealth of texts available for analysis, the researcher seeks criteria for selection. The choice of texts to be examined is determined largely by competition success and by tent acclaim. Given that public response is the raison d'être of performance, the researcher must consider how this supremely important element fixes a particular song in the public mind as well as in the mind of its composer/performer. Songs performed at the Calypso Monarch show need special attention because that competition, maligned though it is, enjoys the greatest prestige of any calypso show. Here it is that performers make a special effort by way of costume, props and a range of theatrical devices to have their lyrics understood and appreciated. Looking at the special interest generated by competitions on the whole and also at the fact that before 1996 "offensive" songs – especially those which won the Monarch title – seem to have avoided controversy until Ash Wednesday, one concludes that many people acknowledge the Calypso Monarch show as the calypso show of the year, and, except for the party songs "jammed" ad nauseam on commercial radio or presented in video format on television, the calypsos performed at the national Calypso Monarch competition may well be the only calypsos many people hear in a particular year. This argues for a closer look at the songs performed not only at the Calypso Monarch show but also at the qualifying semifinals, the Calypso Fiesta. Attention should be paid to the songs performed at the Young Kings and the Calypso Queen competitions, which both feature many worthwhile calypsos.

Researchers need to consider as well the fact that many eminently serious, well-composed songs with pleasing melodies and with good correlation of word, tune and beat remain as silent songs. *Silent songs* range from those which are never performed to songs which do not seem to have received attention although performed at the highest levels. The subcategory also includes those songs performed unsuccessfully at the tent and those which languish underexposed on albums. Dougla's "Split Me in Two" (1961) is the supreme example of a silent song which won the Calypso King crown, the most prestigious award in Calypso. Marvin's "The Way", the national unity song which partnered the controversial "Jahaji Bhai" to a second-place finish in 1996, and Gypsy's "Unity" (1998), which succeeded his controversial prize-winning "Little Black Boy", are also excellent examples.

Important and highly exposed songs can be relegated to the subcategory because audiences choose to ignore them. This happens when the calypsonian sings unpleasant or unwelcome truths. Dougla's "Split Me in Two", for example, discussed the predicament of the dougla in a society bent on ethnic polarization, and, although the song won him the greatest prize in calypsodom, including a victory over the otherwise unbeatable Sparrow, it was ignored by the "pure" of all races. David Rudder's "Hoosay" (1991) was largely ignored because it demolished our false representation of ourselves and presented us with a more realistic but more unflattering reflection:

Not in this house
Not in this garden of Eden
Oh how we danced to the beat of this lovely lie
Until a man [Abu Bakr] opened a door
And showed us our other side
And all our meccared illusions walked right on by

Now Trinis know what is Uzi diplomacy
Now Trinis know what is SLR [self-loading rifle] love
In these troubled times under the stars above.

A silent-song situation is also created when audiences prefer to listen to other songs by an artiste whom they have classified in a particular mode and are collectively unable to hear when he or she ventures outside the limits of their perceptions. Colin Lucas's "Doh Hate" (1995), which advises the citizenry of all ethnicities to applaud and follow the positive examples of successful citizens rather than hate them, suffered because Lucas is perceived as the "Dollar Wine" man; the singer who is rapturously received when he advises audiences to gyrate and oscillate is hardly heeded when he tells warring members of ethnic groups to imitate and emulate but "doh hate".

The Media

In the Caribbean, oral culture and literary culture intercept each other, and calypso research cannot underplay the role of the media in stimulating composition. Calypsonians are and have long been avid readers of print media. A statement in the locally owned *Argos* newspaper inspired the Duke of Normandy's popular calypso of 1919:

Argos newspaper, latest telegram
Argos newspaper, latest telegram
Germans surrender under the British commander
Germans surrender under the British commander.

Attila the Hun's famous "Mr Nankivell's Speech" (1938) begins with the couplet "Hand me the *Port of Spain [Gazette]* / to read Mr Nankivell's speech again". These two examples demonstrate that calypsonians are aware of their indebtedness to conventional media for "the big story" which they then editorialize and broadcast from the calypso stage.

When the newspapers carry stories which calypsonians find unfair, they riposte in song. Attila's "Reply to the *Daily Mail*" (1946) refutes as "a dirty lie and a calumny" the front-page article of the *Trinidad Guardian* which reproduced the sensational allegation that "bands of negroes robust and bad / Were violating white women in Trinidad". This allegation was first carried in the

English newspaper the *Daily Mail*. The *Guardian*, mouthpiece of the English plantocrats and merchants, was perceived as antiblack and antipopulist, and, although the song does not accuse them of this, it is the subtext on which the direct accusation is constructed. In 1961 when Sparrow was in full flight as the world's leading calypsonian and also the leading calypso propagandist for the People's National Movement, which was opposed by the English and French Creole plantocrats, the *Guardian* saw fit to predict his defeat in the Calypso King competition (Regis 1999, 12). Sparrow's "Thanks to the *Guardian*" (1962) chastizes that newspaper in language characteristic of Sparrow of the period:

> They have a big stupid editor
> Only printing special letter
> Plenty plenty people write in favour of me
> The criminal ignore them completely
> Now and then he'll pass a good one
> That sneaky son-of-a-gun
> But good or bad without any doubt
> It good for me, is Sparrow they talking 'bout

Gypsy, on the other hand, was challenged in the media well before the 1997 competition for his "Little Black Boy" and so was able to employ his matchless improvising skill in a special stanza on the "little black boy" of its critics in the media. He thought it necessary to present the following preface to a tent performance of his song: "As a writer sometimes you write a song you like to write, love to write, and sometimes you write a song you have to write. As a singer sometimes you sing songs that you love to sing and then again sometimes you sing songs that you have to sing. The next song I'm about to do falls in the second category" (taped proceedings of a tent performance in 1997). This brief introduction is an example of the kinds of improvisation afforded in a live performance. It is doubly important because it confirms that Gypsy was describing a familiar and familial situation and was singing from the depths of his personal pain rather than discussing a situation alien to him. He then performed the regular stanzas of the song and added as an encore the following:

> Ah read a article on the newspaper the other day
> Ah didn't like what the little Black boy say

The little Black boy misinterpret my song
No way in the world could I ever be wrong
The things that he say, well it could never be true
I'm a racist? Who could I ever be racist to?

. . . .

Little Black boy, education is the key
But you can't use it writing stupidness 'bout me

The next year provided other evidence of the relationship between calyp-sonians and the conventional media. Iwer George's trite "Bottom in the Road" (1997–1998) was contested by the Trinidad and Tobago government of the day and by special interest groups well before the start of the 1998 season. Iwer, a competent composer when so inclined, penned an explanation and "apology" for the controversy generated by his song:

Ah never sing to degrade nobody
   Bottom in the road
Since Ah sing 'bout this Indian lady
   Bottom in the road
Radio stations come out to ban me
   Bottom in the road

Interestingly, he was able to profit from the sales of the controversial original as well as from the sales of the seeming apology. What is important about "Little Black Boy" and "Bottom in the Road" is that they inform us that calypsonians are very aware of media focus. They are also keenly aware that they consti-tute an unconventional press sometimes in opposition to the conventional. They are also aware that they act as the medium for those unrepresented by mainstream press, which is seen as subservient to the state. Valentino's "True Opposition" (1980) begins like this:

We have no opposition in the houses of Parliament
So politically is we who have to comment
On this government

Media intervention and calypsonian response, then, have to be considered in any viable study of the calypso together with calypsonian perception of and playing to audience appreciation.

After researchers have approached Calypso research as discussed above, there remain five simple-seeming steps:

- Pay close attention to the calypsos and their performances.
- Read and listen to the discourse surrounding the songs, if any.
- Return to the song texts themselves.
- Analyse and discuss.
- Repeat all the steps above.

Conclusion

This chapter proposes a responsible methodology for continued research on calypso. It is a well-known truth of ethnomusicology that popular culture transmits values and attitudes of (segments of) a society, and this knowledge informs the appropriation of the calypso in recent research, especially in political and social anthropology. Given this scenario, there is need for proper analysis of the calypso if conclusions based thereon are to withstand rigorous academic scrutiny.

In surveying the academic and artistic landscapes, this chapter reviews the work of early methodologists, especially Rohlehr, who has designed a viable model of procedure consistent with his perception of the calypso as a literary form which grows out of the private and collective experiences of the urban underclass. Rohlehr recommends a multidisciplinary approach which harmonizes literary criticism, social history and biography. Using this model as a basis, this chapter proposes its own cross-sectional and longitudinal approach which analyses individual songs in light of others composed on the same theme or "moment" and also in light of the performer's own body of work. The interview, which is the major instrument of this approach, is frankly assessed. The chapter also suggests a logical formula for selecting the songs to be used in general thematic analysis and presents the notion of the silent song. Finally the chapter recommends a five-step procedure which, if implemented, will provide an informed view of the calypsos under examination.

Chapter 9

Textual and Discourse Analysis

Barbara Lalla and Valerie Youssef

A range of analytical techniques are available for deriving as much as possible from text and discourse. Whatever approach is customary in a particular subfield of literary or linguistics research, a different technique may yield more, depending on the nature of the material.

Analysing Text

Analysis of a literary text involves examination of its general *structure.* This requires identifying its components. Its ultimate constituents (such as events, in the case of narrative) must be ordered in some describable way, and this order is determined and stated. Because these components must also be linked if the discourse holds together, the bases on which they are linked can also be stated. For example, events may be ordered chronologically or to bring out causal relationships. Narrative gaps and their functions are also significant, and the researcher gives thought to the purpose of gaps and to whether constituents of the discourse are conjoined or some embedded into others, whether their arrangements are sequential or parallel, and whether some constituents of the text adhere to each other to form larger constituents, producing a hierarchical set of relationships not unlike those of sentences.

Because a great deal of discourse (especially narrative discourse) is retrospective, temporal organization requires mapping, and chronological inversions or other departures are also noted and their significance evaluated. Such departures, indicated by tense, may coincide with causal linkages and affect plot definition, while shifts in aspect may foreground or background situations. When analysing Caribbean discourse, the importance of rigorous attention to tense and aspect cannot be overemphasized in a literature infused with its past and preoccupied with remembering and re-membering.

Observing the linguistic mechanisms by which effects are achieved requires close attention to *language* at every level of description, to phonological effects and their orthographical representation, vocabulary choice and sentence structure, devices such as metaphor and irony, and images. Merle Hodge's (2007) detailed analysis of Lovelace's language exemplifies this approach.

Apart from events in a narrative, *participants* have roles and motives that move the action along, as well as responses through which they become better known to us. Such participants are frequently defined by their voices and even discourse types. The behaviour of characters is understood within a context constructed in the text itself. The *setting* of the action comprises propositions about location in time and place and propositions about circumstances underway against which the events unfold.

Outside the text is its own *context* – those circumstances that frame the text itself and are part of the discourse to be analysed for that added meaning that context confers. This includes the socio-historical background of the work and the literary setting of its age. The author's biography may illuminate the significance of authorial experience of the social circumstances identified. Exposure to the author's opus may reveal important trends in style and content. Then it is important to assess the relevance of feminist, postcolonial, postmodernist or other *theoretical approaches* to the material contextualized. Indeed, discourse analysis is generally associated with postmodernism. Earlier philosophies are characterized by particular ways of viewing the world, while postmodernism insists that there is no one way but a multiple, shifting, fragmenting reality in which (dominant) interpretation is constructed through the perspective of the powerful.

A *historical* sensitivity is thus essential not only to context but to analysis of language. Understanding language history facilitates interpretation of a text from previous centuries. Researchers working with such texts must familiarize themselves with the earlier sound structure of the language and attend to orthographical representation. Anyone familiar with earlier English writers knows that understanding phonology facilitates appreciation not only of rhyme schemes and metre but of puns. In such circumstances also a historical dictionary reveals nuances of meaning that would otherwise be lost. Similarly, familiarity with earlier syntax sensitizes readers to subtleties of reference and to changes in form or function of pronouns or prepositions that affect meaning in the text.

Close links exist between historical change at one level of linguistic description and at another – some phonological forms of words survive while meaning changes radically (e.g., English *gay*), while some word meanings remain unchanged while the phonological shape of the word changes beyond recognition. Jamaican *busha*, "overseer", has travelled through *oberseer* to *obusheer* to *busheer* to *busha* while retaining the same meaning. The understanding of various literary devices (rhyme, alliteration, puns and so on) depends on such information.

Consider, for example, some *weird* and *eerie* situations in *Macbeth* and in Jamaican songs recorded by Monk Lewis (1834). Shakespeare's weird sisters are so called not only because they are weird in our modern sense but because they were felt to determine human destiny, the Anglo-Saxon *wyrd* having actually meant "fate". On the other hand, in an old Jamaican song, a master ridiculing his slave as looking *eerie* enough already, what we might now loosely call "weird", is probably responding to the man's desire to look *irie* (Jamaican Creole), to look "unusual in a stylish way". The different pronunciation may have come about through some alternative manifestation of the Great Vowel Shift, an English sound change that raised long vowels like [e] to [i] and diphthongized high vowels like [i] to [ai].

Also, established genres may be innovatively applied. Maureen Warner Lewis (2005) demonstrates African patterns in Caribbean song, like the interchange between many voices or the adjustments of pitch by one speaker to suggest this multivocality – an African ancestral form many readers may miss. If a call-and-response pattern is invoked in a Caribbean text, the critic must be aware of it. Conventions relating to large units of text – such as forms of letters, sermons, wedding speeches or wills; or patterns that define literary genres like the ballad, romance or folk tale – evolve in their original cultures and in their crossing into new cultures. These developments can be accurately discussed only if the stages in their history are known.

Some analysis of discourse is fundamentally comparative, for example, postcolonial criticism. It is meaningless to discuss Caribbean responses to nineteenth-century imperial fiction without adequate exposure to that fiction and impossible to assess a text as counterdiscursive without knowing the discourse being "countered". Indeed, we cannot locate ourselves in relation to anything we have not defined. The Caribbeanness of whatever we analyse, or the Caribbeanness of the position from which we view whatever we analyse implies a distinction from something else – whether a clear boundary delimits this something else or whether there is blurring or slippage.

A related consideration is the location of that consciousness that drives the discourse. It may be a created consciousness, as in the narrator in fiction or the persona in a poem. The *angle of viewing*, or orientation of this consciousness to the experience conveyed, may be variously defined. Spatial or temporal location or distance in relation to events or experiences, involvement as a participant or detachment as an observer (reliable or not), ideological position-ing in relation to the views or circumstances relayed – all these determine the view projected and require analysis for valid interpretation. In particular, the power distribution among participants in the discourse, as implied through the language, demands scrutiny. In traditional British literature, the notorious rejection of Falstaff at the end of Shakespeare's *Henry IV*, part 2, "I know thee not, old man", invites a thoughtful eye on *thee*. The audience may well reflect on whether this is a familiar, intimate use of the second person or a more distant, ceremonial use, and, in the process, the audience assesses historical change in the pronoun paradigm. A postcolonial rereading of traditional British literature like Thackeray's *Vanity Fair* ([1877] 1994) may involve considering the role of *dozen* in Mr Sedley's thoughts on his son's attraction to Becky: "Better she, my dear, than a black Mrs Sedley, and a dozen of mahogany grandchildren" (p. 47). What are the mechanisms by which colonial discourse dehumanizes local peoples?

So the critic who employs linguistic or discourse analysis searches out the bases on which power is distributed and the mechanisms by which this privileged view is conveyed, constructed or perpetuated through operations of language. Ideological perspective may be gendered, just as attitudes to ethnicity may be encoded in discourse. Discourse demonstrates privilege in the power to name, to represent common sense, to create official versions, to represent the legitimate social world (Barker and Galasinski 2001, 56). Analysing discourse enables one to disturb entrenched positions. Analysis of ideological perspective facilitates a refocusing, a zooming in on the oppressive way of seeing the world to interrogate this way of seeing. Just as ways of seeing are constructed and perpetuated through discourse, they may be revised or brought to light through discourse analysis.

So the critic must also be prepared to track discursive adjustments that transform ways of seeing and knowing. The shift to a Caribbean point of view and the employment of the Caribbean consciousness by artists with the necessary experience effect a remarkable transformation in understanding the Caribbean world. A number of devices effect perspectival shift. *Metaphor*, for example, adjusts perspective to a new angle of viewing. Over the past two decades, following on the appearance of Lakoff and Johnson's (1981) *Metaphors We Live By*, the study of metaphor has exploded beyond traditional discussion of figurative language to cognitive–linguistic analysis (e.g., Gibbs and Steen, 1997). In discussions of metaphor, the distinctness of literary and linguistic enquiry emerges at surface and dissolves at greater depth. Another mechanism for adjusting orientation is the shifting of *code choice*, which activates an alternate voice. We must establish and trace movements between the linguistic codes in which a text is executed. In transforming orientation, Selvon's pioneering of the Creole narrator in the mid- and later twentieth century is a landmark in Caribbean literary history. The Caribbean consciousness looks out at the world and into itself, displacing the authority of the non-Caribbean gaze.

For sensitivity to code shift, we must be well versed in the linguistic characteristics of both codes to discern subtle movements between them and enjoy delicate plays on meaning where one phrase has different implications in different codes. Also, the ideological implications of code choice and the political significance in choices of representation are crucial both to literary and linguistic history in the Caribbean and other comparable cultures. Roshni Mooneeram (2009) notes how literary artists and scholars have influenced processes of standardization in western European vernacular languages, as language codification and the evolution of literary canons constituted symbiotic processes. Similarly, the development of a Caribbean canon has involved increasing inscription of Creole in authorizing the voice. Moreover, our intertwined linguistic and literary history alerts us to comparable developments in other canons, opening opportunities for uniquely Caribbean critique of, say, British literature.

Representation

Representing the Caribbean voice phonologically is a challenge because it usually involves orthographical practices of standard English, Creole pronunciation spelled according to English rules even where these rules are archaic or illogical. Moreover, the anglophone Caribbean voice may be Vincentian or Guyanese in any variety between the versions of standard English (and anglophone Creole spoken in that territory). Similar options exist in francophone territories, and some territories (like St Lucia) have English- and French-lexicon Creoles along with their official languages. So there is in fact not *one* Caribbean Creole voice to represent.

Caribbean literature represents the Creole partially to retain its non-Creole-speaking audience, but this partial representation remains convincing in view of the continuum of varieties between standard and Creole. In the interaction between oral and scribal traditions, described by Gordon Rohlehr as an oral–scribal continuum (1992a, 68), orature and literature seamlessly interact. The analysis of Caribbean scribal discourse is thus fraught with considerations of intended audience, writer competence in Caribbean language, authorial perceptions of speakers of different codes (and any ideological orientation implied by this) and so forth. Thus, in modern Caribbean letters, the association of standard with writing and of nonstandard with speech is collapsible. Indeed, Caribbean discourse, riddled with continua of one form or another, is by nature slippery and best defined through close reference to its linguistic and socio-historical complexity.

Caribbean discourse is itself discussed from varying angles. Ideological positioning, an orientation to perceived reality that amounts to a way of knowing, emerges through textual and discourse analysis but also through attention to *metadiscourse*. Metadiscourse comprises authorial or narratorial discussion of language in a particular setting, the expression by a central consciousness of his or her own struggle with expression, comments on the language ability of characters and so on. Such discourse reveals describable language attitudes and reflects evaluations of how the discourse categorizes or represents experience, betraying positions from which the Caribbean is viewed or from which the Caribbean consciousness views others.

All literary discourses draw on others, and *intertextuality* takes many forms, from extended reference or rewritings like Maryse Condé's *Windward Heights* (2003) to expansions that fill gaps and adjust perspective, like Jean Rhys's *Wide Sargasso Sea* (1966). It also involves interactions of form, what Norman Fairclough (1995) terms *interdiscursivity*, in which a new literature draws on traditional patterns and conventions of another canon – as John Hearne does in framing fiction revolving around a slave ship in the sea story genre (*The Sure Salvation* 1982). Analysis of Caribbean literary discourse and Caribbean analysis of other literary discourse requires scrupulous attention to intertextuality.

This multipronged approach to text and discourse analysis has as its goal the derivation of meaning. Interpretation constitutes statements about the global meaning of the text, and we come back to the question raised in defining qualitative research: How do we determine validity? What are our guidelines for deriving accurate information and drawing reasonable conclusions? Here too, we draw on operations of language.

We draw our conclusions on a number of bases. Some are *assertions* – explicit statements or claims; others are *inferences*, which rest on implicit information. Interpretation through inferencing means rigorous evaluation of the implicit information we collect. Indeed, we scrutinize all logical processing relating to the text and its circumstances, identifying and weighing *presuppositions* – propositions that must be true if a sentence is to have truth value, that is, to be true or untrue. We must consider *entailment*, information regarding categories, in order to reasonably assign characteristics based on the classification of persons or phenomenon. We must examine *connotations* – information that is based on association and that is often culturally defined.

Much of the knowledge required for such processing depends on other existing information, on a mental framework we call prior knowledge. Critical interpretation through inference, the collection and processing of implicatures, is only possible through prior knowledge. All information exists in relation to other information, and prior knowledge assists in processing new information, providing a mental framework for integrating new facts. There is a *schema* – organized knowledge about particular elements or phenomena in the world (culturally constrained) and their frequency. Circumstances with the highest frequency shape our default assumptions. To gather implicatures from a text, the reader may draw on information about the world of the author.

Finally, one dimension of interpretation is *evaluation*. We ask ourselves whether or to what extent the text achieves its apparent aims and whether it convinces us. In evaluating the success of the work, such considerations as credibility arise. Often, credibility is connected with a sense of realism, and this requires extreme caution. For representation to be successful, it must seem real. However, in discussing literary discourse in the Caribbean, it is essential to be realistic about realism. We can apply the caution by Geoffrey Leech and Mick Short that "the main problem . . . is that talk of realism always seems to involve measuring a work against some absolute standard of reality – something out there of which a writer could, if he wished, give an exact xerographic copy" (1981, 151; and see chapter 4 of this book on representing the Caribbean voice).

In Caribbean discourse reality is highly negotiable. Kincaid's description of Antigua actually denies the reality of what she presents in highly categorical statements. Unreality pertains not only to the façade of paradise which the tourist's vision imposes on corruption but to the actual "real" beauty of the physical landscape which is presented as a stage, a setting in which real and terrible events unfold (1988, 77). Realism is essentially notional, constructed of such elements as (1) credibility and objectivity (which can only be assessed in connection with the writer's profile), (2) authenticity and verisimilitude (which rest on analysis of the text itself) and (3) vividness (which depends on the profile of the audience, as elements of the discourse must be directed to effect strong perceptual impressions) (Lalla 2005).

The representational discourse remains distinct from the discourse it purports to be: in practical effect it can never reflect the breadth of regional discourse nor the detail of a national variety. It is an illusion of realism – a reminder for the uninitiated and a signal that summons to the mind of Creole speakers a Caribbean voice of flexible proportions, regulated more or less automatically by the competence of the audience.

So textual or discourse analysis requires meticulous attention to all levels of the language of the text (employing where applicable a historical sensitivity to language change); structural characteristics of the text; the social, cultural and literary context of the text; metadiscursive commentary that may throw light on further information, such as language attitudes; and intertextual relationships that convey further meaning. A crucial dimension of analysing Caribbean literary discourse is assessment of (1) mechanisms for inscribing orality, (2) the significance of interface between oral and scribal characteristics and (3) the authenticating role played by intersecting codes. The dominance of certain discourses relative to others has implications for choices of theoretical approach.

Only at the end of such thorough analysis of the literary discourse will it be possible to interpret (through inferencing), to suggest global meaning such as critics discuss in terms of theme. Moreover, it is only by networking texts in the total discourse of the author that we can infer authorial position or generalize on the writer's style, as distinct from stylistic characteristics of a particular text.

Approaches to Analysing Discourse

There are two broad kinds of nonliterary discourse analysis: *content analysis* and *linguistic analysis*, and the two should not be confused. The first is now being widely used in the social sciences, and even in the medical sciences, as the type of ethnographic research that records participants in different social, social–psychological and societal dilemmas speaking to their cares and concerns is increasingly interrogated. It is also used in media to analyse trends and tendencies. Content analysis deals in the information content of an interview rather than its structure. It most usually quantifies words of the same base or common themes or concepts running through a text or series of texts. These items are coded and broken down on a number of different levels and subsequently analysed conceptually or relationally.

Discourse analysis in linguistics is all about *how* something is said rather than merely what is said, and this concern goes across all of the subtypes of conversational and other discourse analysis types. This concern with the manner in which talk is formed is now being used in the social and medical sciences also. The difference from strict linguistic approaches often entails setting up distinct discourse formats suited to the milieu under investigation, for example, the extensive work of David Silverman and Anssi Peräkylä (1990) in medical sociology on medical interview formats employed in HIV/AIDS counselling. This was applied successfully in the Caribbean context, although typical formats established for UK and US contexts did demonstrate some differences (e.g., Youssef and Silverman, 1993).

The *how* of communication, studied through discourse analysis, adds insight into intended meaning by careful consideration of the lexicon used, its connotations, use of a broad range of figures of speech, the particulars of the grammatical structure of sentences (e.g., active versus passive) and other focusing devices in the sentence such as extraposition and clefting. It may entail study of conversational features such as openings and closings, hedges and fillers, turn-taking devices, and the like. It may also entail study of discourse structure overall or narrative structure in the case of storytelling in ways identical to those described in the first part of this chapter. The way in which a person says something to another or writes an article in the newspaper, if carefully analysed, can display that writer's exact set towards the addressee(s), as well as a mindset or ideology and an attitude to a condition or situation beyond the words. This is the particular value of this analytical technique which is labour intensive, deriving maximal information from small chunks of text.

There are several different ways of analysing discourse, depending on the nature of the text to be analysed. It would be fair to say, however, that all forms of discourse analysis have a concern with the structure of the discourse overall and with the structure of the individual sentences or utterances within it. In all cases there is attention to the lexicon also. These elements would not be described in isolation but in relation to the effect that they have in facilitating or retarding specific communicative intents. In the case of public discourse, there is a strong focus on the ideological underpinnings of the discourse as revealed by its structure.

This section will discuss data transcription and then briefly outline four main types of discourse analysis:

1. Conversational analysis
2. Interactional sociolinguistics
3. Narrative analysis
4. Critical discourse analysis

It is not possible to carry out any form of discourse analysis successfully without transcribing the data. Content analysis must usually quantify items as they occur to show overwhelming trends and tendencies in semantic focus. As a result the first task after collecting the data is to select an appropriate transcription style. For the most part regular orthography may be used for this purpose, the only exception being, of course, when nonstandard dialects demand a consistent representation that must be worked out without an orthographic system and also when it is necessary to establish a phonetically sensitive transcription system. Conversational features such as pauses, hedges and fillers are always included within a regular orthographic transcription, however, as are indicators of pitch, stress and volume. Today, of course, the tendency is to make video recordings as well as audio for maximal accuracy of interpretation of nonverbal as well as verbal cues. This writer prefers to focus on the audio recording and the verbal, as it is almost impossible to achieve multigrained analysis of both verbal and nonverbal communication effectively at the same time. Moreover, representation of the nonverbal without a visual cue can be ambiguous: raising the eyebrows, throwing up one's hands can convey myriad emotions, depending on context. This medium simply does not allow for the accuracy of interpretation that can be gained from a voice recording.

If a researcher neglects transcription style and is haphazard or inconsistent in its application, analytical problems invariably arise further on in the process. Even with the use of a transcriber, which does not do the work for you but plays a short piece of the audio file and then rewinds to allow relistening to an appropriate point, the work is exceedingly time consuming. An hour's audio material can take between six and twelve hours to transcribe accurately. Ten minutes of transcribed talk, though, can reveal all the researcher might want to find out about gender relations in a mixed-sex group of students interacting on a university campus (e.g., Youssef, 2001), and six focus group interviews transcribed in detail can furnish a researcher with material for meaningful publication for several years. Work by Sue-Ann Barratt (in progress) pinpoints gender perceptions among young Caribbean students which establish them as markedly different from their metropolitan counterparts in their traditional perspectives and points the way to a continuing separateness of development despite perceived stereotypes of neocolonialist mind control.

While a research assistant may be employed by the more seasoned researcher, the latter then loses out on understanding and facility with the data, as a written transcription cannot replace the audio file with its nuances of meaning supplied by speech modulation for focus and emphasis in the speech stream.

In *conversational analysis* (CA) there is a natural preoccupation with features particular to spoken interaction. The way that turns of talk are constructed by all parties to the interaction, whether there are overlaps or pauses between or within utterances, how openings and closings are constructed, whether silences occur and to what ends, all these are the stuff of CA. Ever since Harvey Sacks, Emmanuel A. Schegloff and Gail Jefferson (1974, 696) set up a "simplest systematic for the structure of turn-taking", the rules for conversation established therein have been taken as a measure against which to assess other conversations, even though there has been considerable disagreement on the exact nature of the rules. It is clear that ordered turn taking of the type described by Sacks and colleagues is very much the stuff of formal interactions and that groups of friends, for example, very often interrupt and overlap one another in the spontaneity of their discourse. There are several different types of conversation even within a single language and culture, so there is still much work to be done in this arena, and the Caribbean field is wide open. Kathryn Shields-Brodber (2001b) has done some interesting work recording conversations on a call-in radio station in Jamaica where a doctor responds to callers' queries and concerns.

It is important to make a distinction here from conversation depicted in literature. As noted in the first section of this chapter, much literature, especially fiction, represents conversation, but practical demands (such as that of maintaining the reader's attention) require realism to be tempered by other considerations like relevance. Hedges, stammering, nonessential repetition, false starts and so on have no place in literary dialogue unless required for characterization of the speaker, but they can be significant cues in conversation in their own right. In other words, the creative writer continuously makes choices regarding representation of direct speech that actually distinguish it from genuine speech, yet the writer must find ways of maintaining credibility. David Chariandy (2007), the author of *Soucouyant*, represents direct speech current in Trinidad and Tobago as distinct from direct speech current among people of Trinbagonian extraction living in Canada:

"How old you is, child?"

"Seventeen, Mother."

"And what some boy who have seventeen year think he know about oil and Empire?" (p. 175)

He preserves the distinction between this and archaic speech embedded as a fragment in folktale:

> Old skin, 'kin, 'kin,
> You na know me,
> You na know me . . . (2007, 134)

Interactional sociolinguistics operates close to CA but is concerned particularly with cross-cultural interaction encounters not only when those encounters are interethnic but also when they cut across characteristics like gender within a single culture or society. It is concerned with the broad norms of conversation and how these may differ and lead to misunderstanding. Women in English-speaking societies, and arguably universally, are held to prefer broadly collaborative communicative styles, whereas men prefer competitive. This affects conversational structure as men interrupt women more in conversation and do not always respond readily to questions put to them by women (Holmes 1995). They may also fail to provide supportive minimal responses in conversation. It has been argued that men and women grow up in gendered groupings such that they do not have an opportunity to adapt to each other's norms and such that miscommunication and overriding the other is not intentional but a result of different perceptions as to the meaning of particular conversational signals (Maltz and Borker, 1982; Tannen 1996). Turn-taking procedures then are directly affected by cultural norms, and differences among them can cause conversational difficulty because each party to the conversation assumes that his or her norms are of the same basic kind as the other's. The researcher in cultural studies may have a strong concern with this area and may wish to investigate Caribbean conversational styles rather than assume that they hold to the Western norms most often described. Picong has been investigated informally by Rohlehr (2007b), but verbal duelling characterizes African American male interactions also, and it would be worthwhile to examine the similarities and differences across the Caribbean in this arena. In recent years the analysis of different speech events in the region has developed considerably, but most studies have been carried out by foreigners, and more local studies are very much needed.

Narrative analysis of oral discourse pertains specifically to storytelling or the description of an observed event. William Labov and Joshua Waletsky (1967) set up a schema of the typical discourse structure in oral narratives of personal experience, and it has been used much as has Sacks and colleagues' as a starting point or sounding board against which to measure a wide range of oral narratives. Narratives may be coded in a number of ways, but Labov and Waletsky worked largely with the following: AB = abstract statement segment, OR = orientation segment, CA = complicating action, EV = evaluation, RE = resolution, and CO = coda. Kathy-Ann Drayton (2009) has analysed the story-telling of young children in Trinidad and reports similar patterns. It is arguable that this structural schema or others may transfer to writing also, particularly among students and other societal subgroups who have had little experience of working with the written word. The existence of a possible working frame allows for the recording of oral narratives across the Caribbean region and their comparison and contrast to this US-derived norm. It is of course also possible to examine such narratives from the perspective of temporal sequencing.

Each one of the above techniques can be used then to analyse oral data depending on the genre, the nature of its subject matter, whether it is interactive and whether it cuts across cultural boundaries. It may be that a combination of analysis types is selected. What should guide the choice of a particular discourse analysis type is the nature of the particular interaction under study, its precise characteristics, and what emerges from the data set itself. An analysis type should never be imposed on the data set, but the data set itself should determine the type of analysis selected.

Critical discourse analysis and feminist poststructuralist discourse analysis may be applied to both oral and written discourse. They are both analysis types concerned with working out power through discourse, the first focusing heavily on the ways in which domination and subjugation are enforced and the second on the ways in which dominance can shift and change depending on context, participants to an interaction and individual positioning. Historically, critical discourse analysis had its origins in systemic functional linguistics, which is concerned with linking form and function. It is defined by Rebecca Rogers as "the systematic study of ways of interacting (genre), ways of representing (discourse) and ways of being (style)" (2004, 56). An investigation of genre focuses on the organizational properties of the discourse in relation to its purposes; an analysis of discourse involves looking at the thematic properties of the text, including cohesion devices, lexical choice, metaphor, politeness and interactional features. Style includes grammatical features such as active and passive voice, tense, mode and aspect, transitivity, and pronominal usage.

This area would also include style shift and characteristic features of language variation. There are several approaches to this field, all differing somewhat according to individual emphasis and the genre type analysed. In discussing the notion that critical media literacy should be taught in schools, for example, Fairclough (1995) argues that all students should be able to answer questions on text design, which would essentially carry a focused analysis of the features listed in this paragraph, but should also understand what is entailed in text production – what he describes as "the media order of discourse" – and finally the wider sociocultural processes of which the text is a part (1995, 202).

A greater contextualization of discourse analysis into the particular socio-political, socio-educational or socio-institutional milieu which it represents and supports is evident. In the context of Caribbean discourse, the use of critical discourse analysis and the further development of feminist poststructuralist discourse analysis would allow for greater insight into the precise nature of postcolonial power construction in a number of important social milieux.

The researcher in Caribbean cultural and literary studies derives substantial meaning from a text only through profound analysis of its linguistic and discursive operations, whether this text comprises primary or secondary material. Although little developed in the region thus far, the insights offered by discourse analysis and the applications of these and other approaches in literary linguistics and discourse analysis hold great promise for critical interpretation that is firmly grounded in the text.

Chapter 10

Comparative Analysis

Elizabeth Walcott-Hackshaw

The attempt to characterize comparative study is an act of comparative analysis in itself. Defining the discipline has evolved largely because of the ever-expanding, seemingly all-encompassing nature of cultural studies. There is now greater overlap between cultural studies and comparative studies; the methodologies employed by many cultural studies scholars and researchers necessarily involve comparative approaches. At its heart comparative studies is interdisciplinary and cross-cultural; it explores a wide range of cultural and historical discourses that span several disciplines, including literary, linguistic, religious, technological, political, scientific and aesthetic. Comparative researchers may also draw from both within and across cultures to explore the multiple discourses and practices of a particular society, group of people, geographical region or historical period. However, the comparatist's main task is not simply to point out similarities and differences in a particular culture, group or aesthetic but to try to unearth and understand the various layers of discourses and practices in the particular object of study. Comparative research may also examine and address the process of cultural change and its effect on the individual or collective. This interdisciplinary approach demands both plasticity and precision. There should be flexibility in both theoretical and methodological options, given the cross-cultural nature of the project. However, the success of the study depends on an accurate application of theoretical frames; the expansive nature of a study should not lead to a formless, obtuse result.

One of the primary tasks of any researcher is to define the nature of the project, for an ill-defined study often results in unsuitable methodology. The researcher engaged in a comparative study requires a rigorous yet flexible approach in the choice of methodology. In fact, there is no methodology particular to comparative research: its multidisciplinary nature often demands a mixed methodological approach depending on the subject matter. However, there is a comparative perspective that allows for more open, creative methods. Comparative researchers in the social sciences show a greater preference for quantitative rather than qualitative analysis; for cultural comparative studies, the researcher may use a qualitative approach. These methodological issues are critical when designing a multidisciplinary study.

Most researchers are engaged in some form of comparative analysis, since intellectual curiosity often fosters comparisons. Furthermore, this curiosity has been fed by the far-reaching effects of the Information Age and the globalization of knowledge. There is a new landscape for twenty-first century comparative research with no shortage of quantitative data to facilitate original analysis. The only cautionary note is that, with the plethora of information, refining a study may prove to be more challenging. However, comparative analysis has become critical in our ability to understand the world of the twenty-first century.

Researchers in the field of Caribbean literature and culture have long been engaged in comparative research and analysis; the region naturally lends itself to comparison as a result of its dynamic multicultural character. Cross-cultural poetics and counterdiscursive practices have played an intrinsic role in much of what is produced by writers, artistes and scholars of the Caribbean region. Recently, two notable comparative studies have emerged from Caribbean scholars using visual representations to explore socio-political and historical issues in the region. In *An Eye for the Tropics: Tourism, Photography and Framing the Caribbean Picturesque* (2006), art historian Krista Thompson analyses, with a critical lens, the tropical images and representations of late nineteenth- and early twentieth-century photographers and artists. Patricia Mohammed's *Imaging the Caribbean: Culture and Visual Translation* (2010) traces the history of visual representations in Haiti, Trinidad, Jamaica and Barbados over the last five hundred years. The two works draw material from several disciplines and methodologies including history, literature, art, gender studies and cultural studies.

Comparative Literature

There have been several fundamental debates on the method and scope of comparative literature. In the early twentieth century, the French school of comparative literature advocated a more empiricist approach to the discipline. It was important to study the influences and origins of the text. Gathering as much factual information about the work was as important as the text itself. The historical context also played an important role in the researcher's ability to draw conclusions about the text. This positivist approach differed in many ways to the postwar American school of comparative literature. Although both French and American schools felt the need to extend the comparisons of works beyond national boundaries, the American comparatists prioritized textual analysis and content. Unlike the French researchers, there was less dependence on paratextual data and evidence. One example of this flexible, broad approach to comparative analysis of literary texts is Erich Auerbach's classic *Mimesis* ([1946] 1968); in this work Auerbach explores the representations of Western realism from the *Odyssey* (1996) to Virginia Woolf's *To the Lighthouse* ([1927] 1987). Although Auerbach's focus is on Western literature, the essays transcend temporal and national constraints, setting it apart from other comparative literary texts of that period. The widening comparative approach also encouraged an interdisciplinary comparative perspective that in many ways was a forerunner to cultural studies. In recent times and as a result of the popular interest in cultural studies that emerged in the 1970s and 1980s, there has been a greater move away from nation-based comparative literature to a more cross-cultural approach. Gayatri Chakravorty Spivak discusses this twenty-first century vision of comparative literature in *Death of a Discipline* (2003). Rather than lament the limitations of more traditional comparative literary studies, Spivak proposes a new way forward, a way in which linguistic and cultural diversity is respected. Spivak also probes the political effects of reading and writing about other cultures. In a review quoted on the publisher's website, Judith Butler summarizes Spivak's argument and comparative approach:

> Gayatri Chakravorty Spivak's *Death of a Discipline* does not tell us that Comparative Literature is at an end. On the contrary, it charts a demanding and urgent future for the field, laying out the importance of the encounter with area studies

and offering a radically ethical framework for the approach to subaltern writing. Spivak deftly opposes the "migrant intellectual" approach to the study of alterity. . . . She asks those who dwell within the dominant episteme to imagine how we are imagined by those for whom literacy remains the primary demand. And she maps a new way of reading not only the future of literary studies but its past as well. This text is disorienting and reconstellating, dynamic, lucid, and brilliant in its scope and vision. Rarely has "death" offered such inspiration. (Butler, http://cup.columbia.edu/book/978-0-231-12944-2/death-of-a-discipline/reviews)

It is interesting to note that many university sites describing comparative literature programmes emphasize this cross-cultural approach. The Berkeley comparative literature programme is described as a vast canopy that covers "concerns about literature including the relationship between literatures within national, historical, theoretical, and thematic contexts, as well as the relationship between literature and other disciplines (philosophy, politics, art, etc.)". There is also an emphasis on the fact that the comparative researcher focuses on the study of literature from different cultures, languages, genres, historical periods and literary movements. Like Spivak, Steven Tötsöy de Zepetnek, in his definition of comparative literature, places emphasis on the inclusion of the other:

In principle, the discipline of Comparative Literature is *in toto* a method in the study of literature in at least two ways. First, Comparative Literatures means the knowledge of more than one national language and literature, and/or it means the knowledge and application of other disciplines in and for the study of literature and second, Comparative Literature has an ideology of inclusion of the Other, be that a marginal literature in its several meanings of marginality, a genre, various text types, etc. Historically, it is true that Comparative Literature demonstrated a focus on European literatures and later on European and American literature. . . . At the same time, however, the discipline paid more attention to "Other" literatures than any of the national literatures. (1998, 13)

Critical theory and cultural studies have changed the way in which literature is read, interpreted and culturally translated, paying greater attention to what was once perceived as outside of the more traditional borders. In *Comparative Literature: A Critical Introduction* (1993), Susan Bassnett traces the development of comparative literature in the 1990s, mapping the many ways in which the discipline continues to expand beyond these early nationalistic, Eurocentric concerns. Bassnett explores the future of comparative literature and the changing reading patterns and approaches as a result of the growth of translation studies (TS), gender studies and Orientalism.

In spite of the varying debates on the scope and definition of the discipline, language skills have always been a fundamental issue. Traditionally comparatists have been fluent in at least one other language beyond their native tongue. A researcher choosing to compare non-national works would usually possess an excellent reading level in the nonnative language. It was believed that, beyond the basic grasp of narrative content, without the necessary linguistic skills in a nonnative language, it would be difficult for the researcher to appreciate the subtleties of form and narrative techniques. Understanding the author's language also gives the researcher a greater capacity for cultural translation and comparison. Although it remains preferable to possess strong reading skills in the non-national work, translations of the original texts have become a route for those researchers who do not possess reading skills in the nonnative language; however, a researcher able to work with the original text rather than a translation has a greater advantage for effective comparative analysis, particularly if the subject of comparison is the translation itself. This issue of multilingual literary comparisons is often important to researchers in comparative Caribbean literature.

Recently more Caribbean works have been translated into English, particularly from the French- and Spanish-speaking islands. Writers like Maryse Condé (Guadeloupe), Dany Laferrière (Haiti) or Gabriel García Márquez (Colombia) have had their works translated, creating a broader comparative landscape. Translations have made significant contributions to create "conversations" among Caribbean literary works; however, these translations often privilege English speakers. *The Oxford Book of Caribbean Short Stories* (1999) is a compilation of English, Spanish, French and Dutch stories. All of the stories appear in English and not in their original language. Although this privileges English speakers, the inclusion of these works in translation, in particular the stories from the Dutch Caribbean, widens the breadth of comparative possibilities for Caribbean researchers. According to the editors of the collection, Stewart Brown and John Wickham, "Our original brief was to compile a truly pan-Caribbean collection. . . . For all sorts of reasons, not least the linguistic insularity of the British, there was little cultural interchange between the different language communities of the Caribbean through most of this century" (1999, xiii–xiv).

Contemporary studies in comparative literature often compare works of literature in relation to other disciplines, including religious studies, ethnic studies, art, music, digital culture, film and performance. However, as Zepetnek notes, the pluralistic nature of the discipline requires a certain level of creative methodology: "Comparative Literature has intrinsically a content and form which facilitate the cross-cultural and interdisciplinary study of literature and it has a history that substantiated this content and form. Predicated on the borrowing of methods from other disciplines and on the application of the appropriated method to areas of study . . . the discipline is difficult to define because thus it is fragmented and pluralistic" (1998, 13). With interdisciplinary studies the comparative researcher should have theoretical and methodological knowledge about the discipline selected for the comparative analysis. A researcher engaging in a comparative study between a film and novel is not necessarily involved in film studies but rather studying the narrative in film form. Nevertheless, the researcher cannot simply ignore the nature of the medium and its particular discourse: the film's soundtrack, special effects, cinematography, editing and audience response make the experience of film essentially different from that of a written work. These elements significantly impact the way in which the researcher will attempt to analyse the narrative of the film. Familiarity with, or preferably fluency in, the disciplines to be compared becomes crucial to the efficacy of the project, be it film and literature, literature and music, or any other cross-disciplinary discourse analysis. A comparative analysis of the film *Sugar Cane Alley* (1983) by the Martinican director Euzhan Palcy and Joseph Zobel's novel *La Rue Cases-Nègres* (1950) on which the film is based could be organized around the director's emphasis and interpretation of particular thematic concerns in the novel versus those of the author. The analysis could also discuss the way in which the sepia tones of the film create a particular atmosphere and period in Martinican history that Zobel attempts to create in the narrative.

Comparative Literary Skills

The pluralistic nature of comparative literary analysis requires researchers to develop and refine a wide range of skills in order to produce a rigorous and successful comparative study. These include sophisticated cognitive and reading skills, a refined critical sensibility and a highly developed concept of genre, especially where literary genre is the subject of the study. The nature of genre can be viewed from wide and narrow lenses. In the wider frame, genre is divided into categories: whether the text is a novel, play, film, short story or novella. However, on the micro level, researchers need to consider genre within its context: literary, historical, political and cultural. *Comparative genre analysis* requires knowledge of these contextual frames and the ability to distinguish characteristic features of the genres to be compared.

Comparative literary skills deepen researchers' understanding of intellectual and transnational issues as they engage in cross-cultural analysis and approach materials from an interdisciplinary and international perspective. A basic yet crucial question for any comparative study is the question of its design, which requires a careful selection of primary material. As with any research project, poorly selected material will produce an unsatisfactory result. But for the researcher engaged in a comparative study, ineffective selections can be detrimental to the health of any project. The comparative researcher does not want to force unnatural fits with tenuous connections and leaky arguments. The material must be probed and prodded and then placed against other subjects of inquiry that undergo a similar process. Only after possible research questions and potential arguments have been formulated for the possibilities of comparative analysis should the researcher proceed. However, there is also a creative aspect to the selection process that moves beyond procedure and is purely the result of intellectual curiosity and the indefinable, enviable quality of a lush imagination.

The benefit of the freedom afforded in the discipline of comparative literature to create an international, interdisciplinary study also poses the challenge of structure and research design. Without a careful map plotting the project, a study will likely be too wide in scope and lack probing analysis. A comparative perspective should be one that sees the borderless possibilities of comparative analysis while keeping in mind the practical requirements of clear, logical, persuasive scholarship. It may be helpful to alert students undertaking such research to the fact that several fundamental areas require attention in comparative analysis. According to Kerry Walk of the Harvard Writing Center, these basic areas include the frame of reference, grounds for comparison, thesis and organizational scheme (1998).

- The *frame of reference* creates the context. The frame of reference may consist of an idea, theme, question, problem or theory; a carefully defined group from which you extract two for special attention; or biographical or historical information. The best frames of reference are constructed from specific sources rather than one's own thoughts or observations. Thus, in a paper comparing how two writers redefine social norms of masculinity, it is usually best to take into account established positions before proposing one's own theory.

- The *grounds for comparison* need a clear rationale, and the choice should be deliberate and meaningful, not random.

- The *thesis statement*, or argument, is fundamentally linked to the grounds for comparison and to the frame of reference. The grounds for comparison anticipate the comparative nature of the thesis. It is also important to state how the different selections for the study relate to each other. Do they extend, corroborate, complicate, contradict, correct or debate one another? For example:

  "Whereas Camus perceives ideology as secondary to the need to address a specific historical moment of colonialism, Fanon perceives a revolutionary ideology as the impetus to reshape Algeria's history in a direction toward independence."

- The *organizational scheme*, or design, is critical to the effectiveness of the study. In a literary comparative analysis, it is possible to organize the thesis thematically, where several texts are discussed based on the thematic canopy. There is also the possibility of comparison on an author-by-author basis. For example, in *The Sense of Community in French Caribbean Fiction* (2008), Celia Britton analyses the theme of community using the French philosopher Jean-Luc Nancy's ideas as a frame of reference and a text-by-text organizational scheme. The opening chapter is entitled "Restoring Lost Unity in Jacques Roumain's *Gouverneurs de la rosée*", chapter 2 examines "Past, Future and the Maroon Community in Édouard Glissant's

Le Quatrième Siècle" and chapter 7, the final chapter, addresses "On Not Belonging: Surrogate Families and Marginalized Communities in Maryse Condé's *Desirada".* In all, Britton designs a comparative study using seven French Caribbean works around a central theme.

Critical Reading Skills

One of the most fundamental qualities of a comparative researcher in literature is strong reading skills. This is often something that is taken for granted in literary studies. Roger Shattuck elegantly describes the pleasures of reading as well as the sensitivity and sensibility of a good reader. Underlining the importance of maturation, he articulates the ways in which time and personal experience affect our appreciation and rereading of literary works: "Literature has two advantages over wine. A good book ages forever; and you can read it as often as you wish without diminishing its substance. The devoted reader is like a wine lover whose dream has come true. His stock will never spoil or be consumed. He can sample, enjoy, and share his cellar without depleting his reserve; it will grow as he grows. He need never go thirsty" (1984, 311). Refining reading skills requires a temporal frame that allows tastes to develop as we become more sensitive to textual layers and varying contexts, discourses and registers. Implicit in Shattuck's idea is readers' own awareness of how and at what point they enter a work, their cultural expectations, their personal anthologies and the paratextual issues. The approach to critical reading as opposed to reading for pleasure is obviously different; a researcher often enters a work with the intention to glean and gather information for the particular study. However, an essential part of reading is also the ability to be sensitive to one's own ideological frames and research agendas and still be able to read with what Shattuck terms an "innocent eye": seeing what the work itself has to offer. The good reader's appreciation of a text is dynamic, never static and should not be impaired by poor insight.

Basic skills that facilitate reading critically include the ability to recognize figurative language and rhetorical devices, narrative voice, symbolism, influences, and archetypes. Critical thinking skills allow for a more profound reading of the work when discussing theoretical issues. This critical literacy is one of the most important elements in developing an advanced sensitivity to theoretical and critical material; this skill facilitates a clear command of the argumentation in order to pursue a dialectic and cognitive approach to the material. Young researchers may fail to question perceived *idées reçues* and as such never fully grasp, question or formulate a personal response to the established argument. Without such a response, the researcher is apt to integrate theoretical approaches that do not necessarily elucidate, enrich or even apply to the research topic. In the ever-expanding broad research area of New World studies, the comparative design is crucial. Nick Nesbitt's *Voicing Memory: History and Subjectivity in French Caribbean Literature* (2003) is an example of a unique portal into the area. Nesbitt deftly manipulates Antillean poetry, literature and theatre, but also Haitian Vodou, visual arts, American jazz and West African musical traditions. As is the case with becoming a good reader, critical literacy is developed over a period of time as the researcher adopts a more questioning, critical stance.

Critical literacy is a crucial skill for cross-cultural analysis; it gives the researcher an ability to read the material from an interdisciplinary, even international, perspective. This perspective also facilitates an understanding of transnational relations. According to Reed Way Dasenbrock (1992), the central movement for cross-cultural reading and interpretation moves from the presumption of sameness to the recognition of difference. Dasenbrock outlines several of these stages:

- The uninformed reader will begin with a "prior theory", and "interpretive charity" that assumes the new person or text we encounter is like us (same worldview, behaviour patterns, values, aesthetic principles and so on), but also with the receptive attitude of desiring to learn across cultures.
- The reader encounters "interpretive anomalies", differences that make us suspect the new person or text is not like us in significant ways, and our "prior theory" of similitude is wrong, incomplete and in need of adjustment.
- We construct a sequence of "passing theories" – short-term theories of interpretation – as we gather more and more information, adapting our inferences so that our interpretive theory better fits the new person or text we're trying to understand.
- The powerful cross-cultural text provokes readers to construct these "passing theories"; such texts are often designed to do this – that is, they are not written for readers just like their authors – and the "best" writers do this kind of writing well.

- Gradually, readers change their interpretive systems to accommodate culturally different people or texts. As readers gain more experience with such cross-cultural encounters, they communicate interculturally across difference.

Comparative Literature and Translation Studies

Translation studies focuses on the theory and application of translation and interpretation. The interdisciplinary nature of TS causes researchers to draw on several areas, including comparative literature, linguistics, philology, philosophy and semiotics. With the increasing cross-cultural, international focus of comparative literary studies, it has become increasingly important for comparatists working in translation to have an understanding of the theory and process of translation, including age-old debates of fidelity versus transparency. Since translation is an act of interpretation, it is important for comparatists to be aware of the possible ways of approaching a literary work. Another significant issue is the manner in which translators translate the culture of the work without embedding their own cultural values or world view. There is always the need to resist such appropriation in cross-cultural discourse.

In *Translation Studies* (2002), Bassnett explores the problematics of translation by examining the history of translation theory. Bassnett looks at several issues including coding and decoding and the problems of equivalence and untranslatability. One of the main differences between comparative literature and TS is the former's original emphasis on studying texts in their original language since it was believed that certain cultural concepts were not translatable. Bassnett's textual analysis tackles these core issues by making comparatists working in translation cognizant of the limitations and possibilities of translation. Reading in this way is not a passive process; by becoming aware of the issues of translation, readers become more self-reflective about their frame of reference, cultural position and organizing principals vis-à-vis the literary work. Translation studies has opened the way for comparative literary and cultural studies widening cross-cultural communication and by extension cross-cultural communities. In the early stages of the twenty-first century, the field of comparative literature is rich with possibilities enhanced by an ever-expanding language community.

Chapter 11

Translation Studies

Jairo Sánchez-Galvis

Implications of Translation

As mentioned in the previous chapter, one of the ways to carry out comparative research is precisely through translation. Researchers interested in translation studies (TS) investigate translation phenomena, translation theories and their applications. TS is an interdisciplinary field that gains insights from various branches of linguistics, psychology, philosophy, sociology, communication studies, comparative literature and cultural studies, among other disciplines. Thus TS uses a great variety of research methods, from qualitative inquiry to quantitative measures. The appropriate method would be determined by the specific research project that is carried out, from the study of metaphors to the development of software for automatic translation. TS is increasingly relevant to the Caribbean context because of the great number of interlingual exchanges that take place on a daily basis both within and outside the region. Also, the particular linguistic and cultural situation of the Caribbean – with languages and cultures from every region of the world influencing each other in a relatively small geographical space – presents an ideal scenario for translation research.

In order to offer an idea of the type of research carried out in TS, we will first outline the "map" of the discipline as established in the second half of the twentieth century and later expand briefly on its latest research interests.

The Map of Translation Studies

Although translations have always been an essential part of human communication, TS as an interdisciplinary field was only established in the later part of the twentieth century. In 1972, James Holmes set out a map of the discipline distinguishing two main branches which he called *pure* and *applied* TS (2004). Bolaños considers these terms to be "clearly reminiscent of the so-called 'exact sciences'" and proposes to call them *theoretical* and *practical* endeavours respectively. As Bolaños states, "exclusively 'pure' research endeavors that do not take into account the reality of translating can be of very limited use for advancing the discipline. Furthermore, all practical translational endeavors . . . necessarily have a theoretical foundation, albeit not always at the highest level of conceptual elaboration" (2008, 4–5).

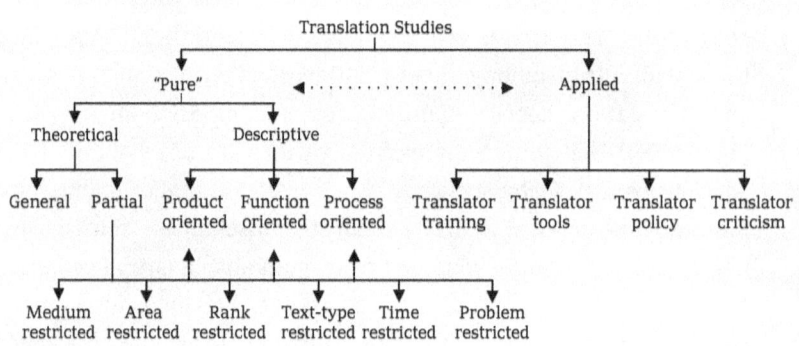

Figure 11.1 Adaptation of Holmes's map of translation studies (see also Holmes 1972)

Pure areas of research include the description of the phenomena of translation (*descriptive translation studies* or DTS), and the establishment of general principles aimed at explaining and predicting such phenomena (*translation theory*). Translation theory can be *general* if it tries to establish theories that are valid for every type of translation or *partial* if it aims at accounting for specific restrictions, like those shown in the map in figure 11.1.

Medium-restricted theories account for machine translation (a computer program receives an input and produces a translation), human translation and the interactions between humans and computers to produce translations. *Medium* also refers to whether human translation is written or oral, and, in the latter case, whether it is consecutive or simultaneous. (Many theorists, however, nowadays consider the oral branch, interpretation, to be too different in nature from written translation, suggesting a new area of research altogether called *interpretation studies*.) A useful project in this field could explore machine translation specifically for Caribbean literary texts.

Area-restricted theories are limited to specific languages and culture, for instance, translation in the Caribbean from Spanish into English or vice versa. Literary texts are charged with culture, and researching the translations produced from them can give insights into the distance from one cultural group to the next.

Ranks refer to linguistic units of analysis, for example, the word or the sentence. However, subsequent to the work of Holmes, translation theories have moved to the higher rank of the text as a unit, or *text-rank analysis*. Thus, a whole novel can be the unit of analysis, even if it can be divided into smaller subunits. A research project based on lower ranks could try to find how certain words or sentence structures appearing in different literary texts are translated and the implications of the choices made by the translators.

A theory of literary translation or a theory of translation of tourist brochures would be *text-type* restricted. We should note, however, that text types are not mutually exclusive, and their boundaries are far from clear cut (Snell-Horby, 1988). A possible research project dealing with text types could study how poems from the French and Hispanic Caribbean have been translated into English.

Time-restricted theories try to account for translation phenomena in a specific historical period. Studying translations produced during the colonial era would be an example of this type of restriction. For the Caribbean, a theory of the evolution of translation trends from the colonial period to the postindependence era would also be time restricted in nature.

Finally, solutions to translation problems can be theorized in this last branch of the map. Problems such as the concept of equivalence or variance and the translation of metaphors or proper names can be analysed. In our Caribbean context, one of the most interesting problems to tackle would be the translation of regional varieties or dialects.

A particular theoretical research project can have several restrictions. We can try to produce a theory of the translation of metaphors (problem) from English to Spanish (area) in poems (text-type) produced in the Caribbean (area) in the nineteenth century (time). Such a theory would require insights from comparative literature, historical linguistics, sociology, dialectology and history.

The next branch of the map groups together pure DTS, which can be product oriented, function oriented or process oriented. *Product-oriented* DTS looks at existing translations, aiming to describe what relationship holds between a source text and a target text, a source text and several target texts (several versions of the same text into a target language or various target languages), or a group of source texts and target texts. The study can be *synchronic* (i.e., studying translations produced during the same historical period) or *diachronic* (i.e., studying translations of the same text in different periods). According to Holmes, "one of the eventual goals of product-oriented DTS might possibly be a general history of translation" (2004, 185). For those interested in this branch, it is worthwhile to point out that a history of translation in the Caribbean is still to be written.

If product-oriented DTS concentrates on texts, *function-oriented* DTS concentrates on contexts. It focuses, therefore, on how texts were received in a specific place and time by the target culture, including which texts were translated – and which were not – and the effects such translations had in shaping the receiving system. In the case of the Caribbean, one could study the reasons why some authors are exported and translated while others are only known in the region, or one could analyse the flux of translation within the region or with the rest of the world. Product-oriented DTS had received much more attention than function-oriented DTS at the time Holmes wrote his article. However, later developments have integrated function as an essential part of TS. Holmes termed this branch "socio-translation studies", but a more appropriate name nowadays would be *cultural studies–oriented translation* (Munday 2008, 11). This is perhaps the branch that has received the most attention in recent years.

A further branch of the pure DTS concentrates on the process of translation, that is, what happens in the minds of translators when they are carrying out the task. As mentioned earlier, TS is generally referred to as interdisciplinary: developments in psychology and in cognitive science inform *process-oriented* DTS. One of the ways to study the translation process is by means of think-aloud protocols. In these protocols translators are asked to verbalize whatever comes to their minds when they are translating. This verbalization is recorded, transcribed and later analysed. This process can serve to determine which translation strategies are more common or effective, or, if there are inconsistencies, discrepancies or mistranslations, to explain why they happened.

It is important to mention that the findings of DTS (product, function or process) can be fed into the theoretical branch to yield either general theories of translation or, most probably, partial ones (Munday 2008, 11). At the same time, the theories (general or partial) can be put to the test and studied in the descriptive branch.

Applied TS uses the theoretical and descriptive findings of the pure branch to improve translation practice and to explain translation phenomena. At the same time, it feeds the pure branch with new insights, which is why a dotted line with arrows connects both branches.

To exemplify the issues dealt with in the applied branch of TS, we will examine translation aids and translation criticism. With translation aids, both for training and professional translators, Holmes refers to lexicographical and terminological support, on the one hand, and grammars, on the other. Work on these aids has generally been carried out by linguists not necessarily interested in translation, leading Holmes to emphasize the differences between comparative grammars for language learning and those required for translator training.

Translation aids include developments such as translation memories and other computer-assisted translation tools or translation environment tools. A *translation memory* is a database that, when faced with a new text, looks for similarities with previously translated texts, helping the translator attain consistency. Translators working for transnational organizations such as the Caribbean Regional Information and Translation Institute in Suriname, which translate documents for the Forum of the Caribbean Group of African, Caribbean and Pacific (CARIFORUM) and CARICOM, are sometimes given translation memories so that their translations maintain terminological uniformity.

Depending on the type of document translators are required to process, they need specific software solutions, as happens when translating a web page, localizing (that is, translating for a specific country or area) a new shampoo brand or producing a second-language track for a video game. In short, as technology advances, more research will be needed to bring appropriate solutions to new translation challenges.

Applied TS also involves translation criticism, which is still nowadays carried out mainly by nonexperts who judge translation "errors" or omissions or give their subjective uninformed impressions of a translated work. Of course, there will always be a subjective component in translation criticism, but the aim of this branch is to bridge the gap between translators and critics so that the latter can reduce the intuitive element in their work and gain insight on translation issues. For example, the concepts of *faithfulness* and *fluency* are still deeply rooted among critics (Venuti 1995, 1–12) and are thus the main standards against which to measure the quality of a translation. But these concepts present some problems. First, the very definition of faithfulness varies depending on the approach to translation one assumes. In translating advertising, for instance, one can be faithful to the function but might have to change the form considerably. Second, making a text read fluently as if it had been written in the target language (a strategy called *domesticating*) is not necessarily the best practice. Many theorists argue that domesticating is against the very essence of translation, whose goal is precisely to bring something foreign to a new context and not just to hide foreignness. Finally, both faithfulness and fluency rest on old-fashioned conceptions of translation and of the translator. In previous centuries, the "original" was seen as a sacred, higher text and the translation as a mere attempt to reconstruct it. This notion brought about the idea of the translated text as an inferior entity, in which something was always lost, and of the translator as an imitator, who should be invisible. As we will see in the next section, these ideas have undergone radical changes since the latter part of the twentieth century.

New Developments in Translation Studies Research

From the time of Holmes's map, TS has established itself as an interdisciplinary field with dedicated centres in many universities. Work emanating from collaboration among translation scholars, linguists, psychologists, philosophers and so on has changed both the research interests and methods used in the discipline. Depending on the issue being tackled, the researcher will need different theoretical frameworks and practical tools.

As mentioned before, the branch termed cultural studies–oriented translation is perhaps the one that has received the most attention in recent years. TS has moved from the study of how to translate words or sentences (*comparative linguistics*), through how to translate texts (*text linguistics*) to what happens when we translate discourses. Discourse should be understood here as texts produced with a certain purpose by social beings in specific socio-historical contexts. As such, it cannot escape ideologies, power relationships and other constraints.

In this framework, TS has concentrated on the various relationships among translation, culture and power. Under this general heading we can study, for example, the link between translation and gender. Within TS, feminist activists research the metaphors of translation and the female in order to deconstruct them. For instance, in seventeenth-century France the translation method called *belles infidèles* indicated that, like women, a translation can be either beautiful or faithful, but not both. The French, culturally powerful at the time, decided that beauty was more significant and thus called for unfaithful translations moulded to suit their taste (Simon 2005, 10). Feminist translation research also investigates how women have been erased from HIStory, what role translation has played in continuing the trend and, more importantly, what steps can be taken through translation to subvert it. Feminist translation activists (both men and women) manipulate translations to reduce gender bias. For them, translation is always a political act, and it is the duty of the translator to use this power to change inequalities. Research in gender and translation in the Caribbean is blooming in the twenty-first century, though mainly from the francophone arena.

Another view of translation as a political act comes from postcolonial theories of translation, which are especially relevant in the Caribbean context. They concentrate on researching how translation has strengthened the ideo-logical structure of colonial rule, how it has helped either erase otherness or conceptualize it as inferior or, in the best-case scenario, as "exotic". Asymmetry of power is at the centre of postcolonialism and translation. The fact that most translations into English tend to read "the same" even if the source texts come from diverse backgrounds shows a tendency to domesticate to the local taste. As with the *belles infidèles*, the cultural and economic powers determine what type of translation strategy to use when translating into a given language, but the result tends to be the dominance of the powerful and the effacing of the other. However, research into the structure of translated discourse can give new authority to translators to subvert the status quo. *Foreignizing translations* (translations that stay close to the source text, instead of adapting it to the receiving culture) have always been an option but are still nowadays viewed with some apprehension, especially because they do not sell as well.

Some forms of rewriting can also be analysed and researched as a type of translation. For example, Jean Rhys's *Wide Sargasso Sea* (1966) has been interpreted as a postcolonial translation (in the etymological sense of the word: "carrying across") of Charlotte Brontë's *Jane Eyre* (1847). Other examples from the Caribbean include *Moses Ascending* ([1975] 1984) by Samuel Selvon in regard to Defoe's *Robinson Crusoe* ([1719] 1983) and Aimé Césaire's *Une tempête*, a radical response to Shakespeare's *The Tempest* (Sumillera 2008, 26). Rhys's masterpiece has been the source of many research projects and papers because of its linguistic complexity. One such paper details how three translations of the novel into Spanish were produced (Sumillera 2008, 35):

"My momma die when I was quite small and my godmother take care of me." (Rhys 2000, 60)

T1: Mi mamá murió cuando era muy chico y mi madrina me crió. (Rhys 1981, 75)
[My mum died when I was very small and my godmother brought me up.]

T2: Mi mamá se murió cuando yo era muy pequeño, y mi madrina cuidó de mí. (Rhys 1982, 98)
[My mum died when I was very little, and my godmother took care of me.]

T3: Mi madre murió cuando yo era pequeño y mi madrina se hizo cargo de mí. (Rhys 1998)
[My mother died when I was little and my godmother took care of me.]

Sumillera tracks the use of French Creole, patois and Caribbean English Creoles and compares the three translations – T1 produced in Cuba, T2 and T3 in Spain – finding evidence of how each translator deals with the variation in Rhys's text.

As mentioned in chapter 10 of this volume, "Comparative Analysis", film adaptations of literary works are analysed under studies in comparative literature, but they can also be analysed using the methods proposed by TS, especially when the adaptation crosses the linguistic barriers, as is the case with Mike Newell's 2007 adaptation of *Love in the Time of Cholera*.

From the sociolinguistic perspective, inequality of power is also present in the translation of regional variants. Most translation theorists agree that expressions in the regional dialects of one language are not equivalent to expressions in the regional dialects of another and therefore advise against translating a dialect from the source language into a dialect in the target language because such translation would activate connotations not necessarily present in the source text. However, the only other option is to translate the text into the standard. This again effaces variability and otherness and contributes to the stigmatization of regional dialects. Translation research is still in the process of finding new ways to tackle this problem. In film, Jean-Louis Robinson's research project analyses the Merchant Ivory film adaptation (2001) of Naipaul's novel *The Mystic Masseur* (2002). Since the story takes place in Trinidad, Robinson (2011) concentrates on cultural items and instances of Trinidadian Creole as they are subtitled into Spanish. He then proposes a Creolized subtitled version in Spanish.

Sociolinguistics has also informed TS research methodologies, in particular with respect to corpus analysis. Researchers can find translation trends or produce theories on how a specific linguistic aspect is translated between two languages by means of large corpora of either translated texts or parallel texts (where parallel texts are not translations but rather texts produced independently in each language to serve a similar purpose). Through sociolinguistic tagging of texts, studies can be carried out, for example, on the language used by women or men under certain circumstances and how these specific uses are retained, lost or enhanced in translation. The use of corpora or translation shows how qualitative approaches and quantitative research are increasingly relevant in TS.

As we have seen in this brief sketch, TS is a vast area of study, and its interdisciplinarity makes it as challenging as it is interesting. Being a relatively recent discipline, there are many topics which young researchers can approach. Caribbean researchers are in a particularly advantageous position since translation (between languages or within one language and its varieties) is, for many, part of everyday life (Craig and Sánchez-Galvis 2007), and relatively little research has been produced in the region. Caribbean history also presents exciting opportunities to study the relationships among translation and gender, identity, politics and (post)colonialism, so that we are able to better understand the effects of those relationships in our present time.

Chapter 12

Playing with Sound and Visual
Literature and Film in the Anglophone Caribbean

Jean Antoine-Dunne

The interrelationship between film and literature is as old as cinema itself, and the academic study of this relationship began virtually at the inception of the new art. Cinema's versatility led to increased interaction between film and teaching in many disciplines. Oksana Dykyj (2011) points out that "it was pedagogical innovation rather than film research that led the way for the classroom presentation of films in literature, theatre, philosophy, and art history courses. Film was introduced as an innovative way of teaching, and as a means of encouraging the study of adaptations of novels and plays. The use of film allowed the inclusion of popular culture in treating traditional topics like genres and myths." The engagement with film in such interdisciplinary work may often skirt the fact of film's distinct aesthetic, and film is still seen in some circles as a kind of poor relation in the world of academia. The fact that early filmmakers used literary works to provide storylines and narrative development to the newest art of the twentieth century might on a superficial level appear to validate such ideas. The importance of film and film theory to literature suggests, however, that film has had a pervasive impact on how writers think about the written word and about the relation between artist and audience. Even when filmmakers use literary works as the original impulse for their films, recent studies of film adaptations point to cultural transitions and variations in form, for example, and raise issues that go beyond simple questions of authenticity.

This chapter will focus on questions of cultural and ideological differences in the adoption of a literary work by a filmmaker. It will also look at the ways in which writers have thought of film as a vehicle for cultural transformation or as giving rise to an aesthetic that enables new meanings or ways of seeing the Caribbean experience. These writers often incorporate filmic passages, formal structures or even concepts specific to film into their literary works.

What recent studies have sought to do, taking their cue from these two lines of thought – that is, (1) film montage as linked to literary form and (2) film language as bearing a parallel though distinct relationship to verbal language and structure – is to establish a mode of enquiry that on the one hand sees the adaptation of literary works into film as a distinct form of scholarly enquiry and on the other hand conceives of the literary text as having a kinship in terms of form and figure with the film work. This chapter explores these two modes of enquiry as they may be fruitfully deployed in both the study of literature and the fields of cultural studies and film studies.

What we now call *film adaptation* began with early silent cinema. But that dependence on novel and drama to provide material for film production developed into a symbiotic relation between film language (as in cinematic form) and literature. The idea that cinema is a distinct language derives from early semioticians and aestheticians such as Sergei Eisenstein and Christian Metz and produces different conceptualizations about the overlaps and differences between a language of words and word structures and a language of shot, frame, camera angle, *mise en scène* and, above all, editing (Metz 1974, 1986; Eisenstein [1942] 1990).

Montage as the art of editing both within and beyond the shot, in terms of the assemblage and sequential development of a film, could be seen as equivalent to the techniques employed by a nineteenth-century writer like Dickens (Eisenstein [1942] 1990, 165) or Pushkin (48–54) or Maupassant (21). This equation between film montage and literary form nonetheless emphasized the fact that film and literature employ different perceptual apparatuses. Film is an art of time in that objects appear to move in time through a process called *eidetics* – that is, the capacity of the retina to hold an image so that information is added to the material that precedes it and appears to create a moving line. This is but one theory that seeks to explain the phenomenon of apparent movement in film.

Two works by French philosopher Gilles Deleuze have been important to contemporary theories of perception: *Cinema 1: The Movement Image* ([1986] 2005) and *Cinema 2: The Time Image* (1989). Certain film analysts have focused on the way that film's formal sequential build-up of images is perceived by the viewing subject. In other words, how is meaning received and processed through the construction of images that form a unified whole? Film scholar David Bordwell and philosopher Nöel Carroll (1996) have been to the forefront of what has been called a neoformalist approach to film analysis. They insist that the construction of the film work and the perception of the film image should remain paramount in our understanding of film and in particular the art of cinema.

Studies in perception include several analyses of point of view, as in George Wilson's *Narration in Light* (1986), which examines how film creates deviant perspectives to intensify suspense and to build the psychological profile of a character. But there are several other strands of film theory such as the school called apparatus theory that derives from Christian Metz and semiotics and that combine Lacanian psychological studies with that of linguistics to provide quite powerful readings of films. Perhaps the most important essay to have emerged from this school is Laura Mulvey's "Visual Pleasure and Narrative Cinema" ([1975] 2001). This work is central to any enquiry into the way processes of identification are managed through the pleasure principle, in particular *scopophilia*. The idea of a film directly in league with the male patriarchal gaze has been countered by women filmmakers such as Trinh T. Minh-ha who create for other women and who also reverse the idea of male scopophilia by making men the object of their gaze (see Ging 2004).

Mulvey's work remains important because it foregrounds ideas of identification and desire as essential ingredients in spectatorship and further forces the film scholar to focus on questions of ideology and world view – both that of the director and that of the viewing public. It makes us consider that no film is innocent and insists that we account for the ways in which the pleasurable act of watching and the narrative strategies that mobilize this pleasure engender unconscious meanings that cluster around each and every projection of a film at any moment in time within specific cultural frameworks.

Thinking about cultural readings and ideological underpinnings affects the ways in which we conceive of the relation between a film and its literary counterpart. It should be noted, however, that films are not only translations of written texts; on occasion films engender written works, as, for example, Michael Thelwell's adaptation from screen to novel (1980) of *The Harder They Come*, the film directed by Perry Henzell (1972). The word *translation* is used here to emphasize that, while one work may spawn another, cultural differences as well as the capabilities of a particular medium make the two works (literary text and film) distinct in many ways. Robert Stam and Allesandra Raengo (2005), for example, differentiate between some of the categories in which the film work may be explored in relation to the literary work, including ideas of authenticity, cultural difference, perspective and narrative structure.

The use of film occurs quite frequently in modern literature. One may find evidence of this in the work of Virginia Woolf, for example, in particular the novel *To the Lighthouse*, and in the work of Samuel Beckett. This chapter focuses on anglophone Caribbean writing and its absorption of film forms and on the adaptations of Caribbean literary works.

The Exotic Other

The novel *Wide Sargasso Sea* (1966) provides a concrete example of cultural difference in the adaptation of a novel to film. It has been thrice adapted, once by an American, once by Michael Gilkes who named his work *Sargasso* (n.d.), as well as a television adaptation (Maher 2006). This fascination with the novel by a white Creole Dominican artist is testimony to her genius but equally foregrounds the many debates that have encircled her work and her position as a Caribbean artist, as evident in the *Wasafiri* debates between Kamau Brathwaite (1995a and b), Peter Hulme (1996) and Denise de Caires Narain (1998). These debates – many of which focus on Brathwaite's statement in *Contradictory Omens* (1974) that Antoinette as a white Creole could not understand nor be friends with the black Tia, given the historical setting of the novel – provide a context for a discussion of the cultural and ideological interpretations of the novel in these two cinematic productions of the work, since they are films that suggest widely divergent readings of the same novel. On the one hand, the American film *Wide Sargasso Sea* (Duigan 2003), represents the Caribbean as brash, exotic and sexualized through the impact of colour and the camera's mapping of lush foliage and the filming of the female body. *Sargasso*, by Caribbean scholar and critic Michael Gilkes, seeks to remain faithful to Rhys's Caribbean revolutionary perception in differentiating between ways of seeing both landscape and the black subject. In particular Gilkes's film seeks to interpret the figure of the Martinican Christophene as a powerful and dynamic presence in whom vestiges of African belief remain alive and culturally important to black and white in the Caribbean. It further explores the complex relationship between Tia and Antoinette as specifically and uniquely derived from a history of slavery in the Caribbean.

Language and the Body

Joebell and America (Lovelace 2005) offers a different example of a writer collaborating with a filmmaker, thus perhaps ensuring a closer affinity to the written text and providing greater authenticity in the film work. Lovelace's rhythmic prose and keen ear for nation language are sustained in the film version. What is more, the characterization of Joebell as someone whose sense of personhood is retained within and despite the struggles for economic success is reinforced in the film's final scene, where Joebell is seen walking happily with his love in Trinidad. The notion that foreign metropolitan places represent some form of upward mobility is made more complex, and ideas of victimhood are challenged by the use of close-ups and the focus of the camera on the body, gestures and facial expressions of the Caribbean male. This use of the camera leads to the suggestion of an inner voice, discipline and awareness of self despite the superficial poses of the protagonist.

Is Just a Movie, Lovelace's 2011 novel, may be seen to be an extended version of this short story in several ways: the novel engages with film in a very direct way and uses the metaphor of film ("is just a movie") to signify the illusions that dominate the mind and psyche of the Caribbean subject. This is not new and has been used by Naipaul, for example, with great success (see Macedo 2003; Warner 2000; Antoine-Dunne 2004, 2011; and also Mary Lou Emery's *Modernism, the Visual, and Caribbean Literature* [2007]). However, Lovelace's novel goes beyond metaphor in its use of the filmic trope by using a system of montage fragments to knit together the separate stories within the text. This contrapuntal system (see Antoine-Dunne 2004) maintains a sense of unity despite the fragmentation of stories that move almost erratically in time and space. At times the spiralling story lines appear somewhat bewildering, but the transition to a form of magical reality through the novel's leap to film in the chapter entitled "Resurrection", forces the reader to make linkages that connect the whole in keeping with the basic theories of film montage. In this chapter, a woman, Dorlene, who is about to be buried, comes alive again. Her resurrection triggers a carnival which celebrates the appearance of Caribbean unity and what seems to be the realization of decades of utopic desire. But the dream/vision of calypsonian narrator, Kangkala, which is narrated as if it were a movie sequence, provides the true "reality" of this moment and reverses the reader's perception of what is real and what is imaginary. This is achieved through the construction of a discourse on the efficacy of verbal language.

A close analysis is useful here. The sequence begins with the introduction of sound as words that engender images through the rhetoric of the politician Evrol Chance (p. 286), which is immediately undermined. The medley of sound moves into an orchestration of singing, praying, drums and calypso that is the voice of the people "touched by a new spirit" (p. 289). This "resurrection" (p. 289) is given expressive shape as communal unity through famous mas man Peter Minshall whose carnival mas has come to be associated with the colours black and white and whose words "My God, Calypsonian, this is the mas. Boss, this is it, The River, mas in black and white. Look at the beauty, look at the majesty! Look!" (Lovelace 2011, 289) trigger what is in effect a visual fugue.

The calypsonian, who is also a narrator, is "struck dumb" and begins to "see" differently (p. 290). His vision is of Grenada and occurs through the creation of echoes that engender echoes or sounds from the past. The narrator recalls

> the noise of death as we sat in a circle with bowed heads hearing the radio playing over and over again the Becket calypso that was big in that season, *Vincy mas: whole night we fêting, whole night we jamming* . . . while the bullets sang through the hibiscus hedge and the women huddled in fear crept through the doorway of our shelter to go indoors to relieve themselves in that pitiless afternoon of our shame. (Lovelace 2011, 290)

The synchronous build-up of images and the sound and "jamming" (calypso and song) moving in parallel lines at this juncture suggest the facile fête-loving attitude of Trinidadians who live their lives on the surface while tragedy happens around them. In this sense their lives are indeed lived as if they are permanently watching a movie. The images in opposition to each other (fête versus bullets), as in classical dialectical montage (see Antoine-Dunne 2004), "leap" into something else as the "movie" progresses. This is traditionally understood in montage theory as the leap to a new image-idea, as explored by Eisenstein in his many writings. This principle of the efficacy of individual thought and imagination in the creation of a global image was first discovered by Russian filmmaker Lev Kuleshov in the early part of the twentieth century. In effect, Kuleshov understood that cinema is as much about editing as it is about shooting a film. He realized that the filmmaker must take account of the fact that spectators will fill in the gaps of information in their processing of visual images and will do so by accessing their own personal experience or memory bank. The final meaning in any sequence of film is, therefore, achieved through a combination of the filmmaker's manipulation of images and sounds that direct the viewer to a possible conclusion and the unique conceptual frame of individual perception. The filmmaker must in effect calculate how a particular combination of images and sound will affect the spectator.

In Lovelace's novel (2011) the unfolding, burgeoning images generate confusion. Experience as a collection of images derived from external or hegemonic forces seems to coincide here with the construction of a narrative as in a movie. However, the narrator recognizes that "my voice is not my own". This recognition undermines the whole apparent transformative experience of Dorlene's resurrection. The true "leap" or transformative event occurs instead when Kangkala becomes Everyman in a move that synchronizes several layers of the history of revolution and repression in the Caribbean: "And I was seeing me everywhere" (p. 290). His vision is therefore also like a movie in the sense that he is reshaping experience and like the cinema spectator realigning the experiences that he sees or imagines through his own memories of the past. He becomes both filmmaker and audience inasmuch as his version of reality dominates the story at this point and his reconstruction of the images of the past enables or authorizes a new narrative of history that approximates myth in its capacity to reflect a deep but incomprehensible truth.

This truth is born out of the confusion of "words of speeches" that reverberate in the "tomb of my head; but no song" (p. 291). Political systems, hegemonic institutions, global forces such as that deployed by Ronald Reagan in 1983, are equally part of this medley of confusion. In such moments words are futile and the visual achieves a new potency:

Who could have forecast the dirge of machineguns wailing in the hills above the harbour, or imagined the people they call *the masses* holding their belly in grief, singing *God bless America, thank you, my Saviour President Mister Reagan, for taking away this curtain of fear, thank you for helping us take back our minds from the confusion of so many rulers of the Central Committee and the party bureaucracy* . . . I could feel words in my head, but my voice had no sound. (Lovelace 2011, 291–92)

What cinema, and in particular silent cinema, represents here is the power of the visual to engender emotional and psychological effect and to create new concepts and myths out of apparently conflicting images and events. The idea of cinema as a new form of myth making enables Lovelace to reinforce the idea that history is traditionally a collection of stories told from the perspective of the powerful and that art must find new ways to recount the experiences of the subjugated.

In this sense, Lovelace is referring us to early theorists who sought to understand cinema as a medium that has a physiological effect that leads to emotional and psychological affect. In particular cinema as a projection of images and sounds in time generates thought through the body in a manner that is comparable to the play of music on the body (Eisenstein 1994). Kang-kala's visionary understanding of the language manipulation at the heart of history's lies legitimizes a new approach to language, one based on the potency of the visual.

Lovelace's attempt to reproduce the impact of cinema on the imagination both in its positive and negative effects is in keeping with writers such as George Lamming, Kamau Braithwaite and Derek Walcott, whose incorporation of modernist ideas, for example, those of Kandinsky and T.S. Eliot (Pollard 2004), has led to quite unique theories of sound–visual relations in Caribbean writing. Critics such as Jean Antoine-Dunne, Annie Paul and Kim Robinson-Walcott have written on this matter (see Bucknor and Donnell 2011). The literary work of the generation writing around the time of independence movements sought simultaneously to valorize ideas of difference and to claim Caribbean modernism as a distinct phenomenon as well as to incorporate the lessons of European modernism, in particular those of the surrealists who experimented with sound and image in paintings exemplified in René Magritte's *The Art of Conversation* (1950; and see Meuris 2009).

Many Caribbean writers have sought to identify a particular mode of thinking in Caribbean artistic expression and have been influenced by the ideas of modernist painters and thinkers. Wilson Harris's "History, Fable and Myth in the Caribbean and Guianas" (1999, 152–66) explores the paintings of Caribbean artist Aubrey Williams as extraordinary examples of the ways in which movement, as that of the eye, can evoke both sound and vision and act as a trigger for a leap into a new psychic domain, one in which the threshold between spirit and body becomes a point of negotiation for new ways of experiencing what it means to be a Caribbean person.

Williams's paintings work on the level of bodily perception – that is how the body responds to sound and to visual images. Colours become a mechanism for demonstrating and evoking the intensification of experience unleashed by the way the eye moves or is moved by the play of form and the musicality or rhythm inherent in such play. His fascination with the music of Russian composer Dmitri Shostakovich exemplifies this idea. He sought in his series of paintings on the music of Shostakovich to show that sound and image are deeply intertwined at a visceral level and that seeing and hearing are experienced in a way that is almost identical. The paintings are, of course, a response to Williams's own perception of the music, that is, how his mind and body acting in tandem experienced the music as something that he could sense in a visual way. This principle is at the heart of the kinds of experimentation with sound and image that Caribbean writers have undertaken over the past five decades.

The work of Derek Walcott, in particular *Another Life* (1973), *The Prodigal* (2004), *Omeros* (1990) and *Tiepolo's Hound* (2000), are expressions of a concern with the identity of sound and image. Walcott's desire to "paint in dialect" (2000, 53), referenced throughout this work, is developed in his theory of light. The painter Dunstan St Omer, who is at the core of *Another Life* (Gregorias) and *Omeros* (Seven Seas sees with his ears) in its centring of the Caribbean Homer (St Omer), noted in an interview with Monsignor Patrick Anthony (in the 2011 film by Antoine-Dunne) that, for Walcott, Caribbean light is prismatic. Looking at paintings by St Omer, this sense of the cubist impact on the interpretation of light takes on a philosophical dimension, captured in Walcott's lines from *Another Life* (1973) in which St Omer's raw capacity to capture the multiple layers of St Lucian existence is opposed to Walcott's own perceived failure to capture the true light and life of the Caribbean. Walcott's "Where did I fail?"

(58–59) is followed by his admission that the visible world "hinders" him in his attempt to represent reality. He fails because he seeks in "every surface" what he calls "the paradoxical flash of an instant / in which every facet was caught / in a crystal of ambiguities" (58–59). For Walcott, then, his painting is unable to capture the transitions and complexities of the visible in the way that the poetic metaphor potentially can. What these lines invoke is the movement of light and the elusive shapes and forms through which a particular land or sea acquires a unique and specific expressive force. Walcott's lifelong quest to capture this "true light" finds its resolution in *Tiepolo's Hound* (2000) and *Omeros* (1990). On the level of discourse, *Tiepolo's Hound* seeks to add movement to sound and visual image through a succession of journeys and to explain the difference in the perception that shapes an image through the use of Pissarro who, as an artist native to St Thomas, carried the light of the Antilles with him and transformed impressionism and by extension European art.

Tiepolo's Hound also attempts to make an equivalence between painting and the spoken word. Some proximity may be found with Glissant's observation in *Caribbean Discourse* that "The only way ... of maintaining a place for writing (if this can be done) – that is, to remove it from being an esoteric practice or a banal reserve of information – would be to nourish it with the oral" (1989, 101). For Glissant, language must be an expression of diversity to move it beyond the universalizing influence of sameness, or what Walcott calls blandness. But since both writers have paid homage in their writings to the language of their respective European traditions, simply using dialect could not be the answer. Rather, it is that relationship with the world in its recognition of diversity that Glissant advocates. In using Pissarro as a painter whose interpretation of light and transference of light created a bridge across the boundaries of cultures and shaped a new aesthetic through the impact of different ways of seeing, Walcott is giving concrete expression to lived local experience as something that is shaped by culture and impacts on the whole person. Light becomes a metaphor that suggests a collection of cultural and geographic elements that shape how an individual sees the world and impacts that world.

Light signifies at another level a relation between cultures, and this is reinforced through the idea of movement as travel and transition. This use of light suggests also the power of illusion or "play", as in the trick of light. The connection again is with movement or, more precisely, vibration. Movement is at the very core of the long poem *Omeros* and is linked to an idea of change or transformation through light. Light encapsulates both sound and image in that both evoke meaning through a process of vibration (sound vibrates). In this sense there is a similarity between Lovelace's thinking through of the effect of sound on the body as it engenders images and Walcott's idea that light as captured by St Omer in prismatic forms signifies both the ambiguities and the complexities of the Caribbean experience and their effect on the fertile imagination of those who live in these islands. The landscape breeds presences because light playing on landscape gives an appearance of realities that exist beyond time and Enlightenment logic. Cinema as an art that manipulates concrete reality is akin to the imagination of the Caribbean artist in his or her interpretation of this light. Light then comes to signify a particular gift of seeing, linked to local folklore and a specific and unique vision of the world. The rootedness of the poetic word in the lifeblood of Caribbean mythology and imagination is figured in the opposition between "floating" and "rooted" on page 266 of *Omeros*. In these verses the image of a lily connotes whiteness, here associated with the Irish Maud, who has lived and died in St Lucia and who has sought in her embroidery to give concrete expression to the various cultures that have migrated to the Caribbean. Walcott yokes together Irish mythologies and black African Caribbean beliefs in the image of the "cool mud" that recalls the Circe myth and equally the accommodating culture of the island as he seeks to find the right metaphors to explore the development of his own poetic syntheses. The reflective surfaces of water become like magical mirrors as the light creates ever changing shapes on the pond's surface. Here light is analogous to writing and poetry's constant permutations and (mental) reflections. The ever-changing light and appearances on the surface of a pond enable a meditation on language's burgeoning meanings, "the clear concentric / rings from a pebble, from the right noun on a page" (Walcott 1990, 266), and his own desire to send ripples from St Lucia to the wider world. This language, within which Walcott discerns a rooted tradition linking him to Europe and to Africa, is evoked through light as in the "resinous woodsman" who "walked without noise, / a shaft of light angling the floor of the forest / without shaking the ferns, his soles quiet as moss" and who goes his way "soundless as light" (1990, 61).

Frances-Anne Solomon also uses movement to interpret the collection of poems by Grace Nichols (1983) in her film *I Is a Long Memoried Woman* (1990). She too combines the unique capacity of the moving image to enable deeper and more concrete reflections on experience and the impact of such experiences on the human psyche. As Gwyneth Cumberbatch (n.d.) reflects in her online review, the depiction sucks the viewer into the "stubbornness and tenacity" of black women, and the dance reflects the "moods and actions" and the agency of black women from Nanny of the Maroons to the present through choreographed movement.

A reading of the poems in the collection by Nichols immediately gives rise to the impression of movement at several levels, so that choreography as linear expressive movement in space is a singularly apt way of interpreting this work. The female voice that speaks is permanently on the move, from Africa to the New World. As cane worker she is constantly forced to "move on". As migrant she is on the move. Time moves and the black woman is also "the fuel / that keep them all going" (Nichols 1983, 49). The female black body speaks of constant pressure because of these experiences, so that film as an art form that can give concrete visibility to the body is again a resource for Solomon in her interpretation of the poetic work.

Sexual Difference and Sexual Desire

What these works suggest is a desire among Caribbean writers and filmmakers to find a form that goes beyond verbal language and that enables the viewer/ reader to see, hear and experience what is specific to the Caribbean. The writer Shani Mootoo has made a number of short films, each of which provides, unwittingly, a commentary on some aspect of her novel writing. The film works are very literary in their use of metaphor and for this reason provide easy parallels between film and literature. The themes are equally about diaspora and the finding of home in a distant place, same-sex desire, and language difference. Sexual desire, for example, may be imaged through an unfolding flower that through camera focus seems to resemble the female genitalia. This is a more loaded use of flower imagery than, say, the flower in *Cereus Blooms at Night* ([1996] 2001), which gives off an exquisite night-blooming flower, is borne by a cactus-like plant and acquires significance as a sign of illicit same-sex love and desire.

Mootoo's work as a filmmaker and visual artist has impacted on her writing in other ways, in particular in the novel *Valmiki's Daughter*. Here the distancing of the narrator is achieved through a strategy of the movement of the camera, and we are manipulated as readers in the same way we are manipulated as film spectators. This sense of insider/outsider relations is quite important in cinema and is one of the more heavily theorized practices. The filmmaker is working with that which is visible but seeking to give expression to inner reality or consciousness. *Valmiki's Daughter* opens with a prologue in which Viveka is seen on a bed by her father. It foregrounds that the novel is about "seeing her for who she is, as if for the first time" (Mootoo 2008, 4). It then moves to a panoramic view of San Fernando through a playful strategy in which the reader's eye is invited by the omniscient narrator to see via a camera-like movement that dictates what is seen as well as the perspective and positioning of that seeing. We are led as observers to a voyeuristic encounter with Viveka and her meeting with the girl abandoned by her parents because she is a lesbian. The eye is made to trace the geography of San Fernando, situating the event within a specific place and cultural context. This is part of the strategy of playing with both inner and outer reality and with public and private lives which is at the heart of the narrative.

Part of the effect of this chapter is to assault the reader's senses and to project the tangibility of the Caribbean through sensuous play via a moving line, so that the seer as "tourist" can be assailed by a "cacophony of sound, and a cacophony, yes, of smell" (Mootoo 2008, 7). The playfulness available to the artist through camera movement is evident in Mootoo's 1993 film, *The Wild Woman in the Woods*, a work that suggests the author/filmmaker is using the camera to toy with the viewer and also to map the psychic landscape of a place. The establishing shot of the city of San Fernando also maps a social and a gender history: the beggars sleeping on the pavement and the sentry guard raping the woman with his eyes as well as the love of cricket that binds are all part of that mapping (Mootoo 2008, 10–11). This moving filmic line also contextualizes the monied social structure within which Valmiki (a doctor) and Viveka live. By the time that the camera zones in on the doubles vendor, we are already aware of the social stratification and also the racial differences that dominate the lives of the protagonists and that also provide the social mores that have caused Merle Bedi to become an outcast in this place, described by the narrator as a "well-seasoned, long-simmering stew" (p. 25).

Mootoo's interests lie in using film's metaphoric power to enter into the hidden spaces that are in many ways shaped by Trinidadian society and more specifically Hindu Indo-Trinidadian society and its material and cultural biases. This desire to enter into hidden spaces expresses itself in several ways within the body of the text and most particularly in the doubling that occurs as a result of Viveka's repressed desire. She fantasizes and indeed sees the ghost of her dead brother and inhabits his phantom presence. She suffers from repressed memories because she knows dimly about her father's affairs with women and his secret life in the forest. This forest is a metaphor, echoed in her films, for hidden sexual desire and the refusal to face up to one's homosexuality as in *The Wild Woman in the Woods* (see McCormack 2011).

The impact of literature on film metaphor has been variously explored in several works. But perhaps the impact of film on poetic metaphor needs further study and may prove to be a useful tool for researchers. The use of film form in the poem *Omeros* is mentioned by Edward Baugh in his 2007 *Derek Walcott*, and a number of essays on this subject include "Towards an Audiovisual Caribbean Aesthetic" (Antoine-Dunne 2004) and two essays in the 2011 *Routledge Companion to Anglophone Literature* (Paul 2011, 626–35; and Antoine-Dunne 2004, 591–98). Antoine-Dunne addresses Walcott's use of montage as a poetic principle that incorporates the idea of synchronous time and movement to effect a dialogue between history and the individual and to complicate ideas of how the Caribbean is seen from outside and how it sees itself.

Mapping the Psyche of the Caribbean through Film Forms

Caribbean writers have sought to define what it is to be a Caribbean national through concepts of race as in Négritude, language as in Créolité or philosophical ideas derived from Deleuze and Guattari in the extended meaning of the rhizome. Film's combination of individual idea and concrete reality enables new ways of juxtaposing the psychological effects of enslavement and indentureship with that of the desire for nationhood and autonomy. Harris takes an epigraph from Eisenstein's *Nonindifferent Nature* (1987) as the guiding principle of his novel *The Mask of the Beggar* (2003). It directs our attention to the importance of conflict as the base of montage and the ways in which montage as a form can enable the expression of particular historic realities (also based on conflict) that have led to the creation of what is now Caribbean culture. Montage as perceived by Eisenstein creates a leap to a new idea – a moving outside of self. The Caribbean as a layering of historic experience within which the novelist can chart the labyrinthine course of human evolution in one space is evoked through a dialectical leap from fragmented reality to human oneness. This is no utopian idea but one that demonstrates the parallel atrocities to be found in the lives of Lazarus, Quetzalcóatl, Trotsky and contemporary movements of peoples who are turned into refugees by the human desire for control and power.

Walcott uses a similar technique found in classic contrapuntal montage, where individual lines of sound and visual, or light and dark, are each infused with an identical idea and move towards the creation of what Eisenstein has called, throughout his work, a global image. Walcott's depiction of modern horror includes an image of the Alps and an uncovering of layers of human suffering through the clash of echoes (sound) in *The Prodigal*. Memory works in opposition to visual beauty to give free expression to the vestiges of ethnic cleansing and racism. But this is just one line in a developing idea. Other lines include that of human destruction in Mexico, Serbian racism and hypocrisy, the fall of Lucifer, white Anglo-Saxon Protestant racial stereotypes in America, and his own imaginary life filled with images from European fairy tales. These are bound together by the overarching idea of death, decay and disassemblage caused by the death of his twin brother. In ways that are very obvious, Lovelace's use of contrapuntal montage in the formal structure of *Is Just a Movie* and his summoning of memory as submerged vision through the simulation of film is an echo of what Walcott does in *Omeros*. But it is perhaps Brathwaite who has been most daring in his use of film form to give shape to the pain of humanity through the ages and to use the Caribbean experience to globalize such suffering.

Brathwaite experiments with the use of visual play and montage forms in his invention of Sycorax video text format (Rohlehr 2010b, 356; Antoine-Dunne 2004, 126–52). The imagistic play of text as a mechanism for the creation of ideas is not unique (Selby 2009), but Brathwaite's poetry is linked to his theory of sound as outlined in his *History of the Voice* (1984). A good example of his theorizing of sound–visual relations through filmic movement may be seen in the book of poems *X/Self* (1987), where psychological mapping is suggested by montage forms and the shape of words on the page and the size and choice of font. In a manner reminiscent of the metaphysical poet George Herbert, he positions the text on the page to mimic the shape of an idea, like a missile, or visualizes the shape of hurt in *Born to Slow Horses* (2005). In this way his theorizing of the forces of capitalism in opposition to what he sees as residual communal structures or the effect of enslavement and racism on the psyche of the Afro-Caribbean individual becomes immanent on the page.

Despite the antagonistic discourses directed at European capitalism and economies, it is important to note that both Walcott and Brathwaite as modernists are concerned with situating themselves in relation to something called a tradition via T.S. Eliot. Charles Pollard (2004) notes that both writers appropriate Eliot, but the uses to which they put his ideas are radically different. For Brathwaite the call to tradition is transformed into a mission to establish the black Caribbean writer with his "individual talent" around a "matrix of texts" that form a "little tradition" (that includes T.S. Eliot) and that give a sense of "cultural coherence" to his work while at the same time orienting "his tradition around a particular viewpoint" (Pollard 2004, 53). But both writers are working with a sense of their relation to Europe (Pollard quoting Breiner, 53). Walcott insinuates himself into a tradition spanning back through English literature (Shakespeare, Milton, Eliot among others) and Anglo-Irish literature (Yeats, Synge, Joyce, Beckett). At the same time, he is locating himself throughout his essays and poems within the emerging tradition of New World writers (such as Marquez, Perse, Borges, Glissant, Chamoiseau, Brathwaite, Harris). What Caribbean writers, including Erna Brodber, who names one of the chapters "The Moving Camera" in her 1980 novel *Jane and Louisa Will Soon Come Home*, seem to share is a sense that the visual in its various manifestations as text or as pictures in the mind or imagination can be placed at the service of a form of textuality that takes into account several levels of experience and in particular the aura and vestiges of history and religious belief that live within the everyday existence and experiences of the Antilles. Brodber, it may be argued, uses a montage system to fragment experience so that the past exists in the present in her 1980 novel, in a manner quite similar to Brathwaite. In both writers the play of form gives expression to the domain of spirit and the dead.

The relation between film and literature as well as that of the visual in literature cannot be exhausted in an essay. Writers such as Jamaica Kincaid have shown that an author can collaborate with a filmmaker in diverse ways and for deeply political reasons. The use of excerpts from Kincaid's text *A Small Place* (1988) as the narrative for the voice-over in Stephanie Black's *Life and Debt* (2001) is a case in point. Here the images of Jamaica, both as idyllic space for the tourist and economic landscape decimated by IMF intervention and free trade policies, operate alongside ironic narrative.

The use of the close-up provides a powerful psychological and emotional tool for political analysis in Black's film. The words, however, give both particular and universal application to these images. Said's *After the Last Sky* ([1986] 1998) demonstrates the plastic nature of sound or words aligned with visual image. Black's documentary proves his thesis.

Increasingly, collaboration between visual artists (including filmmakers) and writers is becoming the norm, and filmmakers and writers are finding new ways to express their concern with the limits of verbal language or even visual language. Such interventions and interfaces point the way to more direct modes of communicating ideas and suggest that film forms can enable Caribbean writers to shape new avenues of expression through which the concreteness of lived experience is mapped not onto but into language.

Film form and philosophy also suggest that language can be made to enter into the realm of spirit and psyche through the power unleashed through the break up and reconstruction of space, as in the fragmentation of word, page and text. This accessing of the potential available through the manipulation of time and space, as in the visual fugue of early cinema, provides a powerful tool for the writer who is working with ideas of fragmentation, rupture and reconstruction. The Caribbean has made ample use of such lessons.

Part 2

The Research Process

The second part of this text addresses the postgraduate student researcher who must identify a topic, produce a research proposal as a foundation and frame for the thesis or dissertation, execute this plan, refine the full product and eventually defend it.

If the research is for an MA research paper, the student will be required to read as widely as the time frame allows, summarizing and focusing the literature in terms of themes covered and undertaking an independent though small-scale study which suggests itself out of the reading as capable of fuller exploration. The creative writer who seeks to become *officially qualified* via a master of fine arts (MFA) must produce an actual creative work to be assessed and examined by a team of seasoned writers and may explicate aspects of the work in an oral presentation. The research thesis demands more research, involving a review of the state of knowledge in the relevant area and independent research for critique or interpretation of the subject. The PhD student must, additionally, make a significant contribution to knowledge, through methodologies that include strong theoretical underpinnings and that achieve independent findings and an original position. Students who seek to upgrade from MPhil to PhD registration should note that extensive scope and originality comprise salient features of an upgrade presentation.

All such projects, however, share certain components and stages of research. Research is motivated by some problem or issue and defines an issue or set of issues to be analysed. An important starting point is identification of a viable topic and of a core question around which the research will cohere. The "Caribbeanness" of the research may pertain to the topic itself or to the approach to the topic. Because the multicultural nature of Caribbean research implies a process of research that recognizes alternative interpretations, the relationship between the researcher and the topic must be clearly articulated from the outset, establishing an ethics and politics of research.

Next there must be a design or rationale for conducting the research, shaped by disciplinary constraints and based on the nature and significance of the issues to be addressed. Proper consideration of the topic should prompt a hypothesis to be tested or a thesis to be developed or interrogated. The research must then be located in relation to other work in the area, and its scope and limitations defined. After assessing current thinking on the subject, the researcher should review the literature and frame the chosen topic in the relevant theoretical orientation. Ann Gray distinguishes method from methodology, associating method with different research techniques for constructing data and interrogating its sources and explaining methodology in terms of "the overall epistemological approach adopted by the study" (2003, 4). In the humanities, and particularly in literary studies, theoretical underpinnings of research have generally been granted far more attention than method, but a system for gathering sound content and analysing the information collected must be carefully defined if a solid study is to be achieved. Once the design is drawn up, it will be time to prepare the research proposal, an essential tool not only for the postgraduate student working towards a degree but for any researcher seeking funding for research or publication.

Only in executing this proposal, however, does the researcher actually collect, process and analyse data, and only then can one evaluate the material according to the criteria set up. The interpretative goal is fulfilled by identifying such criteria for evaluation, applying practices and policies of interpretation, and interpreting sources in light of historical context and knowledge of the period and society being studied. Many students believe that at this point the thesis is virtually finished. They tend to say, "I have it all in my head." But it is of no use whatever there! The last stage of the study, the production, is essential if the project is to be realized.

Chapter 13

Topic and Focus

Valerie Youssef

Choosing and Plumbing a Topic: The Process

Caribbean research in the humanities in literary, discursive and cultural contexts challenges us with its capacity for further exploration of human diversity and potential. The range of possible topics to be tackled is manifold, and one challenge is to become and to remain focused. There are so many subareas that have hardly been explored that one can productively be pulled from subfield to subfield, buoyed by the fascination of approaches and methodologies to be tried and tested in the crucible of Caribbean multiculturalism. At a point, however, it is absolutely necessary to resolve the issue of "What next?" and to go at what is decided upon with a fair degree of single-mindedness.

The first matter to be established by a researcher is a *workable* topic. This means

- one that interests the individual,
- one that can be achieved, and
- one that has not been tackled before, at least from the angle you propose.

The researcher may have a broad area of interest, for example, twentieth-century Caribbean writers, but will need to narrow and focus that topic appropriately. It may be necessary to ask, "What do I already know about my topic?" "Where are the gaps in my knowledge?" "How can I fill those gaps?" If the gaps can be filled just by reading further literary criticism of the works you are studying, then this is not the best topic because there is no *information gap* to fill. Questions which we need to ask ourselves when embarking on a new project in literature might include the following:

- Is there a Caribbean writer, genre or theme that has been little investigated thus far or, alternatively, little studied from a particular angle?
- Would a comparison of two writers be revealing?
  - If so, do they need to be linked in some way?
  - Would it be useful to examine two writers from the same territory writing from different perspectives or points of view?
  - Would a comparison across two countries provide more research prospects?
  - If the study is comparative in nature, should it cross linguistic barriers?

Sometimes a researcher identifies an area of study and reckons that the topic will "come", when the reality is that the topic will define itself only in the context of further focused reading. Coming out of undergraduate study, young scholars will now need to go back and reread, noting again, in a more profound way, the *style* of the writer in question and reconsidering broader concerns beyond the narrative. Consideration is necessary as to whether there is a particular *theme* that is of concern or a particular *approach* to the writing which has not been taken before.

A common feature of *style* in Caribbean writing is the choice of language variety in narrative and in dialogue. This is just one aspect of the larger stylistic frame of the writer under examination. The level of use of the Creole vernacular has to be considered as well as its effects. Sometimes it is necessary to read without presupposition and consider the effects of a writer's use of each language variety. Why does the writing have this effect? Does every writer use the vernacular in the same way? Superficially this may appear to be the case, but it is unlikely to be true. There is some useful discussion of this complex area in chapter 11 of this text. In everyday life throughout the Caribbean, Creole and standard English may be blended together, so it is likely that there will be subtle nuances of difference in the use of language by different writers and within a single writer's work different characters will blend varieties differently. If this is the case, what does it say about them?

And what about the text's perspective? Several Caribbean writers, including both Samuel Selvon and V.S. Naipaul, have written about the experience of Trinidadians who migrated to England in the middle of the twentieth century. As the migrants experience harsh, challenging conditions and deal with them in ways that are sometimes presented comically, sometimes in a very different vein, what is being unmasked about this foreign society and the protagonists' attitudes to it? Are they rewriting colonialism, undermining it, unmasking the attitudes of those who uphold it?

Another consideration is that of overall *approach*. What theoretical frames may best be applied to the text? For example, is C.L.R. James's writing best viewed through a modernist or postmodern lens; does it reflect a colonial or postcolonial sensibility? Sometimes there is a tendency to interpret terms by what the parts of the word suggest, so that postcolonial writing, for example, might mean something written after colonialism officially finished. It is only when scholars do serious reading that they recognize the concern to unmask colonial attitudes in writings of that era as well as to reinterpret the world from the perspective of those who were formerly colonized. Even more challenging are issues of whether one can pin down the shift from colonialism to postcolonialism or whether this is something which shifts and blurs with every writer, depending on his or her own experience and attitude. What is clear is that there are Caribbean approaches to postcolonialism which have been articulated by twentieth-century Caribbean scholars but which demand further plumbing.

Research is concerned with asking questions, but it is necessary to check these constantly to assess their continuing meaningfulness and relevance. After that, more reading is required of existing critiques to discern how far these questions have already been answered. Issues dealt with in literary works are not only matters of mere fiction but an alternative mode to political writing for examining socio-political issues. Far from being unfocused or irrelevant, research in the humanities shows itself to be pertinent to global issues of the interrelationships among humankind.

As individuals read, they refine their own perspectives. One may hold oneself to be impartial when one is not. In addition, theoretical frames have their own biases which can problematize a particular field. Any new theoretical position is forged in the fire of subjective experience and evaluation. When Foucault's modernist thinking evolved into postmodernism, for example, it did so not in a rejection of the restrictedness of binary thinking as a whole, but in relation to Foucault's own experience as a gendered being and his absolute belief that there should be recognition of alternative sexualities. Is there one ultimate interpretation of a topic or one best kind of analysis? Are there issues raised that can be incontrovertibly dealt with? The answer must be negative, but the exploration is nonetheless critical.

Focusing the Topic

At this stage it is appropriate to raise a series of questions:

1. What topic demands exploration?
2. Is it narrow and focused enough?
3. What is the central concern of the research? Is it about the writing itself, the way it is achieved, or is it also about the author's purpose and approach to the topic?
4. Is there an intellectual problem to be investigated?
5. Beyond the writing and its critiques, is other information needed? If so, what is it and where might it be found?
6. How will this additional research strengthen the literary investigation?
7. In what sense is the proposed research original?

If one is researching literature, the primary data is, of course, the text itself, but nonetheless what arises with regard to questions 5 and 6 is that some real-world investigation may need to be undertaken to comment better on the literature. It may be necessary to delve into archives to find out more than the writer reveals in the primary text. There may be persons still alive who can shed light on a particular time or event. This will bring breadth to the work but may involve some judicious interviewing not initially considered.

The kind of research proposed may fall under the following broad headings:

- Exploratory
- Descriptive
- Analytical
- Argumentative

These headings are taken from Tony Bastick and Barbara Matalon (2007, 2–3) in a research methods text for quantitatively oriented research students, but they certainly have significance for the humanities. It is useful to reorder them in terms of level of complexity and to amplify them for the humanities, considering whether, as we go further into our research, the nature of the study actually changes:

1. Descriptive
   The focus here is accuracy and all-encompassing description.
2. Exploratory
   a. Facts are gathered and questions answered as to how and why the facts are as they are.
   b. The findings are explained.
3. Analytical
   a. The components are analysed to establish an overall meaning.
   b. It may be requisite to compare or root out causes and consequences.
4. Argumentative/critical
   a. The aim is to interpret an issue and to argue an opinion based on research.
   b. All sides of an argument must be presented with sound evidence.
   c. A position is to be articulated with referenced support.

Clearly, any study can encompass two or more approaches, but it is useful to consider from the outset which are to be attempted. It is possible to take a single Caribbean writer and see how an approach develops. An individual about to become a researcher may have enjoyed the writing of, say, Jennifer Rahim in one work or more, in prose or poetry or both, and simply do a descriptive work answering the question, "What is she writing about and how does she achieve her aims?" In dealing with narrative fiction or poetry, that description can hardly remain at a surface level because the investigator immediately becomes deeply involved with point 2b above, taking the descriptive facts depicted and explaining them. Questions might include the following:

- What is the purpose of this description?
- Why is this story being told in this way?

The investigator needs to plumb another level, comparing the writings and searching out common themes or common dilemmas which reveal a deeper layer of meaning. Finally, at the fourth level, one reckons with the reality that there are perhaps multiple readings of these works, that, as Rahim's understandings mesh with our own, our interpretation will be subjective, differing from another's interpretation just as life experiences are different and shape different understandings. We live after all in a postmodern time which argues that there is no one truth but only different constructions of reality tied to subjective experience.

At this stage of the process it should be possible to write the research questions. There is likely to be one main question with the potential for subsidiary ones. This is easier once the topic is focused and consideration given to the kind of study to be conducted. In this chapter, we have selected two examples, one from literature, one from cultural studies, and developed a series of questions around them.

For literature we have selected "Studies of Anglophone Caribbean Migrants in London". This is still broad and shows no particular slant or approach, and it is not clearly literary, so it might be usefully adapted to "A Comparison of Fictional Works on Caribbean Migrants in London: Selected Works of Naipaul, Selvon and Levy". This may be broad still and may need to be narrowed to specific works. There is an issue of depth versus breadth here. In order to delve deeply into a subject, it may be necessary to narrow its range.

Some basic questions suggest themselves:

1. How do the migrants represented in novels X, Y and Z experience their initial time in London?
2. How do they adapt to their new environment?
3. How are their experiences depicted?
4. Why do the writers focus on experience in these ways?
5. Besides depicting a phase of the characters' lives, what are they saying about the quality of these experiences?
6. What philosophical position are they taking in relation to their characters' experiences?
7. What evidence is there for this philosophical positioning?
8. What are the writers' concerns in telling these stories?

It is important to review these questions, considering whether they are answerable and what levels of response they call for: descriptive, exploratory, analytical or argumentative. Having a rough sense of the level of the response required is important. What is clearly still lacking is an overarching question, which should relate to all the subquestions and at the same time define a larger problem that the literature is addressing, albeit in diverse ways.

We might ask, "What are the effects on the human psyche of migrating from a land where one belongs to one where one is regarded as alien, other and, for some, inferior to the native population?" While this question is only a *what* question, it opens itself to several *whys* as well as *hows*. Despite its ingenuousness, it is a question of profound significance for today's world, in which large-scale migration from less-developed to more-developed nations in the quest for some measure of material and educational benefit for the next generation results in alienation and a questionable acculturation of the next generation. This perception indicates the wide relevance of literary study. It is not written for a world of fiction but to address real-world issues which the author is concerned to tackle, and it may well inform our perceptions of the world in critical ways.

At the Criminology Conference held at the University of the West Indies (2009), two qualitative papers were presented, one on rape in Caribbean fiction and one on the media depiction of rape, murder and its aftermath. Following the session both presenters were approached by audience members who felt that these particular analyses had addressed the issues of the day far more profoundly than had the statistically based discussions which characterized the rest of the conference. We are reminded that qualitative research of all kinds studies "things in their natural settings, attempting to make sense of or interpret phenomena in terms of the meanings people bring to them" (Denzin and Lincoln 2004, 2). It is an inquiry process of understanding based on distinct methodological traditions that "explore a social or human problem" (Creswell 1998). It focuses on what people say and do and draws inferences from these activities in profound and diverse ways. That this is achievable through literary analysis is one of the tremendous strengths that the humanities brings to social research and is of particular import for focusing the Caribbean experience.

With attention to methodology, we must now consider the best approach to analysing the texts. A final review is merited to be sure of the set to be examined and the analytical frame used to best reveal its complexities. It is useful to consider whether there may be archival materials which could add substance and weight or whether interviews with the author or those around the author would strengthen the analysis. Triangulation of data is always useful in achieving a rigorously executed study.

Let us now examine a topic from cultural studies which draws on discourse analysis for its methodology and approach: "Gender Bias in Caribbean Media". As it stands, this topic is virtually impossible because it is far too broad and nonspecific. We might ask, "Which media?" "Which Caribbean countries?" "Gender bias against whom? By whom?" "Does gender bias exist?" In a relatively straightforward manner, we may fine-tune it to "Gender Bias in the Trinidad and Tobago Press". However, even that is broad. We can further limit it to two news dailies, say, the *Trinidad Express* and *Trinidad Guardian*, and choose feature articles, editorials, front-page coverage or any combination thereof. Also, *gender bias* will require defining.

Next, an overarching question must be framed. One possibility might be, "To what extent does Trinidad press coverage of gender relations perpetuate bias and misunderstanding?" Once these issues are resolved, the following questions may be considered:

1. How does gender bias manifest in Trinidad and Tobago society?
2. How does bias manifest in editorial columns on gender issues?
3. How does gender bias manifest in the front-page headlines and layout?
4. How does gender bias manifest as a feature in both papers?
5. How is gender bias expressed in feature articles?
6. Is there a balance in representation overall through the range of feature articles?

Again these questions must be analysed for what they demand in terms of relative descriptive, analytic and argumentative responsiveness. A final topic selection could compare the press and its potential gender bias within Trinidad and Tobago to another Caribbean territory with the possibility of ultimately moving even beyond the region.

With topics of this kind, the researcher will have to select both a means of analysis and a theoretical approach. There are several different kinds of discourse analysis which recommend different ways of analysing the language in the text and which also suggest perspectives toward the relationships indicated between the writer or speaker on the one hand and the audience on the other. Broadly speaking, one can examine the language at the levels of discourse structure overall, at sentence level and at clause and word levels, and one can achieve this within the broad frame of critical linguistics.

This can usefully remain a constant across analyses but, depending on one's philosophical set, one may choose to apply critical discourse analysis (CDA) or poststructuralist discourse analysis (PSDA). This will depend upon whether the researcher chooses to see the discourse as manifesting manipulative power through its form and constructing a reality for the reader which suits the powerbrokers who create it or whether power is perceived as fluid, dynamic, continuously reinvented according to the particulars of a given situation. The major proponents of CDA deal in issues of racism, gender inequity, politics and systems which promote prejudice of all kinds, with the understanding that systems of thinking are constructed and perpetuated in society through the organs of power: government, audiovisual media and the press. The proponents of PSDA espouse a more postmodern position, recognizing no fixity in systems or relations but a continuous reinvention of levels of relationship which allows for the oppressed to assert themselves and become empowered, depending on their specific context of operation and the relative support they might have within it. Given the topic above, either position might be taken on the basis of the articles examined themselves and on other contexts of talk one might choose to examine to get a fuller picture of the situation. If one was working in gender studies, one would also need to consider whether one was taking up a particular feminist position and, in order to determine that, not only study but also select a very clear perspective on feminism which has had diverse representations. The chapters on theory and method in part 1 provide guidance on a range of possible approaches and strategies.

Checklist

It is important to summarize briefly the stages that have been suggested above in selecting a topic for study and focusing it appropriately. With any list there has to be some ordering, but this is by no means cast in stone.

Select a broad topic.
1. Refine it in consideration of the scope and depth of the study to be undertaken, individual interest and what has been done before.
2. Consider what kind of coverage appears to be useful in the broad frame: descriptive, exploratory, analytical or argumentative.

3. Construct a research question that expresses the overarching problematic that motivates the study. Then construct a list of research questions to be answered in order to fully address the main question.
4. Consider further the appropriate methodology and the nature of the data.
5. Consider the likely approach to the analysis of the data, given the nature of the subject as it reveals itself and the researcher's philosophical positioning.
6. At all stages assume subjectivity and reckon with it carefully; it cannot be eliminated, but a powerful analysis will ensure the efficacy of your positioning. It is to be noted that the terms *reliability* and *validity* are only applicable in qualitative research when translated to "more appropriate terms, such as, quality, rigor and trustworthiness" (Golafshani 2003, 602).

Chapter 14

Preparing the Research Proposal
Nicole Roberts and Elizabeth Walcott-Hackshaw

The Proposal

Nicole Roberts

This chapter contains considerations for writing a research proposal, that is, laying out a complete design to the full study. The purpose of preparing a proposal is to have an organized plan or design in place prior to actually writing up a full dissertation, thesis or book. Writing the proposal is a crucial procedure which, if done correctly, makes writing up the thesis or dissertation substantively easier. In addition, if the proposal is given due care and attention, then the writing process can be more stimulating and productive. The chapter also presents a short description of some traditional sources of research especially integral during the early stages of research. Finally it ends with a short guide to developing an ethical approach in literary/cultural Caribbean research.

The Process

At this stage a topic has already been articulated and a plan formulated in accordance with that described in chapter 13. Also as stated earlier, the topic should be one that offers a challenge and provides the scope and depth for the study to be undertaken. Figure 14.1 outlines the process for writing the proposal.

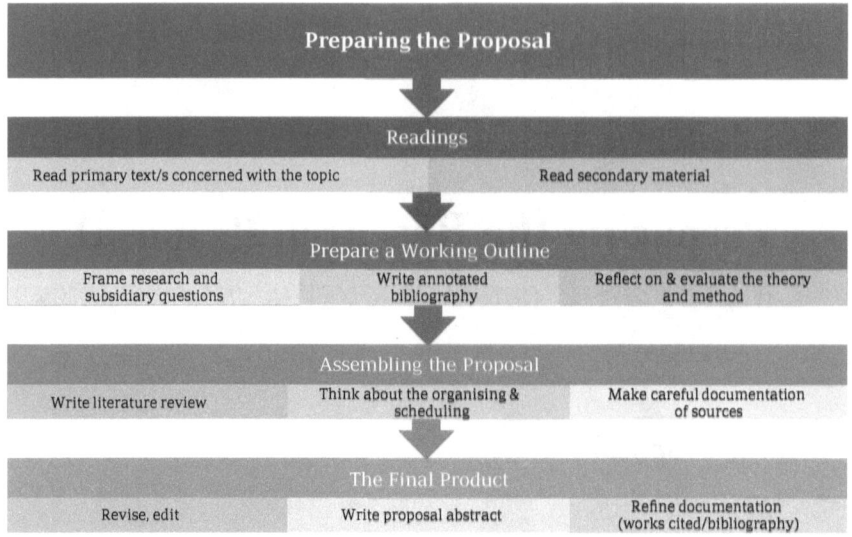

Figure 14.1 Preparing the proposal

It is helpful to remember that this sequence of stages in the research process need not be rigid. Figure 14.1 is simply meant as a guide. For example, it is always helpful to document the sources and material for the proposal together. Documentation is a continual process. When refining documentation, the researcher should cross-check all sources. Care is required to ensure that any material cited in text or notes also appears in the works cited. With all this, researchers working in the Caribbean are advised to keep note of where they have accessed references, to differentiate among those gathered at repositories, those accessed through interlibrary loan, those gathered during a visit to a foreign institution and so on, and to ensure their notes are exact because of the financial implications of travel among institutions. Following a plan such as that outlined above not only leads to the production of the full study but guides the writer in coming to terms with the research in question. Indeed, down the line, there is time to revise and move away from the original idea of the topic – in which case it will be necessary to rethink each of the steps in the above process. A well-structured and cogent proposal will pave the way for the production of the entire work. What follows focuses more closely on the central steps in the preparation of the research proposal.

Introductions generally fulfil a number of crucial requirements:

- They provide a background or frame of reference for what is to follow.
- They indicate a rationale for the study.
- They establish topic and focus.
- They signpost what is to come.
- They establish the writer's ability to deliver.
- They capture the reader's interest.

The introduction to a research proposal should establish the background to the research and identify the central issue. Gripping the reader's interest in the topic and establishing confidence in the writer's ability to take the study forward are essential, but the introduction must also convince the reader that the study is a sound and worthwhile undertaking. So it must provide a rationale, a line of reasoning, an argument in favour of the study. To achieve this, the introduction must clearly contextualize the study. It must give some indication of the impact of the work, and it must respond in advance to questions which the reader may have. Following are research questions with examples of potential reader responses in parentheses:

- Why is this study important? (Will it help to break the silence on AIDS in the Caribbean and other developing countries?)
- How will it contribute to knowledge? (Will it adjust angles of viewing British canonical literature from the traditional Eurocentric to a Caribbean-centred or New World perspective?)
- What was missing, or what were the shortcomings of previous studies in the area? (Does this study move between a theoretical and a global political analysis, thereby adding a new formulation to the method of critique?)
- How best should these gaps be addressed? (Can this study, shaped by a globalization analysis, offer a more rounded and in-depth analysis to the critique of spoken-word poetry?)
- What outcomes will the study provide? (Does it offer specific insight into the intergenerational and gender issues which shape the Dominican American immigrant community in New York and their creative culture?)

All of this means aligning the research and locating it in relation to other comparable work. It is useful to bear in mind that the introduction to the research proposal is distinct from the introduction that will be required for the full study when it is eventually written up. The finished research proposal provides a basis for the introduction to the full work.

While thinking through the research proposal and especially the introduction, it is essential to provide a *definition of terms*. These definitions provide the researcher as well as the reader with clear explanations associated with pivotal concepts in the thesis or dissertation. It is always difficult to assess which particular terms should be included in the listing. It is fair to say that, unless the terms are familiar or obvious, they must be defined but also if they are used in different senses by different scholars, if there is controversy surrounding them or if they stand for key concepts in the methodology intended. The list that is the definition of terms should be relatively short and should refer to authoritative sources and scholarly argument regarding their meaning. Working through the definitions ensures that the researcher understands the terms and concepts which have significant meaning for the study and provides the reader of the proposal with clear guidelines regarding the contexts in which these terms will be used.

Once reading is underway it is useful to maintain an *annotated bibliography*. The standard bibliography details citation information; however, the annotated bibliography is a listing which also includes detailed information about the text. This listing helps the researcher to think through the value of the cited work by adding a descriptive evaluation (or annotation) of the text on which the research can build.

The next step in the process of thinking through and writing up the proposal is defining the *methodology* for gathering and processing information. In so doing, an essential consideration will be those theories which most impact the proposed research. Numerous studies address the many and varied theoretical approaches to the study of literature, culture, film and discourse through structuralism, feminism, postmodernism, Marxism and so on. Theory provides a framework for reading and understanding a text and provides a mechanism for combining what and how the text signifies with what remains extratextual, for example, cross-cultural or gender issues. Gregory Jay and David Miller point out, "In this sense theory is always at work, however inadvertently, in the provision of such backgrounds as biography, genre, and socioeconomic matrix. Even aesthetic, formalist, and rhetorical criticism require a concept of art, an idea of the difference between form and matter, and a distinction between trope and reference before their practices can go forward" (1985, 3).

It is essential, then, to identify the specific choice of a *theoretical frame* for any research. This choice of theory or even a combination of theories (e.g., postcolonial feminism) will affect the reading and analyses of such texts as Shani Mootoo's *Cereus Blooms at Night* ([1996] 2001), Cristina García's *Dreaming in Cuban* (1994) or Edwidge Danticat's *Breath, Eyes, Memory* (1995).

Once there is a clearly defined research problem, as well as main and subsidiary research questions, it will be possible to set out precise steps toward answering the questions and solving the problem. Anyone reading the proposal will want to know

- the theoretical frame intended,
- the sources and quality of evidence to be sought and authority to be consulted,
- the method by which to acquire the necessary, and
- the analytical technique to be employed.

The researcher can only articulate problems within a conceptual system, and that is what a logical structure and theoretical framework are all about. The theoretical framework of the thesis is important because it is the foundation and essentially tells the reader how the research concerns will be addressed. From reading a range of theories, the writer decides which best suit the research. Many critics agree that theory often appears to be a nebulous space. In a sense, we can compare it to a wide-open highway which is not signposted nor is it particularly well lit. The rule which applies in this space is simple: theory is in constant flux. So it is absolutely essential to become familiar with varied theoretical perspectives from which to choose and apply to the work at hand.

To indicate the theoretical framework proposed, the researcher outlines existing theories which are closely related to the topic. Postcolonial feminism may provide a suitable approach to one topic, and continuum theory may be more applicable to another. It is essential not to enmesh the work in too many theories, as good research requires profound and cutting-edge analysis in relation to the theory specified. In short, a *research design* requires a single well-defined and coherent methodology.

As a step to achieving clarity, researchers should ensure that theoretical assumptions and allegiances are as explicit as possible. A logical theoretical framework establishes a specific perspective, a set of lenses through which the researcher views the problem. In this sense, the selection of a theoretical framework is both a clarifying and an exclusionary step in the research process. While it sharpens focus and consequently increases the clarity brought to the problem area, it excludes other perspectives that might be brought to bear on the problem but does so in explicit recognition of those perspectives and details the rationale for their rejection. Later, the choice of method may hinge on this theoretical framework, both comprising the overall methodology.

The research design must include statements regarding the method by which information is to be found. A wide range of research methods is available for data collection and analysis. For example, the study of early development of the romance in West Indian settings may require archival sources, while the analysis of how folktale is woven into the literature may prompt interviewing of elderly informants versed in their community's oral tradition. The investigation of cultural history may call for field study in appropriate sites. The understanding of conversation or written dialogue may require discourse analysis.

Methodology, however, goes beyond methods for gathering and analysing data to include the approaches that govern a study. So, for example, a researcher may state, "In this thesis, we shall attempt a literary analysis of Rosario Ferré's *Maldito amor.*" However, a methodology requires more than this. It also encompasses the philosophical as well as ontological assumptions which underlie the study. In this light, a more comprehensive statement would be: "In this thesis, we shall attempt a decolonial feminist reading and analysis of Rosario Ferré's *Maldito amor* and show it to be a direct text of resistance and response to the conflictual condition of women in contemporary Puerto Rican society." In the latter statement, the methodology is much more focused: first, because the author and text are clearly indicated and, second, because the state of being of women in Puerto Rican society is made explicit. Finally the statement includes the approach to be taken or theory to be applied (decolonial feminist theory). Only thus is a coherent methodology signalled.

Traditional sources of research are increasingly supplemented by new sources. The ability to draw upon diverse sources is essential to becoming a good researcher. Once the topic and keywords (see chapter 15) are identified, the researcher needs to find one or more sources of background information to read. These sources will illuminate the broader context of the research topic and clarify what is known about it. The most common background sources are encyclopaedias and dictionaries from the print and online reference collection. They are wonderful resources to begin the subject searches, and, perhaps more importantly, they are relatively easy to use. There are also a number of online reference databases to encyclopaedias which can be accessed in the search for material on the topic. Once this material is sourced, it may provide background information and more specific readings (books, journals, magazines and so on) listed in the bibliography at the end of the encyclopaedia article or diction- ary entry. These sources cited in the bibliography are good starting points for further research.

Online catalogues, such as OPAC of the Alma Jordan Library at the Univer- sity of the West Indies, St Augustine (available at http://mainlib.uwi.tt/), OPAC of the University of Guyana, NATCAT of the National Library of Jamaica and so forth are excellent places for researchers to find material on their topics. Such catalogues are available at many libraries. A variety of keyword searches enable the researcher to obtain information on available material. It is impor- tant to print or write down the citation (author, title and so on) and the location information (call number and library) and to note the circulation status of the item. After visiting the library and obtaining the item from the stacks, the researcher should check the bibliography in the book or article found for additional useful resources. This technique of closely following up on sources cited in bibliographies generates a large amount of material on the topic.

A number of periodical indexes and abstracts provide citations to articles on the research topic. These indexes and abstracts may be in print, though increasingly many are computer based. Most researchers have heard of JSTOR; however, there are many others, as well as online journals like *Small Axe, Anthurium* and *Tout Moun*. A librarian can assist in identifying the indexes best suited to a particular discipline and topic. A search of the home page of the nearest university library will also lead to periodical articles. Those searches (as with books) can be conducted by the article author, title or keywords.

The Internet is an immense source of information for online papers. But a researcher's job entails much more than simply surfing the web. Although there are many search engines, and many of them produce similar results, there is always that one article or link that may be invaluable. This may be found through only one search engine. For this reason, it is important to use a variety of search engines in conducting one's research. Search engines such as Google, Altavista, HotBot, Lycos or Google Scholar (these are only a *few*) are comprehensive and can yield specific information. It is also productive to combine search terms. Subject indexes (such as Yahoo!, LincOn and Ask) will only provide general information and they should *not* be the main sources. The web is easy, and it gives vast amounts of information in an instant, but you should not allow yourself to be hypnotized by it. It is not the only place to find research material. The web is one of the many tools available for conducting research.

Increasingly, full-text books and journals are available online, stored in varied digital libraries. Varied digital repositories now offer digitized and online published sources. You may also check online indices, which oftentimes provide links to higher education or publishing sites. One most widely known index is the MLA (**Modern Language Association**) International Bibliography, which is an ongoing index of scholarship in literature and linguistics. In addition, there are numerous online portals to literature resources.

Many people choose online reference programmes (sometimes called personal assistant programmes) to help them keep track of documentation. These programmes, such as Zotero, Mendeley, RefWorks and so on are available via downloads either on Internet Explorer or Mozilla Firefox, and they help with the formatting and output of bibliographies and citations. **Familiarity with the use of one of these programmes will be an asset in compiling the bibliography or bibliographies for a thesis or dissertation.** However, while all of these programmes have their usefulness, it is wise to remember that they obtain information for the entry by scanning the web page. This means that errors and duplications can and do occur. **One should** always double-check every entry at the time that it is made. Otherwise there is the risk of a bibliographic output with many errors, which will later **take** time and perhaps considerable effort to correct.

Finally, **successful researchers** consistently record what **they** find and where **they** find it because **proper citing of** sources requires comprehensive, methodical attention to details of documentation.

A *literature review* is an in-depth account of what has been published on a topic by accredited scholars and researchers. Relating the central idea of the study to the relevant literature in the area is essential for any scholarly purpose and for developing expertise in a chosen area of study. As we have seen in the annotated bibliography, the work for the literature review begins early in the research process and develops as the research proceeds. In writing the annotated bibliography, the researcher begins the process of compiling texts relevant to the particular study. For the literature review, the researcher must now give the reader the background or the foundation for the proposed study. For obvious reasons, the literature review will become stronger as the proposal nears completion; however, the researcher refines it even further in writing the final thesis. Although not obligatory, some scholars devote an entire chapter of the thesis to the literature review.

The literature review evolves from a summary of readings on the topic. Writing an outline of the author's main concerns can clarify the context. Paraphrasing these outlines enables a researcher to assess whether the text fulfils its aims and how so. A literature review also requires the researcher to locate the work in relation to other studies in the field and to evaluate its significance. Each item thus requires the type of scrutiny one might provide in a book review, though length of treatment needs tight control. Finally, and perhaps most importantly, the researcher determines whether the item complements or contradicts ideas crucial to the study proposed. This final attribute is important in determining and indicating the relevance of this material to the research.

Some pitfalls in writing the literature review are usefully borne in mind. A verbose review can result from repetition or fuzziness. Precision and clarity of thought is most likely to produce precise and clear language use. For example, in discussing Caribbean approaches to Shakespeare's *The Tempest*, it is important to clarify mentally whether the focus is on creative rewritings, like Elizabeth Nunez's *Prospero's Daughter* (2006), or applications of Caribbean critical theory to the Shakespearean text itself. It is essential to decide whether to comment on rewriting or rereading. Such decisions enable a researcher to focus the search for pertinent material and to assess its relevance to the study. A careful review of unclear ideas and concepts helps the researcher to articulate these accurately and in relation to the main propositions of the study.

A frequent challenge in producing the literature review for a contemporary area of research is that there may be a dearth of published material on the topic. The best way to approach this problem is to use a variety of terms or even alternative terms to conduct the research. If the latter also yields little, then the researcher is best advised to broaden the topic or place it in a context. It is rare for the student researcher to invent a new theory and wiser for the aspiring researcher to join an academic debate, to show the reader the relationship between the proposed study and what has gone before it or to reconfigure existing debates with the possibility of expanding critical theory.

Just as crucial to the literature review are its structure and coherence, which reflect critical evaluation of the works reviewed and their significance to the study. Grouping material that deals with similar issues (like hybridity or creolization) with the possible use of subheadings facilitates evaluation as well as connections to the main ideas of the research. Going way beyond citing of sources, the literature review critically evaluates the papers and texts that comprise significant secondary sources and does so in as engaging a manner as possible.

The proposal is not complete without a *trial table of contents*. Writing the trial table of contents will require serious consideration of the structure of the project. The subsidiary questions produced earlier offer a simple yet useful guide, and the chapters gain focus and coherence through revisiting both research and subsidiary questions. Each chapter will have a guiding question, the answer to which will complete the chapter. At this time, giving each chapter a title helps to complete the frame in which its content is to be organized. Quite a different structure pertains to discourse analysis or cultural studies, where the literature review may be one of the substantive chapters and findings may be another. At least to some extent, structure is governed by disciplinary requirements, and the appropriate guidelines for the discipline must be consulted.

A breakdown for the thesis titled "Salvadorian Women and Social Change: An Analysis of Selected Works by Claribel Alegría, D.J. Flakoll and Manlio Argueta" might look like this:

- Introduction: Women Redefining Identity
- Chapter 1: Salvadorian Testimonial Writing
- Chapter 2: A People's Mind Cannot Be Colonized
- Chapter 3: Woman, the Creator of Her Destiny
- Chapter 4: Religion, Revolution and Counterrevolution
- Conclusion and Findings
- Bibliography

Here the author, Marlene Aguilar-Nahas, has given a title to the introduction. Strictly speaking, this is not necessary but it is acceptable. In addition, selected texts may be included in a chapter heading. With later revisions to the proposal or after beginning to write, chapter titles might be changed or revised. Subheadings might be included and even the placement of chapters may be modified, among other changes.

Given all of the above, in the planning stages of writing the proposal, thinking through a *timetable* for completion is crucial. This means the specific time frame in which to carry out the preliminary work, execute research, analyse data and write the actual thesis. For this exercise researchers must be as reasonable as possible with their own time and that of their supervisors in order to produce a manageable and comprehensive time frame for completing the thesis. Reading, feedback and revision times must be taken into account when the work is to be shared with others along the way or considered by a supervisor. But be advised that the full write-up will probably require later adjustments to this preliminary schedule.

All writers must acknowledge the sources consulted in the preparation of their work. Whether to use the term *bibliography* or *works cited* in a research proposal or in the full study can be decided on the basis of consultation with the supervisor(s). Style manuals (*MLA Style Manual and Guide to Scholarly Writing*, *Chicago Manual of Style*, *Publication Manual of the American Psychological Association* and so on) provide detailed guidance. The proposal will not include a full list of readings for the research. However, it must reflect the quality and quantity of available source material to the reader. Throughout the writing of the research proposal (and eventual production of the thesis), it is essential to carefully document all of the sources read and used. Meticulous attention should be paid to this process, because forgetting to note the full reference for a quotation may mean losing an opportunity to use it if the source cannot be retraced and the debt properly acknowledged.

All documentation manuals provide precise specifications regarding the format for works cited entries for single and multiple authored books, articles in journals, chapters in edited volumes, Internet sources, personal interviews and so on. These manuals give clear guidelines for punctuation, spacing, the use of hanging indent and other matters to be followed by researchers who recognize their ultimate responsibility for proper documentation of the work.

When a clear design for the project has evolved, it will be possible to write an *abstract*. This is usually the first item in the finished research proposal but often the last to be constructed. In many places, this type of abstract is called a *promissory abstract*. It essentially establishes what the researcher promises to accomplish in the thesis. It has specific requirements for length, diction and content:

- It should be approximately two-thirds of a page and certainly no more than a full page.
- It should be expressed in two to three coherent paragraphs.
- Its diction should be pitched for understanding by a wide audience, for it may be read by persons outside of one restricted discipline. It must be clear and must convey interest and significance.
- It must immediately identify the focal issue and then define the scope of the project.
- It must sum up the central points and indicate the central theoretical orientation and method of conducting the study.
- It must predict the outcomes or the significance of the study.

To round off a sound proposal, the writer ensures appropriate style and sentence mechanics throughout the document, as a poorly written proposal invites rejection.

A Checklist for the Research Proposal

A complete research proposal includes the following:

1. Abstract (one page / 200–250 words)
2. Introduction
3. Research question
4. Subsidiary questions
5. Definition of terms
6. Methodology (including theoretical framework, method and brief explanation of structure)
7. Literature review
8. Trial table of contents
9. Timetable for completion
10. Bibliography or works cited

Avoiding Plagiarism

Elizabeth Walcott-Hackshaw

Throughout it all, professional research requires awareness of ethical approaches and choices in writing. Ethical principles must always inform research. This applies to research in any part of the world, and the Caribbean is no exception. Ethical norms in research tend to be guided extensively in terms of authorship, copyright, patents and various other areas. All of them serve ostensibly to protect intellectual property. Strict codes and policies regulate ethics in research. Researchers in each faculty should apprise themselves of the exact codes or rules which relate to their particular field.

Moreover, in developing countries such as the nation states of the Caribbean, it is particularly important that we underscore the value of ethical issues such as the privacy of individuals in recordings and other oral material, the use of personal treasure including photographs of someone being interviewed or indeed Caribbean material which may be the personal property of individuals. In recent years Caribbean artists have become more sensitive to performance copyright issues. Researchers must therefore be meticulous about documenting not only such sources as YouTube videos or podcasts but also the original material within them. An ethical approach must underlie all research. In the humanities, guides such as the *MLA Style Manual* or the *Chicago Manual of Style* can assist the researcher in maintaining an ethical approach throughout the writing of the research paper or thesis. Whichever guide is chosen or required, it is essential to follow closely the rules outlined therein. These guides help the researcher to avoid intellectual fraud.

Plagiarism, the focus of this section, is one such serious academic offence, likely to be severely penalized and liable to tarnish a researcher's reputation. One must be constantly aware of correct documentation procedures to ensure fair use. Being unaware of the appropriate academic conventions does not exonerate a researcher of plagiarism. It is the researcher's responsibility to determine and observe requirements of fair use. Writing a thesis or research paper involves reading and assimilating the ideas of others, but the unacknowledged use of the thoughts of another author is plagiarism. Without appropriate documentation, it is even possible to self-plagiarize and infringe on the copyright a publisher holds over one's own work.

There are two main types of plagiarism:

1. *Plagiarism of ideas*: Taking an idea in whole or in part, incorporating it into a text and not citing the source of the idea.
2. *Plagiarism of text*: Copying a portion of a text without giving credit to the author by enclosing it in quotation marks and providing citation details.

A writer does not create a new idea by simply paraphrasing someone else's words. The reality is that the researcher must always acknowledge and document every source used, whether it is paraphrased or summarized. Just as important is the need to accurately represent the meaning and intent of the author's idea. It goes without saying that it is necessary to use quotation marks in citing a person's exact words.

A Checklist for Avoiding Plagiarism

1. Own your ideas. One of the most effective tools is to write down one's ideas on the primary material. It is best to do so in a timely manner before the original feelings, thoughts and reactions are forgotten. This is also the time to develop arguments and to formulate questions or ways in which the primary material relates to other sources. These first reactions should be recorded before moving on to secondary critical or theoretical material. The main purpose of this exercise is to have a record of the researcher's original thoughts before engaging with the ideas of other researchers and scholars. This method of recording a personal response should continue throughout the entire research process and include the writer's response to secondary material as well. This simple exercise requires a certain amount of discipline, but it also maps a researcher's thought process and the way in which these thoughts respond to and correspond with the thoughts of other researchers in the particular area of study. It allows for ownership. One technique might be to read a particular work and then close it before writing notes on it. One may need to open it to retrieve some of the detail, but essentially writers produce their own notes in this way and should subsequently work from these in writing up. Owning ideas is a critical aim of Caribbean scholarship, born of a need to resist simply adopting the

approaches of others uncritically and in a sense to beat out our own path in Caribbean criticism and analysis.

2. Turn yourself in. Programmes like Turnitin may be used not only by lecturers to check students' essays for plagiarism but also for checking one's own work for errors in documentation of electronic sources. As with any spelling or grammatical check, running a document through a plagiarism programme is an excellent way to avoid committing such a serious offence. Plagiarism checker technology can also help to detect potential self-plagiarism.

3. Get other opinions. This does not mean abdicating one's responsibility for correcting and refining one's own work. Research can be a rewarding process, but it can also be a very isolating experience. The researcher is often pulled into a specialized area that creates specific contexts. Young researchers should remember that, when it comes to incorporating and documenting the work of other researchers, most universities offer assistance through discipline-specific librarians. This allows any questions which might arise regarding documentation to be addressed by an objective source.

In this chapter we have seen that words and ideas really can be stolen. Fortunately, though, most cases of plagiarism can be avoided by citing sources. Clearly acknowledging that material and providing the reader with the information necessary to find that source is usually enough to prevent plagiarism. Plagiarism can be avoided if researchers remain vigilant and maintain an ethical approach.

Chapter 15

Preparing the Thesis
Geraldine Skeete

From Beginning to End

Writing up any research is a painstaking, rigorous and rewarding part of the postgraduate experience. Gathering the research – whether it be quantitative or qualitative data – documenting, transcribing and analysing it, depending on one's area of discipline, are just some of the processes undertaken, and the researcher has to be mindful that the writing up of the research is as important as these preceding stages. It is like having obtained all the required ingredients for a meal that are now spread on the kitchen table: the cook needs to know how to combine them and to employ the best culinary practices in order not to spoil the pot. In this chapter we focus on aspects of *getting the writing started*. This begins with the essential writing guides to draw on prewriting documents like the research proposal. Then, factors in the researcher's academic experience *during the writing-up* stage can positively or negatively impinge on the writing process. In the end different considerations shape the writing of the introductory chapter, developing the argument in the body chapters, and *finishing the writing*.

Beginning to Write Up

Before one begins to write, one needs to have ready at hand – on the desk where one works, preferably – the most recent edition of the required style manual, a good dictionary, a thesaurus and (if required) a grammar text. In beginning the first draft of the thesis after getting feedback on your research proposal, there are three major points to bear in mind: (1) how to introduce the topic, (2) how to develop the argument and analysis throughout the chapters of the thesis and (3) how to conclude the thesis. It means, therefore, that although the introduction and conclusion must be given special attention, every chapter is vital to a good or excellent thesis.

Although the reader encounters the abstract before the introduction, it is written *last* when the entire thesis has been completed. This is by definition a *summary abstract*. However, as pointed out in the preceding chapter, for one's own purposes it is helpful to write a *promissory abstract* before one proceeds with the introductory chapter since this helps both student and supervisor(s) to forecast what is proposed for the thesis.

How many drafts are written before submitting the final thesis to the supervisor and advisory committee depends on the student's writing ability and willingness to take constructive advice and criticism. There is no formula for how many drafts these may be; some researchers need to write only one or two drafts, while others need several.

The most important thing is to begin writing. Jotting down ideas in point form using concept or mind maps can provide a start, but must give way to writing in continuous prose. Some researchers feel they cannot proceed with the writing of the main body of the thesis unless they begin with the introduction; that is, they begin at the beginning. Others feel more comfortable starting with a chapter of the body and working around or backward to the introduction. Ultimately, writing is a recursive process rather than a linear one, so whether one starts at the introduction will be based on the supervisor's advice, personal preference and proficiency, and ensuring that the necessary thematic and discursive linkages are established for a coherent and cohesive thesis.

Experiences in Preparing the Thesis

Where the study is a postgraduate thesis, various factors can impact the writing up of the research: these can be emotional, mental, familial, physical, financial, administrative and, of course, academic. Below are snippets of experiences from a current MPhil researcher, a past MA candidate, a current PhD researcher and a past PhD candidate. Getting feedback from advisors other than one's supervisor, coping with joint supervision, participating in conferences and persevering are the foci of the testimonials. These real accounts demonstrate that others have experienced the highs and lows of writing up postgraduate research and that you, like them, will ultimately prevail, enjoy and succeed.

What they share illustrates how research and writing is a holistic experience, impacted by the academic environment and other scholars within and outside the researcher's own institution. Knowing how to manage and learn from these aspects – and others that pertain to each researcher's unique circumstances – can either tangentially or centrally influence the writing up and outcome of one's postgraduate work.

Feedback from Other Sources

Even though your supervisor may be an expert in the field you are researching, even if the two of you communicate well or may have a good relationship and although she or he may give prompt and valuable feedback in the writing up process – in other words, if you are blessed with ideal supervision – it is still advisable to seek advice and resources from others besides your supervisor. Committee advisors, other graduate students, academics (from within and outside your faculty, school, department or university), informants, family and friends may also read chapters at each stage of the writing and offer suggestions and corrections. These can take place in formal and informal contexts. Assistance may come from these persons or through serendipity – that is, new ideas may open up that you may not have considered before in consulting them. Some researchers find it useful to be part of an organized mentoring circle of persons who meet regularly and provide advice, encouragement and support from the beginning to the end of the process.

Good supervisors often advise their postgraduate candidates to consult with others on specific matters related to the research. Broadening one's resource base and "think tank" in this way can only benefit the writing-up stage of the research process. Because postgraduate work is notorious for being an arduously lonely experience, consulting with others also allows for opportunities for mentoring, sharing and collegiality. The MPhil researcher below, still in the throes and successes of writing, affirms these advantages of getting feedback from those in his academic and non-academic community:

> Ryan: The most important advice I can give anyone writing a thesis is to actively seek feedback from the knowledge base around them. Whether it be with lecturers or other postgraduate students, testing out ideas (even the ones that you think are solid and don't need tweaking) with other academics can open up whole new avenues for your research. Some of the best ideas I've had while writing my thesis would never have come about had it not been for discussions I had with friends and colleagues in my department. Moreover, apart from the obvious academic merit of sharing your thoughts informally with others, talking about your work with the academics around you who have gone through the same hellish process or those who are just now beginning their own journey into academia, can help you vent your frustrations or, conversely, celebrate the small triumphs that coaxing a large body of writing into existence will yield. In the early writing up of my thesis, I often felt lost, adrift among methodological issues, structural problems and even problems of expression. These plagued me far less when I discovered that almost everyone that I spoke to about my woes had gone through similar issues and had useful tips for overcoming them. I think that there is a danger of becoming so wrapped up in your work that the process becomes an insular one, a danger that is antithetical to the academic process. For as much as the final product has to be shared with the academic community, sharing the problems of writing with friends and colleagues along the way will help you develop the tools necessary to sustain your growth as an academic.

Coping with Joint Supervision

Having two thesis supervisors is both challenging and beneficial to a postgraduate researcher. This type of supervision may be necessary if the researcher is engaged in cross- or interdisciplinary studies and may prove ideal for the researcher, who receives the best of what each supervisor has to offer. However, because these supervisors may belong to different disciplines and subscribe to different, and perhaps to conflicting or oppositional, styles or approaches in terms of how the thesis should be written, the researcher may consequently confront problems. Hence, in addition to the need for managing one's own schedule in order to get the work done, it is important to ensure proper management of time as regards consultation with both supervisors and the mass of knowledge gained from both. The former MA researcher below, who pursued a study that bridged two disciplines, outlines the ups and downs of trying to cope with being jointly supervised while at the same time grappling with shortcomings in her writing competence. In spite of the challenges and periods when she felt discouraged, this researcher was ultimately successful in obtaining the degree:

> Pamela: I embarked on my master's degree with enthusiasm, knowing that at the end of the two-year programme the requirement for completion would be a research paper. My research was interdisciplinary in nature; therefore, I required two supervisors: the principal one and another who had specialist knowledge, in separate departments. It is my firm position that teamwork is absolutely necessary for progress and modification of the chapters as a student under joint supervision continues to formulate thought and to critically assess the body of knowledge; hence, effective communication and regular meetings are important. However, maintaining contact via telephone, email, and face-to-face meetings was challenging. It was therefore necessary to ensure scheduling of meetings on a timely basis. Though each supervisor was always available to meet on a one-to-one basis, I felt that I needed all three of us together in conference at times. An effective working relationship as a team was crucial so that there could be open and constructive criticism about the work. This became problematic. . . . As the body of knowledge became enlarged, it was my responsibility to manage my information and my time with my supervisors. I needed to ensure that my own thinking was critical in nature as I formulated this vast body of information into a written context.

Conference Participation and Publishing

Attending conferences and presenting papers assists in writing up ideas, and chapters can be tweaked based on feedback from presentations given. Hence, they serve the same important function as seminars and workshops. That is why supervisors encourage their graduate researchers to participate in conferences so as to gain exposure and advice from international scholars in the field. Ideally, the conference paper should be related to the thesis topic or could be a chapter or section from the thesis.

The role of conference presentation in thinking through and writing up the thesis is expressed in what the PhD researcher below says about her first two conference experiences. She reports that conference presentations help the student write for and be understood by an audience while honing communication skills because other participants may not be in the graduate researcher's particular discipline. Thus, she believes that the conference experience reinforces researchers' awareness of writing for an audience, since one of the ultimate intentions is that the finished thesis should be read by not only those in the discipline but by others in the general public.

> Renée: As a Caribbean postgraduate student, doing a conference abroad made me feel safe, anonymous and exotic. The second impactful event came two chapters, two proposals and an upgrade (to the PhD) later. I attended another conference that was outside of my discipline (linguistics) but related to my thesis. This conference brought an external lens to bear on my write-up so far. . . . From the second conference experience, I was able to deepen a now narrowed focus I had adopted since the upgrade and to write two more body chapters. So, under the guidance of your supervisor, conferences are an essential part of writing up the thesis because they bring fresh, central and tangential perspectives, like fine-tuning instruments to the overall process.

Getting conference papers, chapters from the thesis or other material published in reputable journals or edited volumes even before the research has been submitted for final examination is highly recommended. At *least* two such publications should be under one's belt, as it were, before the awarding of the degree. Besides being important on one's résumé when job-hunting starts, publications – like conference presentations – help you learn to write for an audience, to give yourself voice within the academic community and to share your ideas with a wide readership. Many institutions limit student publication to a certain percentage of the final thesis. It is essential to avoid self-plagiarism through continued original work and through proper documentation. (See "Avoiding Plagiarism" in the preceding chapter.)

This final anecdote by a successful doctoral candidate demonstrates how, despite previous postgraduate work, it cannot be taken for granted that the writing process will be easier when one later embarks on further studies. It is possible that, despite having had prior experience, writing at the postgraduate level can at times be pressure laden. Bouts of doubt and lack of self-confidence may recur. The key, as this past PhD researcher affirms, is to persevere and continue writing. Her account reinforces the dictum that writing is about rewriting and highlights how sharing can boost one's writing, hence making it advantageous to communicate one's feelings and ideas with other postgraduates, no matter what the discipline:

> Judy: I approached the writing up of my PhD thesis without much trepidation, having already successfully produced an MPhil thesis. Surely the PhD thesis document could be completed in a few short months. I soon realized that the writing process would not be any easier or quicker the second time around. I felt demoralized, frustrated and defeated. I questioned whether I was up to the task; had the prior experience taught me nothing? Well for one thing it taught me to persist and so I persevered. I identified what worked and what didn't. An hour during a busy day did not yield good results; I identified blocks of time where I could work uninterrupted for several hours. Did this always mean that there would be words on the page? Maybe not, but the thought process was essential and moved the process forward. Writing is hard work; several rewrites may be needed until the desired result is achieved. For a long time I thought this was unique to me and perhaps my writing skill was deficient. I mentioned this to someone whose writing style I admired, and I was surprised by the response. The writer admitted writing and re-writing to get it right. This in no small way boosted my confidence; this same confidence was often shaken when a bit of work which was submitted to my supervisor for correction was returned. More exasperation: How did I make these simple mistakes? I learned the hard way that editing is a separate process. Never miss an opportunity to talk about your work with others within and outside of your discipline. One of my great joys of the PhD experience was sharing my perspective of the research and writing process with someone who was engaged in the same processes in a discipline which was far removed from my own. Remember that the intangibles of the experience will serve you in good stead in the future; take time to experience these as well.

The Writing Up

The research proposal is important not just to the initial stage of a postgraduate programme – in delimiting the topic and preparing for an initial seminar presentation – but to the writing-up stage as well. The research proposal is a guide or template for the introductory chapter of the thesis since, like the proposal, the introduction should include background information, a literature review, the methodology and a preview of the chapters. The introduction can therefore be subdivided into these sections.

The background information serves, say, as an introduction within the introduction. It provides the reader with an overview of the problem or hypothesis to be addressed. It therefore not only provides the context of the research but sets up or leads into a statement of the crucial issues, based on the major research question and subsidiary questions defined for the proposal. These questions, much like the thesis statement, are vital to keeping the discussion and analysis in the thesis focused and relevant to the research topic. As in the research proposal, the articulation of the central issues must be clear, concise and related to each other and to the topic. Consult chapter 14 of this book to review the writing up of the proposal.

From Research Proposal to Thesis Introduction

The research proposal is an extremely important component of the writing process – it is not a directionless exercise but one that will guide you to satisfactory completion and submission of the research. Because the research proposal will serve as the basis of the introduction to the thesis, its elements can be laced together into a fluent chapter. For example, the subtitles of the proposal should be replaced by bridging sentences to avoid extensive subtitling. The opening pages of the introduction will draw on the rationale that formed the introduction to the research proposal. Here at the beginning of the thesis, the topic needs to be articulated and an outline of its background should be provided. Delimiting the topic is also necessary: indicate the range of your treatment of this topic and declare any important limitations. The thesis statement should be located close to the beginning and must be relevant to the research question as a statement of the central issue. You should indicate the issues that are subsidiary to the central issue. Indicate as well the work done thus far on the topic, and locate your research in relation to that, providing a statement of purpose.

You should demonstrate your knowledge of the relevant theoretical debate(s) that may contribute to your approach, and you must state how this approach will assist in the analysis. An explanation of how you intend to proceed, an identification of the particular methods to be used (e.g., a case study using interviews as well as participant observation), the selected works on which you will focus and the justification for this selection should be given. You must explain the order in which you will proceed and set out the main contents of the study in a logical structure. Note that the requirements of the research proposal correspond to the requirements of the introduction to the full study.

Like the thesis statement and sentences in outlines that were required for essays you wrote as an undergraduate, the thesis statement and the issues you have identified as central, based on your research questions (see chapter 14) constitute a plan or guide that you must necessarily consult from time to time to ensure that your argument is not skewed but remains on track. It may be necessary, however, to change these guiding statements as you write should your argument develop along other lines which seem strong and reasonable.

Introduction

Whether you decide to write the introduction first, last or in between, it must inevitably be written. Since MA, MFA, MPhil and PhD research involves formal academic or professional writing, it is made up of an introduction, main body and conclusion. The introductory chapter is much like an appetizer because it whets the reader's curiosity and interest in what is to come in the body of the thesis. A good appetizer sets up the *anticipation* for the main course. A thesis introduction that is coherent, substantial and well written will have a similar effect for the reader; that is, the introductory chapter should have the reader eager for more. It provides the background and rationale of the study as well as its purpose, the gaps present in extant research and the ways in which the thesis is to fill these gaps and contribute to the field and the approaches through which the thesis would accomplish this – that is, what methodological and theoretical approaches are to be employed in the discussion and analysis of the chosen topic and the justification for these. Although the abstract serves the function of a non-technical summary, readers should be able to ascertain clearly what your thesis is about from only the introduction and conclusion. Hence, the introductory chapter needs to be planned and written with care.

The introduction, like all chapters of the thesis, must have a concluding paragraph. Bear in mind, too, that ultimately each concluding paragraph will serve another function besides recapitulating the main points of your chapters:

bringing your argument at each point to a logical close and serving as means of continuity, as cohesive bridges between one chapter and the next. You can also draw upon the material in the concluding paragraph of each chapter when you arrive at writing your final chapter on conclusion and findings. This material can be restated and expanded in this last chapter.

Its length is also an important factor for consideration. If the introduction is too long, you may need to excise selected information and place it in a subsequent chapter; if it is too short, then adequate guidelines to the study have not been provided. Perhaps the methodology is not adequately explained or the review of literature is too narrow or has not been adequately related to your own study. You may review the notes from your methodology course, consult your supervisor or browse the thesis collection in your university library to get an idea as to the conventions regarding how long the introductory chapter is expected to be. Usually, however, there is no standard length, and the theses stored in the library may have varying chapter lengths. It is worth bearing in mind, though, that a twenty-page introduction is the maximum suggested by some institutions.

After writing the first draft of the introduction and reviewing it carefully, you will be able to determine whether it is an appropriate length. Page and word limits are important considerations in planning and writing the chapters because of three factors: (1) university regulations may stipulate word limits for postgraduate theses, (2) the chapters of the thesis should be balanced both qualitatively and quantitatively, and (3) you must be mindful of reader retention and interest.

A simple mathematical calculation can solve the dilemma of chapter length. Universities stipulate limits, for example, for MA, MPhil or MFA, and PhD theses or dissertations not to exceed twenty thousand, fifty thousand and eighty thousand words, respectively, excluding footnotes or endnotes, bibliography and appendix. If, say, one's PhD thesis has eight chapters inclusive of the introduction and conclusion, each chapter should therefore not exceed ten thousand words. A similar approach can help you set and stay within limits as you develop and analyse the problem or argument of the thesis.

Development of the Argument

Dividing the discussion and analysis of each chapter in the body of the thesis into sections with titles and subtitles allows the reader to follow and digest the argument more easily. This style is most applicable if the chapters are fairly long. This does not mean they are overly long and unwieldy, but rather are the maximum length that a chapter should *reasonably* be. Sections, titles and subtitles enable readers to better locate, assimilate and comprehend chunks of information, and they lend greater cogency and coherency to your argument. Significantly, it benefits *you* as a writer in your own attempt to organize the mass of information and analysis that is a postgraduate thesis. At the same time, it is best not to overdo subtitling because it breaks the flow of the prose and is not always welcome in literary studies.

The nature of one's discipline or topic helps determine how the argument of the thesis is structured and developed. For example, as outlined earlier (chapter 14), theses in literature, cultural studies, film, discourse analysis or visual arts can each analyse the broad topic of "Caribbean Landscapes". Each, however, will treat with the topic according to the data, jargon, discussion, analysis and recommendations relevant to its discipline, and these will dictate the structure, organization and development of the finished product.

Content and Bibliographic Notes

Researchers can choose between footnotes or endnotes for documentation and explanatory notes within the body of the thesis. Some decide that for the reader's sake footnotes are more convenient and make for easier reading; that is, one just has to glance down at the text on the same page rather than rifling through pages to find endnotes. Yet those who prefer to use the latter may counter with the suggestion that the reader can solve this minor frustration by using a bookmark! Like the decision as to whether to start writing at the introduction, the choice of whether to use footnotes or endnotes lies with the researcher, guided by the supervisor(s). Whatever the choice, it is highly advisable to have a personal copy of and adhere to the documentation format given in the most recent edition of the MLA handbook, *Chicago Manual of Style*, the APA style guide or whatever style guide you are required to follow.

Conclusion

The concluding chapter of the thesis serves a significant function and needs to be given much thought and be written with as much care. In this chapter you recapitulate and summarize your main argument and, importantly, present your *findings*; in fact, in some theses this chapter is entitled "Conclusion and Findings". In addition, depending on the discipline, a section on *recommendations* may be required and move the purpose of the thesis forward into some future course of action. As in all other chapters of the thesis, therefore, *analysis* is also required – not mere statements or restatements of what has been said before.

The concluding paragraphs of the preceding chapters are excellent guides to crafting summaries of the main arguments and findings for this concluding chapter to the thesis. These previous concluding statements can be reiterated – but not duplicated – and expanded as you pull your conclusion together coherently and cohesively.

Like the introduction, which provided the reader with the *first impression* of the thesis, this final chapter is very crucial since it leaves an important *last impression*. "Always leave a good taste in the examiner's mouth", is what a teacher once told me and my classmates; it is something I have never forgotten. In this sense, the conclusion is like the dessert.

The conclusion is important because this is the last chance to solidify the argument presented in the thesis by convincing the reader that the research and subsidiary questions have been addressed and answered. It is here that *closure* is brought to the thesis so that the reader will not be left "hanging", dissatisfied with the impression that the study is incomplete or open-ended or that the researcher was indecisive or unwilling or unable to draw specific conclusions from the research material. A bad last impression can negatively impact on the overall view of the thesis and can result in a less than favourable outcome from the examiners. Time, attention and effort are therefore required when drafting the conclusion. Since writing is a recursive process – as stated earlier, writing is about rewriting – several drafts may be required before this concluding chapter is satisfactory.

Its length may be less, the same, or longer than the introduction – usually it is not the latter – but there is no stated page or word length for the conclusion since this will be a matter of the writer's style. Cogency and conciseness, however, should be evident. Brevity is to be preferred over a laborious, long-winded conclusion that would bore or mentally tire the reader.

Rewriting

At the proposal stage, you determined the general time frame in which to complete and submit the thesis (see chapter 14). This schedule constructed at the proposal stage should be revisited early in the writing-up process. With each draft it is expected that your writing, and hence the thesis, will improve.

In the first draft you are attempting to bring all of your ideas together in a chapter-by-chapter form. Each of these chapters will be revised on the basis of feedback from your supervisor before they are integrated into the draft. Although it is a first draft, you must concentrate on producing complete sentences and on making connections among your varied ideas. In other words, you are beginning to make your ideas and your articulation of them cohere. This draft, however, will more than likely contain errors in expression and even in spelling or grammar since perfection is not possible or expected at this stage.

On receiving the first draft back with written and oral feedback from your supervisor, you move on to the production of a second draft without too much delay. This may prove to be a daunting task since, in aiming for improvement, you must go through section by section meticulously. Sometimes mere revision may be needed, whereas at other times you need to rewrite entire sentences, paragraphs, sections or chapters. It is recommended that, before the actual rewriting, you take time to read your supervisor's comments and understand what is required so that you can try to be objective during this rewriting.

Many researchers attempt to skip a third draft, but that is not a good idea. Two drafts are insufficient to produce a good, excellent or outstanding thesis. At this third stage, you must concentrate on any language – spelling, diction, punctuation and grammatical – errors and typographical flubs. Your efforts at editing will be more effective if you allow time between the readings of the various chapters. More often than not, as you keep revisiting and rereading each chapter, you will discover errors, gaps or areas for improvement that you missed on previous readings.

You must be satisfied with your final product. Therefore, you must be prepared to spend significant time on this. As you read and revise, you must ensure that the entire thesis is unified and focused. In other words, the entire product must be cohesive and coherent. In addition, this draft must include the full bibliography or works cited.

The Abstract

The researcher's summary skills are of paramount importance in this last major task of the writing-up process. Now that the conclusion has been written, attention can be paid to the abstract. This should always be the last section of the thesis that is written – hence, it is referred to as the *summary* abstract. On revisiting the promissory abstract written for the research proposal, one will determine how many changes are required – besides the obvious need to change elements such as tense and aspect, for example – depending on the outcome of the research in terms of how closely the findings correlate with one's forecast. A comparison of that initial stage of the research with this final stage may also prove useful in guiding the discussion of findings.

For those readers not acquainted with what the thesis is about, the abstract is like a menu one is given in a restaurant to browse to see what is available in order to make up one's mind about what to order, if one decides to order at all. Hence, the abstract will lay out for readers what is to be offered in the thesis in order to convince them to continue reading. Since the abstract precedes but is not contiguous with the introduction, its positioning alone indicates its importance. Abstracts from tertiary institutions around the world also find their way into databases like *Dissertation Abstracts International* and *Dissertation Abstracts Online.*

The abstract, therefore, needs to be carefully written and revised. The university's thesis guide, including specific guides for each faculty, school, department or discipline, need to be strictly observed. The summary abstract will normally be of approximately two hundred and fifty words in length.

Typically, the abstract serves to outline the *topic* or focus of the thesis, the *methodology* adopted, and the *findings* of the discussion and *analysis* of the topic. Depending on the discipline, if the thesis includes a *recommendations* section or chapter, the abstract must also summarize them.

Included at the end of the abstract are the *keywords*. A keyword as defined by the *Oxford Concise English Dictionary* is "a word used in an information retrieval system to indicate the content of a document", with the latter phrase signalling the abstract's primary function in the thesis; a related definition states that the keyword is "a word or concept of great significance" (1999, 776). So the keywords should name those concepts that encapsulate the main focus of the thesis, and one keyword should also be the name of the author of the thesis. An actual example of an abstract is given below from this author's PhD thesis:

A Discourse of Alternative Sexuality in Anglophone Caribbean Literature
Geraldine Elizabeth Skeete
Fictional discourse is one means by which those whose sexual orientation falls outside heterosexual norms re-appropriate their identity, find agency and voice, redefine gender roles, and attempt to de-stigmatize their sexual behaviours. Diasporic English-speaking Caribbean novelists and short story writers have begun exposing gay/lesbian/queer Caribbean psyches and experiences of literary characters that live within Caribbean settings and also within foreign cultures. The thesis analyses how these authors negotiate language, and story elements like characterization, point-of-view and structure to explore this theme, which is largely taboo in the Caribbean. Literary linguistics, theories on gender and sexuality, and close readings are primarily employed in such an analysis. Irony is revealed as a predominant trope that subverts heterocentrism, heterosexism and homophobia, thereby producing a counterdiscourse on alternative sexualities. Keywords: Geraldine Elizabeth Skeete; counterdiscourse; sexualities.

Be sure to consult your university's thesis guide on the required format of the abstract.

Writing up the thesis, research paper or dissertation from the introduction to the conclusion and then to the abstract necessitates a contemplative, struc-tured approach. As with all academic writing, the process is recursive – rather than linear – in that it involves rewriting and redrafting. The prewriting activ-ity of producing the research proposal is essential and should be formulated with careful attention, although particular changes may be made, where necessary, as the research progresses and when the actual writing up begins. Managing the writing in terms of time, resources and skill is an important task for the researcher, who must also follow university guidelines and constructive advice from the supervisor and other advisors, while maintaining contact with other graduates and participating in various academic fora – all in order not to flounder and founder at the beginning, the middle or the end of the writing. After the writing up is done comes the very significant proofreading and editing stage, which is the focus of the next chapter.

Chapter 16

Finishing and Proofreading

Merle Hodge

inishing and proofreading will involve more than one rereading of your thesis, some of it quite close reading. It is advisable to read for one thing at a time, or one set of related issues, and then to read again with your attention focused on another aspect of the text. Of course, while reading with a focus on one aspect – content, for example – you may notice flaws in another aspect – perhaps language use or documentation. These flaws should not distract from your main focus; mark them and move on with the task at hand.

Details that do not fall within the focus of a particular reading may be highlighted and dealt with when they become the focus of a subsequent reading. Indeed, subsequent readings may be less time consuming if you simply highlight these other details while reading for something else. Highlight them in different colours or number them according to the categories into which they fall. The following sequence of readings is suggested:

1. A relaxed reading or overview of content
2. A close reading to assess the development of ideas
3. A check for the requirements of documentation
4. A final close reading for language use (proofreading)

During your first and second readings you could, for example, highlight documentation or layout issues in blue, or mark them with the number 3, for example, and problems of language use in yellow or with the number 4.

First Reading: Selection and Organization of Content

As noted in chapter 15, the essential content of the thesis is set out in four sections: the abstract; the introductory chapter; the body, composed of different chapters; and the conclusion, the final chapter. Examine the material you have put into your thesis and how you have structured the material into these sections.

A review of content is a good place to start the rewriting of your draft (also discussed in chapter 15), because if, after the first reading, such changes as reshuffling, elimination and expansion of certain parts need to be made, you are likely to be working with a new document. If you begin your finishing with a detailed overhaul of language, for example, you will eventually have to proofread all over again. To generate your content, you have been gathering information and analysing it, all with a particular topic in mind. That topic will also help to guide your first round of finishing, for one of your concerns will be *relevance*: every piece of the material selected for inclusion in your thesis must be relevant to the line of enquiry announced by your topic.

The criterion of relevance must also be applied within individual sections. Three of the sections present challenges to students in terms of content: the abstract, the introduction and the conclusion. Ensure that each section of the thesis contains only those elements of content that belong, that is, are in accordance with the purpose of each section. This is the crucial issue of where to put what. This extends to the question of overlap, the needless repetition of the same material in more than one section. You will also need to review your content for originality: the content of your thesis must be new scholarship. It must not be a mere rehash of material that you have surveyed.

To ensure overall relevance to the topic of your thesis, read page by page with the following questions in mind:

- Does anything on this page depart from the stated topic of the thesis?
- Will the reader recognize the issue around which all of your content revolves?
- Is there one clear controlling idea that ties together all your points, all your arguments and supporting evidence, and all of the discussion in your thesis?

All of the content must be visibly and closely related to one central concern. If the topic has declared a focus on race relations, for example, the discussion cannot veer off, without good reason, into an extensive analysis of gender roles or all the tenets of all the religions of the society in focus. Gender roles and religion may well have some bearing on race relations, but the analysis must select the factors which do.

By the time that you have read through your abstract, introduction, and the first chapter of the body, one should have gained a strong sense that this thesis is being directed by a statement the writer wishes to make about a particular issue. Your reader must be able to see that statement emerging clearly from what you have written. In reviewing your content, remind yourself constantly of your principal research question and its answer. The answer to your principal research question is your central statement. Use this to guide you in identifying any drifting, aimless material which neither expands nor supports your overarching statement. During this editing process, such material must be taken out. No part of your thesis must read like a collection of random thoughts on your area of research or different chunks of material arbitrarily pulled from here and there in the broad field of that research.

Sometimes the problem is that the relevance of a particular point is not evident to the reader. Leave no room for doubt. Check your work for material that could *seem* not to belong. If it has some bearing on your chosen focus, show how: link it properly to the discussion. When you come upon material that you now recognize as manifestly irrelevant and you cannot remember why you put it in, eliminate it, no matter how true or well written it might be.

Ensure the relevance of content within each section.

In the case of the abstract, there are two that you have had to compose – one for your research proposal and another for the final document, the thesis. They are different in purpose and content. Be reminded that the abstract that you submitted as part of your research proposal was a promissory abstract. It was a statement of intent, written before you carried out your research and analysed your findings. It set out what you intended to investigate, what hypothesis you were going to test (if you already had one) and what issues or questions would drive the research.

The final abstract – the one that appears at the front of your thesis – is a different statement. The following example taken from a student thesis is inappropriate as a final abstract:

This research will examine the issues of childhood, adolescence, early adulthood and later adulthood. It will take into consideration matters such as education, aging, marriage and sexuality. This study will illustrate and explore the various authors' representation of the construction of Indo-Trinidadian women's identity to determine whether the construction of this group has evolved over the period of representation. It will make obvious the differences and similarities among said authors' construction of the feminine identity politics. It will also investigate the changes or shift in the identity construct among the specified texts and seek to establish reasons for the construction shift.

In the first place, this is written in the future tense, as promissory abstracts logically are; but the final abstract is composed after the research has been done and the thesis written. At this stage, therefore, the actions referred to are no longer in the future. Then, this abstract sets out a list of implied questions and issues to be investigated. If the thesis has been written, presumably you now have answers. You cannot present the reader with speculative statements such as "to determine *whether* the construction of the group has evolved". By now you know whether it has evolved or not.

Check your final abstract and eliminate any promissory statements you find there. Remember that the abstract attached to your thesis must indicate what you found when you did the investigation promised in your proposal. An abstract accommodates only main ideas. If you have included supporting material such as illustrations, specific details or quotations, these must be eliminated. Ensure that your abstract contains nothing more than the following, each indicated (not elaborated) in one sentence if possible: the subject matter (e.g., texts examined), methodology or approach, theoretical framework and a few broad statements that provide answers to your major research questions.

The introduction is not just another summary of the study. It must not duplicate the abstract, and it is also important to disentangle the content of the introduction from that of the body of the thesis. Check that your introduction is an independent chapter that (a) provides context for your study and (b) prepares the reader to navigate the study. In the first function, elaborating the context, the introduction takes a wider view of the topic; it takes some distance from your study, much like stepping back to see the "big picture" into which it fits. The second function, of providing a guide to the study, necessarily entails zooming in to look inside the body of the thesis – but not in order to rehash material that appears there.

Ensure that the major research question, as formulated in your proposal, is still valid.

Often the main research question turns out to be far too broad, too ambitious. As you explored the field, you recognized, perhaps, that you had to narrow the focus of your enquiry, or even make some change to its direction. If the purpose of your study has shifted somewhat, this is the time and place to refine your major and subsidiary research questions, as suggested in chapter 14. This is your last opportunity to make sure that your statement of purpose for the thesis, which may be fleshed out by research questions or issues investigated, accurately reflects the focus of the final product, so that there is no conflict between what you announce in the introduction and what the reader will find in the body of your thesis.

In the introduction you must indicate the scope of the study: what it treats and what lies outside of its purview. In articulating the theoretical framework, what is needed is an overview of the theory that informs your analysis – its central proposition and the parts of its philosophy that are specifically related to your study. This involves summarizing, not going off into tangential aspects of the theory that bear no relevance to your study. It also involves writing in your own words. If you have simply reproduced chunks of text from sources, then you have some rewriting to do. Presenting theory in your own words, and accurately, convinces those who read your study that you understand the ideas you are relaying.

If your own hypothesis is a theoretical proposition that you have arrived at without reference to any established and documented system of thought, make sure that you have set out the premises and concepts that flow from your proposition. In identifying the theoretical framework, however, you must not be drawn into elaborating your actual analysis. That would be pre-empting, and duplicating, discussion that belongs in the body of the thesis. Remove from your introduction any material that goes into detail regarding your findings, analysis or conclusions.

With regard to the description of your methods of data collection, again, check for any variation from your initial proposal. The same applies to your literature review, which can now be more focused than the relatively broad exploratory reading done at the outset. Is every text in your initial review now strictly relevant to your thesis? Are there any texts that you now need to add? At this point, when you have read so much more, you can more clearly identify and acknowledge the contribution of previous scholarship to your study. Based on your own findings, you are also now well placed to engage in argument with positions taken by other scholars which have some bearing on your study. Is there anything in what you have read that you wish to challenge? This evaluative dimension will add depth to your content.

Information on the historical background to your study may have been given in the introduction, or, depending on length, it may have warranted a separate chapter placed at the beginning of the body. In either case, it must be scrutinized for relevance. If you find it necessary to refer to history at all, you will need to restrict yourself to information which helps develop your specific topic from the angle you have chosen. Make sure that all details you have presented are essential to your purpose and that you have not strayed into facts and figures that have no role to play in the development of your argument in *this* thesis. For example, a topic such as "The Characterization of the Female Protagonist in Indo-Caribbean Women's Writing" will not require you to deliver the complete and unedited history of Indian indentureship in the Caribbean.

Not every literary study calls for biographical information on the author or authors of the works examined. Where details of the author's life story are crucial to the central issue of your thesis, then a selective author biography is in order. This may form part of the introduction, or you might find it more appropriate to place it in the chapter of body which contains material related to it. If the essential biographical information adds up to a large amount of text, it may constitute a separate chapter. It should appear in one of these places only, and all the details given must be relevant to the study. Make sure that you have not used gratuitous biography to pad your thesis. All background information – biographical, social, political, literary or any other history – must be carefully selected, guided by your specific topic and angle.

Make sure that your introduction has properly framed your thesis, locating it with precision in the landscape of specialized knowledge of which it is a part. The introduction must also give directions regarding the internal geography of the body and shed light on any possible obstacles to clarity. It is useful for the reader to have, in advance, a map of the body: this means laying out your breakdown of content into chapters and possibly grouping chapters that constitute larger sections. It does not mean giving chapter summaries or any such thing, but simply identifying the different units of the body and indicating the *focus* of each. In some cases you might want to justify the way that you have distributed the content of the body, including the sequencing of chapters.

Certain other directions are necessary. Some items in the text may be obscure to readers and therefore need clarification beforehand. Check whether you have made an exhaustive list of such items: technical language, abbreviations, terms used in a special way, choice of one term over another or anything else that may raise questions in the reader's mind.

In rereading the body of your thesis, you need to pay attention to the following:

- Is there a clear, coherent line of argument within each chapter?
- Does all the material in each chapter remain faithful to the focus of that chapter?
- Should any material in this section be shifted into the introduction?
- Is there any material in the body that is repeated from the introduction, or from one chapter to another, without justification?

It sometimes becomes necessary to draw upon content presented elsewhere in the same study, in order to support a current argument. Rather than repeating that material, you may refer the reader to the page or pages on which it appears. In some cases, an idea which is raised briefly at one stage has to be expanded at another stage of the development of your study. However, repeating material from one section to another for no visible purpose is unacceptable. It suggests padding or weak organizational skills. Be on the lookout for such repetition and eliminate it.

- Where theoretical material appears in the body, is it applied to your research, rather than just reproduced?

In the introduction, your theoretical framework is presented mainly for the information of the reader. In the body of your thesis, however, one expects to see theory applied, not simply reported for its own sake. Theory is a tool of analysis. Make sure that your study has taken it beyond simple information. Review the body of your thesis with this in mind: references to theory must be properly integrated into your analytical discourse, as part of the task of processing your research material.

Like the abstract, the concluding chapter pulls together the main ideas emerging from your research and analysis. Ensure that it, too, is summary, rather than a regurgitation of chunks of the body; but keep in mind that this is a fuller summary. It offers limited expansion on the findings condensed into the abstract. Other information given in the abstract (identification of subject matter, methodology, and so on) is superfluous at this stage; these are housekeeping matters not expected to reappear in the conclusion. In this chapter you might also declare the contribution that your thesis makes to the field of enquiry. (See the section under Originality, below.) There is room in the conclusion to suggest some possible implications of what you have found and for looking into the future from the vantage point of your research. It is crucial that the conclusion clearly articulate the significance of your work. This may involve, for example, offering some prognosis on developing trends and identifying areas for future research. Each component of the thesis plays a different role, but some of the differences are subtle, and it is therefore important to read with a view to detecting overlap.

A final consideration with regard to content is originality.

- Has your thesis added something new and substantial to your chosen field of research?

This could mean a number of things:

- You may have applied a certain theoretical perspective to a selection of texts or other research material which has never before been analysed from this perspective.
- You may have created new theory or added new corollaries to existing theory.
- You may have offered a new way of seeing an issue previously analysed by others; and this new way might be complementary or in contradiction to the stance of another scholar or scholars.
- You may have analysed material that has never before received any critical attention.

These are some examples. Make sure that you can identify in your thesis an original contribution to your field of study.

- Is there any material in your thesis that has been lifted without acknowledgement (that is, plagiarized) from someone else's work?

Content that belongs nowhere, in any section of your thesis, is material stolen from another document and presented as yours. Plagiarism is unethical behaviour for which there is no excuse – certainly not the claim that one did not know it was wrong. (See chapter 14 of this book.) One may quote verbatim from another text, but such material must be presented as quotation, with the source clearly identified. One may present an idea from another writer's work in paraphrased form, but such borrowing must be accompanied by a reference to its source. Nevertheless, there are limits to the volume of quoting and paraphrasing that may be deemed acceptable. The greater part of your text must be your own, original composition.

Second Reading: Development of Ideas

To ensure focus, make sure that you have developed *one* point at a time. A point may be developed in one paragraph or in a block of paragraphs that may be seen as a section. Each paragraph must display unity, or a single focus. It is easy, though, and not uncommon, for other related issues to wander into the discussion without your realizing it. These issues may be legitimately part of your larger topic but not part of the specific point or main idea that you are developing at that stage. This loss of focus in the course of developing a point is especially liable to happen if you have not been working from an outline. The exercise of constructing a written outline helps you to literally keep your various points apart.

After the thesis is written, it is not too late to construct an outline. As part of editing, identify and jot down the intended focus of each section to verify that you have stuck to that focus. Ascertain where the development of each main idea begins and ends. Pull out from that discussion any idea that is not strictly part of it, and, if that idea is an essential part of your overall argument, develop it separately. The likelihood is, however, that you have already developed it elsewhere in the thesis.

- Does each sentence follow logically, in terms of its content, from the one preceding it?

A lack of focus is one feature of incoherent writing. Although coherence also applies to the relationship between paragraphs, the first level of coherence is in the relationship between sentences. Coherence in the development of a main idea means that each sentence is properly related to the one that precedes it and the one that follows it. Incoherence may take several forms.

- There may be wide gaps in thinking between one sentence and the next, like a staircase that is missing some of its steps, so that there is nothing to take you from the step you are standing on to the next one that presents itself to you.
- In some cases the problem is sequencing – the cart placed before the horse. A sentence may simply be out of its proper place in the development of the point. It may rightfully belong earlier or later in the paragraph.
- A sentence may have no business appearing in that paragraph at all, because it relates to a different main idea.

This scrambled paragraph illustrates the importance of logical sequencing. Before you move on from it, see whether you can restore its coherence.

> It is language use as shaped by ways of seeing (narrative as well as philosophical perspectives) and by linguistic competence. This versatility with regard to language use is of central importance to Lovelace's narrative practice, which, in turn, is informed by his political consciousness. In the West Indian language situation, "linguistic competence" includes the ability to manipulate more than one code as well as different registers of these codes (Youssef 1996). The dimension of "voice" goes beyond language. By his creative use of the language environment in which he writes, Lovelace has made an unparalleled contribution to the development of the West Indian literary voice.

- Is the content of each sentence effectively linked to that of the one preceding it?

While each sentence must lead logically to the next in terms of the thought that each one contains, each sentence should also have, built into its formulation, a link to the previous one. This device greatly enhances the sense of seamless continuity in the development of ideas, or coherence, which means, literally, "sticking together". The link could be a word or phrase that indicates the nature of the relationship between the two sentences; for example, *but*, *however* or *on the other hand* signals contrast or contradiction; *consequently* or *as a result* establishes a cause-and-effect relationship; *for example* or *for instance* introduces illustration or evidence in support of a point. Make sure that your linking expression accurately conveys the relationship between ideas. For example, if you use *subsequently*, you are indicating a different relationship than if you use *consequently*. And you cannot use *however* if there is no contrast or contradiction between the two sentences. A sentence may also be linked to the one preceding it by a reference to, or repetition of, a key term or concept. There is a tendency to use *as such* at every turn as a linking expression without regard for meaning. It has a pompous air but is quite useless as a link between ideas. Find out what this term actually means, and remove it from your work if you have not been using it for that purpose.

Here is the paragraph above, unscrambled, for you to note the backward links (italicized) between sentences.

> By his creative use of the language environment in which he writes, Lovelace has made an unparalleled contribution to the development of the West Indian literary voice. The dimension of *"voice"* goes beyond language. It is *language* use as shaped by ways of seeing (narrative as well as philosophical perspectives) and by linguistic competence. In the West Indian language situation, *"linguistic competence"* includes the ability to manipulate more than one code as well as different registers of these codes (Youssef 1996). *This versatility* with regard to language use is of central importance to Lovelace's narrative practice, which, in turn, is informed by his political consciousness. (Hodge 2008, 97)

Paragraphs, too, must be placed in a sequence that reflects a logical thinking process. They must also be tied together by the same methods as are used to achieve smooth transitions between sentences. Often, the first sentence of a new paragraph is linked back to the last sentence of the preceding paragraph, but that is not a rule – almost any sentence in either of two succeeding paragraphs may carry the words which link them together. Check for abruptness or disjointedness in the flow of your writing, and correct the problem.

You must also review your writing for expansion, because the third requirement for the satisfactory development of ideas is that *ideas must be developed*. There must be a sense of progression in the development of an idea. Each sentence within a paragraph and each paragraph within a section must move the discussion forward, adding to our understanding of a particular point. The obverse is stagnation – monotonous restatement of the main idea in different words or returning again and again to subsidiary ideas that have already been stated, so that the discussion goes round and round or stands still. That is not development. You may have fleshed out a point to some degree, but not enough to make your thinking clear. There is the danger of your arguments being undermined, if you fail to adequately develop a point. A premise that is not properly substantiated does not convince anyone. Undeveloped and underdeveloped ideas can suggest to your reader that you have not fully thought through a point or that you do not have a complete grasp of the subject matter.

Check for sentences and paragraphs that bog down the discussion, taking it no further, only restating the same ideas.

- Make sure that between the beginning and end of each paragraph and each section there has been a clear progression of thought.
- Check your work for passages that might seem cryptic to your reader because a major point is not sufficiently developed.
- Make sure that your main ideas have been effectively expanded.

In developing your ideas, you will, necessarily, have used more than one of the four discourse modes: exposition, description, narration and argument. Ultimately, however, literary analysis requires you to draw heavily upon the skills of argumentative writing whatever the topic. Arguments have to be supported by evidence, which includes logical reasoning. Make sure that you have observed the laws of logic, so that your reasoning does not contain fallacies. You cannot, for example, construct logical arguments based on flawed premises. Sweeping statements, exaggerations and overgeneralizations are a category of inherently flawed assertions, because they overshoot the truth. Examine your writing for statements such as these: "The Indian woman is the epitome of docility and submissiveness." Check your work also for instances of the non sequitur – the conclusion that does not follow from the premise or evidence on which it is based: "Not one of his leading characters, in any of his novels, is black. Clearly this writer is racist."

Ideas developed in the analysis of literary texts are also supported by quotations from the works of creative writers, critics and other sources. As you read over your thesis, check each of the quotations that you have used:

- Does it effectively support the point you are making?
- Is it relevant to the particular stage of your argument?
- Is every piece of the quotation relevant to that specific point; that is, does it have to be so long? See whether there is an essential part of it that does the job, and eliminate the rest.

In the analysis of fictional narratives, you might need also to refer to specific events or episodes in the text. As with the use of quotations, such allusions must be brief and to the point. You are not called upon to dish out large chunks of the plot. That is an immature approach to literary analysis. Indeed, it is not analysis at all, but mere regurgitation. It is a mark of weak academic writing and is often accompanied by a superficial or negligible analytical component. References to the literary text must support analysis, not replace it. Make sure that your thesis is not padded with regurgitated text – verbatim, paraphrased or summarized. Ensure that analysis predominates.

Third Reading: Documentation

- Does your thesis adhere to the required style of documentation?

The documentation style prescribed for literature may vary across institutions but is often the *MLA Style Manual* or *Chicago Manual of Style*. The notes below touch only on some MLA guidelines that are frequently abused or completely ignored. This is not a complete guide to the rules of documentation, and you will need to inform yourself of further details of the style required by your institution and follow it rigorously.

Formatting of Titles

There are two kinds of titles in the category of printed text: a whole publication (book or periodical) and a discrete component of a book or periodical (chapter, essay, article, story, poem).

1. The title of a book or periodical (journal, newspaper, magazine) is not to be enclosed in quotation marks: it must be italicized. Remember to check the abstract, all footnotes or endnotes, works cited list or appendices. Check

all your book and periodical titles to ensure that they are correct and consistent in format throughout the thesis.

2. The title of a chapter or any part of a larger publication must be enclosed in quotation marks – no underlining, no italics.

Go through your thesis and clean up all titles.

Works Cited

Normally you are not required to provide a general bibliography at the end of the thesis that lists everything you have read or everything that has ever been written about your subject. What is required is a list of works cited, that is, only the sources that you have actually named anywhere in the thesis. Check to ensure that every text mentioned in your thesis appears on your list of works cited, whether you have quoted verbatim from a text, paraphrased part of that text or simply alluded to it. On the other hand, texts that are not cited anywhere in your thesis have no place on the list of works cited. If you wish to display on this list a source that is not named in your thesis as it stands, you will need to insert some reference to it in an appropriate place.

Quotations

Any material reproduced verbatim from another text is a quotation and must be presented accordingly. Short quotations are embedded in your text and marked off by quotation marks. Make sure that such quotations fit syntactically into the sentence in which they are embedded. Longer quotations are set off from the body text as extracts, and there are very specific rules for their formatting.

Parenthetical Citation

Make sure that you have identified the source of every quotation and all other material cited in your thesis. Some styles such as MLA or Chicago (author-date) do not use footnotes or endnotes for this purpose. They use the method of parenthetical citation – brief in-text references pointing to entries on the list of works cited where full bibliographical information is given.

Notes

In these styles footnotes and endnotes are used for notes other than the documentation of sources. They are used for the clarification of points, definitions, additional information and other asides that would unduly interrupt the development of ideas in the main text of the thesis. Other styles, however, like the Chicago notes and bibliography option, include source documentation in the notes and require the first reference to any work to be set out in full in a note.

Fourth Reading: Language Use

In this final reading you scrutinize your diction, sentence structure and basic mechanics of English. A thesis is a formal academic document, requiring the use of a formal register of English.

In the first place, you are expected to use the third person. The second person is used in part 2 of this book for a specific purpose – to put you at your ease, to assure you that the guidance offered is specifically for you, the graduate student. This is not the regular posture, however, in writing academic prose. The main feature of the language of formal writing is that it is impersonal. Both writer and audience remain anonymous. The writer does not address the audience as *you*, nor does the writer enter the discourse personally by using the first person pronoun *I* or *me*. In writing that may be described as semiformal, the use of the first person plural is admissible (*we, us, our*), provided it does not refer to you and your personal friends or family, but to a larger collectivity such as your country, your region or the human race. If you must refer to yourself or to your reader (and this practice is really to be avoided), then one solution is to refer to either party in the third person: *the author of this study* or *the present writer* and *readers* or *the reader*. You may also use the impersonal pronoun *one* for this purpose, but there is a caveat: you have to stick to it. *One* cannot be alternated with any other pronoun within a sentence or closely related group of sentences:

> *One has to ensure that one's characters . . .*
> not
> *One has to ensure that his characters . . .*

The passive voice is used more frequently than in informal writing: "Francis *is transported* from his native village, Mayaro . . . to the alien city of San Fernando. In his isolation he *is subjected* to the tyranny of the Chandles family . . . he *is deprived, degraded and treated* as a tool" (Ramchand 1976, 29).

Formal language is objective and dignified. There is no room in formal academic language for emotive language such as exclamations, impassioned rhetorical questions, or individual words and statements charged with the writer's personal feelings on a subject. Check your thesis for this kind of diction. Formal writing expresses the writer's point of view with sober, controlled diction. Similarly, chattiness is to be avoided. Writing becomes chatty not only when it addresses the reader in the second person but also when it admits vocabulary that is more appropriate for relaxed personal conversation: *guy, kid, her dad*. Such expressions may be used in informal writing, but in your thesis you must use their formal counterparts. A comprehensive dictionary or thesaurus will help you distinguish between formal and informal expressions.

Another feature of spoken English that is not admitted into strictly formal writing is the contraction of word groups involving certain verbs, for example:

The characters <u>don't</u> have any psychological depth.
<u>It's</u> obvious that <u>he's</u> shifted allegiance.

Look for informal features in the language of your thesis and edit accordingly.

Make sure that you have made appropriate word choices. Almost every word belongs to a pool of words with similar meaning, called "synonyms". However, not all synonyms are synonymous. One rarely finds two words in any language that have exactly the same meaning. So-called synonyms usually present different shades of meaning, and often only one word fits precisely into a given context. The *Oxford Thesaurus of English* (2009) offers some help with diction by means of text boxes called "Choose the right word". For example, in one box the words *calm, serene, tranquil, placid* and *peaceful* are each defined in detail (p. 113), so as to allow you to differentiate words which may seem to mean the same thing. If, as you look through the thesis, you find that you are unsure of any word that you have used, either replace it with one that you can use with confidence, or seek help in a dictionary or thesaurus.

Another possible source of unidiomatic use lies in the choice of prepositions, which are placed before (or "govern") nouns and pronouns, relating them to another part of the sentence, often a verb. Check for errors such as those identified below. Some verbs have specific prepositions associated with them. Sometimes people (a) attach an incorrect preposition to the verb, (b) use the verb without any preposition, or (c) attach a preposition to a verb which does not take a preposition:

(a) *Readers have been looking forward <u>for</u> the publication of this writer's biography.*
   The group finally arrived <u>to</u> the airport.
   A child who is deprived <u>from</u> good education . . .

(b) *If toxic waste is not disposed Λ properly . . .*
   Writers are accustomed Λ being criticized.
   Women are discriminated Λ in many ways.

(c) *The esoteric nature of these poems denies the reader <u>from</u> the full appreciation of their import.*
   One must avoid the past <u>from</u> undermining the present.

Errors are made also in choosing prepositions to use with other parts of speech:

This is a threat <u>on</u> the community.
It creates an immediate impact <u>to</u> the reader.
A minor was found guilty <u>for</u> possession of illicit drugs.

Because the preposition *by* has some applications in Creole that are different from English, West Indian students are liable to use it inappropriately in English:

He lives <u>by</u> his brother.
There should be freedom of speech <u>by</u> all members of a society.
This story captures a certain fear <u>by</u> the population in the face of change.

Many people are not aware that *to* is the incorrect choice in this construction:

Between 7:00 p.m. <u>to</u> midnight . . .
Between ten <u>to</u> thirteen people . . .

The following is yet another common error involving preposition use:

Many West Indian writers live in metropolitan countries, Λ example, Austin Clarke, V.S. Naipaul, Jamaica Kincaid, Ramabai Espinet and Shani Mootoo.

Make sure that you know how to correct all the preposition errors shown above. Then be on the lookout for unidiomatic usage in your thesis.

In this reading you are also scrutinizing sentence structure. A number of manuals, for example, the *Harbrace College Handbook* (2009), give some guidelines on constructing well-formed sentences, as well as identifying errors of sentence structure. The main sentence structure problems to look out for in your work, and fix, are

- The failure to correctly identify sentence boundaries – fragments, comma splices, fused sentences.
- Groups of words that are not properly integrated into the sentence – for example, dangling modifiers and noun phrases that play no role, being neither subject nor object of any clause.
- Sentence overload – too many ideas packed into one sentence.
- Monotony – a favourite sentence structure repeated too often; too many simple sentences (as opposed to compound and complex); little or no variation in sentence length.
- Wordiness – using more words than necessary, which sometimes leads to redundancy, for example, "race and class *continue to remain* a major preoccupation".

Check the structure of each of your sentences, which is to say the word groups that currently appear between two full stops. Make sure that each contains at least one *independent* clause.

- If there is no independent clause, then what you have is a sentence fragment to correct.
- If you have two independent clauses not joined by a conjunction but separated by a comma, you have a comma splice to correct.
- If you have independent clauses not joined by a conjunction and separated by nothing, you have a fused sentence to correct.

Check your handbook for guidance on how to correct these errors.

If the sentence does contain an independent clause, or more than one, identify the bare bones of each – subject, verb and object or complement. Then examine what is left to make sure that everything else can be accounted for. Each of the other words and word groups in the sentence must be associated with one of these basic parts of the independent clause. A phrase or a subordinate clause must either *be* the subject, verb, object or complement of a main clause, OR *modify* the subject, verb, object or complement of a main clause (see Hodge, 1997, B6).

- Look for sentences that might be carrying too many different ideas. Express some of these ideas in separate sentences.
- Make sure that there is variety in the structure and length of your sentences.
- Check each sentence for words that are superfluous and eliminate these.

Basic Mechanics of English

This is the actual proofreading aspect of your rereading. Strictly speaking, all the other adjustments to the text fall under the function of editing. In each of your readings you may have noticed mechanical errors, but now that the text of your thesis has been stabilized, it has to be scrutinized for any remaining violations of standard English grammar, spelling or punctuation. The following are some areas that require particular attention.

- **Nouns:** See to it that all necessary plural endings and possessive endings are in place and that you have properly differentiated plural from singular possessive nouns. Make sure that you have not decorated nouns that are neither plural nor possessive with *s* or *s* plus apostrophe (see Hodge 1997, sec. C and D).
- **Pronouns:** A pronoun represents a specific noun, and it must reflect the number and person of that noun. Make sure that all your pronouns agree with the nouns to which they relate. Correct number shifts such as the following:

Their needs and <u>that</u> of their children are not being met.
They take charge of their affairs and manage <u>it</u> efficiently.

For shifts of person, pay attention especially to sentences in which you have used the pronoun *one*:

One tends to become frustrated with oneself and those around <u>him</u>.

- **Verbs:** A literary study is written largely in the present tense, so subject–verb agreement will be an issue (see Hodge 1997, sec. E). Make sure that every present tense verb agrees with its subject. Check for unwarranted shifting into the past tense. However, when writing in the present tense, it is sometimes necessary to go into the present perfect tense (see Hodge 1997, G3, for a correct sequence of tenses).

Elizabeth discovers that the old man has died in his sleep.
NOT *Elizabeth discovers that the old man dies in his sleep.*
NOT *Elizabeth discovers that the old man died in his sleep.*

All verb forms which involve the auxiliary verbs *to have, to be* and *to do* in the present tense require subject–verb agreement.

The rule of subject–verb agreement also applies to the past tense of the verb *to be* (Hodge 1997, F8), except when *were* is used for the subjunctive mood (Hodge 1997, F9). Make sure that you have used *was* and *were* in the right places.

Identify past participles (Hodge 1997, Section G) and see that they are correctly formed.

Make sure that you have not used *would* incorrectly (Hodge 1997, F10).

- **Spelling:** You will, of course, make use of a computer spelling check, ensuring that you look out for errors that slip through computer checks, such as mix ups of pairs like *break* and *brake*.
- **Punctuation:** Some punctuation errors are alluded to above under sentence structure. The internal punctuation of sentences also requires your attention. Check the *Harbrace* or other writing guide if you need to find out whether you have correctly used commas, dashes, colons, semicolons, brackets or quotation marks.

Proofreading Checklist for Basic Mechanics

- **Nouns**
  - ✓ Plural endings
  - ✓ Possessive endings
  - ✓ Plural nouns distinct from singular possessive nouns
  - ✓ No unnecessary plural or possessive apostrophes
    (See Hodge 1997, sec. C and D.)
- **Pronouns**
  - ✓ Represents specific identifiable noun

- ✓ Reflects number and person of noun
- ✓ No shifts of person, especially in relation to the pronoun *one*
- **Verbs**
  - ✓ Present tense subject–verb agreement (see Hodge 1997, sec. E)
  - ✓ Tense shifts only where warranted
  - ✓ Proper sequence of tenses (see Hodge 1997, G3)
  - ✓ All auxiliary verbs agree with subject
  - ✓ *Was* and *were* correctly used (see Hodge 1997, F8, F9)
  - ✓ Past participles correctly formed (see Hodge 1997, sec. G)
  - ✓ *Would* used as in standard English (see Hodge 1997, F10)
- **Spelling**
  - ✓ Computer spelling check
- **Punctuation**
  - ✓ Marking of sentence boundaries
  - ✓ Internal use of commas, dashes, colons, semi-colons, brackets and quotation marks

No matter how thorough your research or how brilliant your analysis, your reader will be distracted, irritated and possibly even insulted by a presentation that is sloppily put together and riddled with errors. By contrast, a document that bears the mark of rigorous attention to standards considerably enhances the impact of your work, earning the respect and goodwill of those who read it – especially those who have to read it because their job is to assess it. Give serious attention to the task of finishing and proofreading.

Afterword

It is difficult to overestimate the significance of developing and honing research approaches and methods relevant to Caribbean material and the insights undergirded by the Caribbean experience. Furthermore, although much has been done in the area of Caribbean research and literary production, the possibilities of future work give the region a dynamic quality. In this book we have attempted to guide Caribbeanists through this ever-changing maze. Our own research has shown that (alongside this thrust) there is still need for a wide range of support material, for example, guides to primary source material that build on and go beyond earlier work on Caribbean sources (mainly print and manuscript) to fully reflect the multicultural region, as well as the interface between ourselves and our erstwhile colonizers, our heritage cultures and the new contacts within the postmodern global village. Beginning Caribbean researchers also need guides to the production of scholarly prose that has international currency yet is enriched by the Caribbean language situation, while even our most experienced researchers may appreciate aids to defining perceptions and viewpoints informed but not enchained by Caribbean experience.

It is imperative that such research be contextualized with regard to conceptual organization in a multicultural space so as to allow scholars to explore evolving theoretical frames – to extend debate, to interrogate or dispute established positions, to reconfigure or reapply these positions and track the interplay of ideas involved, and to network multiple ways of viewing and knowing. In some instances one may be able to define some collective position, in others perhaps only glimpse the nuances that shimmer along the lines of fracture between individual perceptions or interpretations. At any rate our theoretical approaches must address a discourse that has developed to the point of having its own canonicity interrogated.

Methods of data collection and field techniques for creative and scholarly writing in the Caribbean must address somewhat different challenges than those encountered in areas that boast a literary and research history extending over centuries. Strategies must be worked out for producing scholarship on literature, on language, on the negotiation of shifts between discourses in translation and comparative work, on discourse in literature, on discourse in media and popular culture, and on the intersections between literature and culture, where a large percentage of the data may be elusive, rare or transient. In circumstances of a strong oral tradition in continuous engagement with the scribal, priceless information survives in the keeping of aging informants and much has already been lost. This fragility of data is exacerbated by a historical situation in which such material has been undervalued or disregarded. At the same time, the collection of primary material may require direct interface with practitioners to whom literary scholarship may seem intangible and useless.

One of the greatest challenges will always be to define a Caribbean circumstance in its own terms – to free it from the shackles which would impose the research findings of larger, more established territories on the Caribbean as if they will necessarily be one and the same. To reverse the scholarly interface, to suggest that the Caribbean has insights for the larger world beyond its shores, can only be effectively achieved via thoroughgoing research methodologies and practices, via literary analyses which are groundbreaking and infallible.

Systems for analysis must be worked out for subject areas which as yet have no established procedures. Connections must be forged that enable us to deal with issues of canonicity in relation to a vernacular discourse and culture and to analyse and evaluate discourse in the context of multiculturalism and hybridity.

The historical context of Caribbean letters, the attitudes and policies that have attended the growth of our literature, has had consequences for production, including, for example, inhibitions in publishing within the region and restrictions on Caribbean language in publishing outside of the region. Similarly the execution of research projects is affected by limitations on funding opportunities and the rewards and recognition of completed work. Where the rationale for research grows out of the Caribbean situation (whether the content is Caribbean or the approach to some other literature is Caribbean), the researcher must design a framework for completion that is practicable in our Caribbean context.

In seeking to chart the course for these kinds of endeavours, our text has drawn together a complex weave of research approaches and concerns, philosophical positionings and modes of representation, which have been tried and found effective in conveying the Caribbean experience. We believe it will be useful as an original Caribbean volume hinged on the representation of Caribbean experience, looking outward from within. Clarity of vision and its effective recording have been our particular concerns.

References

Abrahams, R.D. 1967. "The Shaping of Folklore Traditions in the British West Indies". *Journal of Inter American Studies and World Affairs* 9: 456–80.

Achert, Walter, Joseph Gibaldi, and Modern Language Association of America. 2008. *The MLA Style Manual and Guide to Scholarly Publishing*, 3rd ed. New York: Modern Language Association.

Aiyejina, Funso, ed. 2003. *Self Portraits: Interviews with Ten West Indian Writers and Two Critics*. St Augustine, Trinidad and Tobago: School of Continuing Studies, University of the West Indies.

Alasuutari, Pertti. 1995. *Researching Culture: Qualitative Method and Cultural Studies*. London: Sage.

Allsopp, Jeanette. 2003. *The Caribbean Multilingual Dictionary of Flora, Fauna and Food in English, French, French Creole and Spanish*. Kingston: Arawak.

Allsopp, Richard. 1996. *Dictionary of Caribbean English Usage*. Oxford: Oxford University Press.

Antoine-Dunne, Jean. 2004. "Towards an Audiovisual Caribbean Aesthetic". In *The Montage Principle: Eisenstein in New Cultural and Critical Contexts*, edited by Jean Antoine-Dunne and Paula Quigley, 125–52. Amsterdam: Rodopi.

———. 2010. "Keeping an Eye on Naipaul: Naipaul and the Play of the Visual". In *Created in the West Indies: Caribbean Perspectives on V.S. Naipaul*, edited by B. Lalla and J. Rahim, 111–20. Kingston: Ian Randle.

———. 2011. "Look We Movin Now: Film and the Interface with Literature". In *The Routledge Companion to Anglophone Caribbean Literature*, edited by Michael Bucknor and Alison Donnell, 591–608. London: Routledge.

Auerbach, Erich. (1946) 1968. *Mimesis: The Presentation of Reality in Western Literature*. Translated by Willard R. Trask. Princeton, NJ: Princeton University Press.

Baldwin, Elaine, Brian Longhurst, Scott McCracken, Miles Ogborn and Greg Smith. 2004. *Introducing Cultural Studies*. Harlow: Pearson Education.

Barker, Chris, and Dariusz Galisinsky. 2001. *Cultural Studies and Discourse. Analysis: A Dialogue on Language and Identity*. London: Sage.

Barratt, Sue-Ann. In progress. "An Investigation into the Relevance of Perceptions of Gender Identity to Interpersonal Communication Conflict". PhD diss., University of the West Indies, St Augustine.

Barret, Andy. 2005. "The Information-Seeking Habits of Graduate Student Researchers in the Humanities". *Journal of Academic Librarianship* 31 (4): 324–31.

Barrow, Christine. 1998. *Caribbean Portraits: Essays on Gender Ideologies and Identities*. Kingston: Ian Randle.

Bashford, Christina. 2008. "Writing (British) Concert History: The Blessing and Curse of Ephemera". *Quarterly Journal of the Music Library Association* 64 (3): 458–73.

Bassnett, Susan. 1993. *Comparative Literature: A Critical Introduction*. New Jersey: Wiley-Blackwell.

———. 2002. *Translation Studies (New Accents)*. London: Routledge.

Bastick, Tony, and Barbara Matalon. 2007. *Research: New and Practical Approaches*. Kingston: Chalkboard Press, Materials Production Unit, University of the West Indies.

Baugh, Edward. 2006. "Literary Theory and the Caribbean: Theory, Belief and Desire, or Designing Theory". *Shibboleths: Journal of Comparative Theory* 1 (1): 56–63.

———. 2007. *Selected Poems: Derek Walcott*. New York: Farrar, Staus and Giroux.

———. 2010. "'Maps Made in the Heart': Caribbeans of our Desire". *Journal of West Indian Literature* 1 (2 April): 1–19.

Baxter, Judith. 2003. *Positioning Gender in Discourse: A Feminist Methodology*. Basingstoke, UK: Palgrave Macmillan.

Benítez-Rojo, Antonio. (1992) 1996. *The Repeating Island: The Caribbean and the Postmodern Perspective*. Translated by James E. Maraniss. Durham, NC: Duke University Press.

Bernabé, Jean, Patrick Chamoiseau, and Raphaël Confiant. 1989. *Eloge de la créolité*. Paris: Gallimard; 1993. Translated by M.B. Taleb-Khyar as *In Praise of Creoleness*. Paris: Gallimard.

Boas, Franz, and George Stocking Jr. 1974. *A Franz Boas Reader: The Shaping of American Anthropology, 1883–1911*. United States: University of Chicago Press.

Bolaños, Sergio. 2008. "Towards an Integrated Translation Approach: Proposal of a Dynamic Translation Model (DTM)". PhD diss., Universität Hamburg.

Bordwell, David, and Noël Carroll. 1996. *Post Theory: Reconstructing Film Studies*. Madison: University of Wisconsin Press.

Bottero, Wendy. 2010. "Intersubjectivity and Bourdieusian Approaches to 'Identity'". *Cultural Sociology* 4: 3–22.

Boufoy-Bastick, Béatrice. 2002a. "Measuring Cultural Identity in Culturally-Diverse Societies". *World Cultures* 13 (1): 39–47.

———. 2002b. "A Differential Construct Methodology for Modelling Predictive Cultural Values". *Qualitative Report* 7 (3). http://www.nova.edu/ssss/QR/QR7-3/boufoy.html.

———. 2007. "Culturometrics: Quantitative Methodology for Measuring Privileged Qualitative Judgements". *International Journal of the Humanities* 5 (10): 1–10.

———. 2009a. "A Culturometric Analysis of Fear of Crime in Trinidad". *Caribbean Journal of Criminology and Public Safety* 14 (1–2): 1–48.

———. 2009b. "Educational, Economic and Social Influences on Cultural Heritage in Trinidad". *Policy Futures in Education* 7 (4): 368–78.

———. 2010. "A Culturometric Exploration of Intrusions of Globalisation on Transnational Identities: The Jamaican Example". *Journal of Identity and Migration Studies* 4 (1): 91–109.

Boyce Davies, Carole, and Elaine Savory Fido, eds. 1990. *Out of the Kumbla: Caribbean Women and Literature*. Trenton, NJ: Africa World Press.

Brande, Dorothea. 1934. *Becoming a Writer*. New York: Penguin.

Brathwaite, Edward Kamau. 1974. *Contradictory Omens: Cultural Diversity and Integration in the Caribbean*. Kingston: Savacou.

———. 1984. *The History of the Voice: The Development of Nation Language in the Anglophone Caribbean*. London: New Beacon.

———. 1986. *Roots*. Ciudad de la Habana: Casa de las Américas.

———. 1987. *X/Self*. Oxford and New York: Oxford University Press.

———. 1995a. "A Post-Cautionary Tale of the Helen of Our Wars". *Wasafiri* 22 (Autumn): 69–78.

———. 1995b. "Days and Nights or Jean Rhys and Cynthia Wilson". *Wasafiri* 22 (Autumn): 79–81.

———. 2005. *Born to Slow Horses*. Middletown, CT: Wesleyan University Press.

Bressler, Charles. 2002. *Literary Criticism: An Introduction to Theory and Practice*. New Jersey: Prentice Hall.

Britton, Celia. 2009. *The Sense of Community in French Caribbean Fiction*. Liverpool: Liverpool University Press.

Brodber, Erna. 1980. *Jane and Louisa Will Soon Come Home*. London: New Beacon.

———. 1994. *Louisiana*. London: New Beacon.

———. 2003. *The Continent of Black Consciousness: On the History of the African Diaspora from Slavery to the Present*. London: New Beacon Books.

Brontë, Charlotte. 1847. *Jane Eyre*. London: W. Nicholson and Sons.

Brontë, Emily. (1847) 1985. *Wuthering Heights*. Edited by David Daiches. London: Penguin.

Brown, Enid. 2001. "Martinique, Guadeloupe and French Guiana (Guyane) in English: A Partially Annotated Bibliography". N.p.

Brown, Stewart, Mervyn Morris and Gordon Rohlehr. 1989. *Voiceprint: An Anthology of Oral and Related Poetry from the Caribbean*. England: Longman.

Brown, Stewart, and John Wickham, eds. 1999. *The Oxford Book of Caribbean Short Stories*. Oxford: Oxford University Press.

Brunsdon, Charlotte. 1997. "A Thief in the Night: Stories of Feminism in the 1970s at CCCS". In *Stuart Hall: Critical Dialogues in Cultural Studies*, edited by David Morley and Kuan-Hsing Chen, 276–86. London: Routledge.

Bucknor, Michael, and Alison Donnell, eds. 2011. *The Routledge Companion to Anglophone Caribbean Literature*. London: Routledge.

Campbell, Angus, Philip Converse and Willard Rogers. 1976. *The Quality of American Life*. New York: Russel Sage Foundation.

Campbell, Mavis. 1989. *Back to Freedom: George Ross' Diary and the Voyage of the Jamaican Maroons from Nova Scotia to Sierra Leone*. Dover, MA: Majority Press.

Cassidy, F.G., and R.B. Le Page. (1967) 1980. *Dictionary of Jamaican English*. Cambridge: Cambridge University Press.

Cassin, Frieda. (1890) 2002. *With Silent Tread*, edited by Evelyn O'Callaghan. Oxford: Macmillan.

Césaire, Aimé. 1969. *Une tempête, d'après la tempête de Shakespeare: Adaptation pour un théâtre nègre*. Paris: Seuil.

Chambers, Iain. 1997. "Waiting on the End of the World?" In *Stuart Hall: Critical Dialogues in Cultural Studies*, edited by David Morley and Kuan-Hsing Chen, 201–11. London: Routledge.

Chariandy, David. 2007. *Soucouyant*. Vancouver, BC: Arsenal Pulp Press.

Cheshire, J. 1982. "Linguistic Variation and Social Function". In *Sociolinguistic Variation in Speech Communities*, ed. Suzanne Romaine, 153–66. London: Edward Arnold.

Chuang, Rueyling. 2004. "Theoretical Perspectives: Fluidity and Complexity of Cultural and Ethnic Identity". In *Communicating Ethnic and Cultural Identity*, edited by Mary Fong and Rueyling Chuang, 51–68. Lanham, MD: Rowman and Littlefield.

Clarke, Richard. 1998. "Notes towards a Taxonomy of Critical Approaches to the Study of Caribbean Literature". Seventeenth Annual Conference on West Indian Literature, University of the West Indies, Mona, Jamaica, 6–8 April, 1–14.

———. 2002. "Androgyny and Miscegenation in *The Crying Game*: The Case for a Performative Model of Gender and Race". In *Gendered Realities: Essays in Caribbean Feminist Thought*, edited by Patricia Mohammed, 297–313. Kingston: University of the West Indies Press.

Cliff, Michelle. 1996. *No Telephone to Heaven*. New York: Plume.

Condé, Maryse. (1995) 1998. *La migration des cœurs*. Paris: Laffont. Translated by Richard Philcox as *Windward Heights* (London: Faber and Faber; New York: Soho Press, 1999).

———. 2003. *Windward Heights*. New York: Soho Press.

Cook, John. 2005. "Creative Writing as a Research Method". In *Research Methods for English Studies*, edited by Gabriele Griffin, 195–211. Edinburgh: Edinburgh University Press.

Cooper, Carolyn. 1993. *Noises in the Blood*. London: Macmillan.

Craig, Ian, and Jairo Sánchez-Galvis. 2007. *A Translation Manual for the Caribbean (English-Spanish) – Un manual de traducción para el Caribe (inglés-español)*. Kingston: University of the West Indies Press.

Creswell, John. 1998. *Qualitative Inquiry and Research Design: Choosing among Five Designs*. Thousand Oaks, CA: Sage.

———. 2003. *Research Design: Qualitative, Quantitative, and Mixed Methods Approaches*. Thousand Oaks, CA: Sage.

Crosbie, Paul. 2001. *Kwéyòl Dictionary*, edited by David Frank. St Lucia: Ministry of Education.

Cudjoe, Selwyn Reginald. 1990. *Caribbean Women Writers: Essays from the First International Conference*. Amherst, MA: University of Massachusetts Press.

Cumberbatch, Gwyneth. (n.d.) Review of *I Is a Long Memoried Woman* by Frances Anne Solomon. Accessed June 2011. http://ledaserene.ca/web/index.php?option=com_content&task=view&id=41&Itemid=50.

Danticat, Edwidge. 1995. *Breath, Eyes, Memory*. New York: Vintage Books.

Dasenbrock, Reed Way. 1992. "Teaching Multicultural Literature". In *Understanding Others*, edited by Joseph Trimmer and Tilly Warnock, 35–46. Urbana, IL: National Council of Teachers of English.

Dash, Michael. 1989. Introduction to *Caribbean Discourse: Selected Essays*, by Édouard Glissant. Charlottesville: University Press of Virginia.

——. 1998. *The Other America: Caribbean Literature in a New World Context*. Charlottesville: University Press of Virginia.

——. 1999. "Caribbean Modernism". In *Enterprise of the Indies*, edited by George Lamming, 195–96. Trinidad and Tobago: Institute of the West Indies.

Davies, Carole Boyce, and Elaine Savory Fido, eds. 1994. *Out of the Kumbla: Caribbean Women and Literature*. Trenton, NJ: Africa World Press.

Dawes, Kwame. 1999. *Natural Mysticism: Towards a New Reggae Aesthetic*. Leeds: Peepal Tree.

Dayfoot, Arthur Charles, and Roscoe M. Pierson. 2004. *Bibliography of West Indian Church History: A List of Printed Materials Relating to the History of the Churches in the English-Speaking Caribbean (and Bermuda) with Annotations and Notes on Locations*. London: Hansib.

D'Costa, Jean. 1984. "Louise Bennett's Dialect Poetry: Problems of Variation along a Creole Continuum in a Literary Text". In *Studies in Language Ecology*, edited by Werner Enninger and Lilith M. Haynes, 135–58. Weisbaden, Germany: Steiner.

D'Costa, Jean, and Barbara Lalla, eds. 1989. *Voices in Exile: Jamaican Texts of the Eighteenth and Nineteenth Centuries*. Tuscaloosa: University of Alabama Press; reprinted 2009, paperback.

de Caires Narain, Denise. 1998. "English Gardens and West Indian Yards: The Politics of Location (One More Time)". *Wasafiri* 28 (Autumn): 37–38.

De Four, Linda C. 1993. *Gimme Room to Sing: Calypsoes of the Mighty Sparrow, 1958–1993: A Discography*. Port of Spain, Trinidad: Linda Claudia de Four.

Defoe, Daniel. (1719) 1983. *Robinson Crusoe*. New York: Scribner.

Deleuze, Gilles. (1986) 2005. *Cinema 1: The Movement Image*. London: Athlone Press.

——. 1989. *Cinema 2: The Time Image*. London: Athlone Press.

Denzin, N.K., and Y.S. Lincoln 2004. *Handbook of Qualitative Research*. 2nd ed. Newbury Park, CA: Sage.

Deuber, Dagmar. 2010. "Modal Verb Usage at the Interface of English and a Related Creole: A Corpus-Based Study of Can/Could and Will/Would in Trinidadian English". *Journal of English Linguistics* 38: 105–42.

Dickens, Charles. *A Tale of Two Cities*. London: Penguin.

Donnell, Alison. 2006. *Twentieth-Century Caribbean Literature: Critical Moments in Anglophone Literary History*. London: Routledge.

Drayton, Kathy-Ann. 2012. "'How yuh make a story': Narrative Development in Young Trinidadian Children". In *The Child and the Caribbean Imagination*, edited by Giselle Rampaul and Geraldine Elizabeth Skeete. Kingston: University of the West Indies Press.

Dykyj, Oksana. 2011. "Cinema Collections in Academic Libraries". Accessed May 2011. Books.google.ie/books?isbn-0313316589.

Eagleton, Terry. 1996. *Literary Theory*. Oxford: Blackwell.

———. 2000. *The Idea of Culture*. London: Blackwell.

Edmondson, Belinda. 1999. *Making Men: Gender, Literary Authority, and Women's Writing*. Durham, NC: Duke University Press.

Edwards, John. 2009. *Language and Identity*. Cambridge: Cambridge University Press.

Edwards, Norval. 2001. "'Talking about a Little Culture': Sylvia Wynter's Early Essays". *Journal of West Indian Literature* 10 (1 and 2 November): 12–38.

———. 2008. "Tradition, the Critic, and Cross-Cultural Poetics: Wilson Harris as Literary Theorist". *Journal of West Indian Literature* 16 (2 April): 1–30.

Eisenstein, Sergei M. (1942) 1990. *The Film Sense*. Edited by Jay Leyda. London: Faber and Faber.

———. 1987. *Nonindifferent Nature*. Edited and translated by Herbert Marshall. Cambridge: Cambridge University Press.

———. 1994. *Towards a Theory of Montage*. Edited by Michael Glinny. Vol. 2 of *Selected Works*. London: BFI.

Elder, J.D. 1966. "The Evolution of the Traditional Calypso: A Socio-Historical Analysis of Song Change". PhD diss. University of Pennsylvania.

Emery, Mary Lou. 2007. *Modernism, the Visual, and Caribbean Literature*. Cambridge: Cambridge University Press.

Espinet, Ramabai. 1991. *Nuclear Seasons*. Toronto: Sister Vision Press.

———. 2003. *The Swinging Bridge*. Toronto: Harper Flamingo Canada.

Evans, Sandra. 2010. " 'Sometimes I Interpret for the Interpreter': The Dynamics of Interpreting in Magistrates' Courts in St Lucia". Paper presented at the Society for Caribbean Linguistics 18th Biennial Conference. Amaryllis Beach Resort, Barbados, 9–13 August.

Fairclough, Norman. 1989. *Language and Power*. London: Longman.

———. 1992. *Discourse and Social Change*. Cambridge: Polity Press.

———. 1995. *Media Discourse*. London: Edward Arnold.

Faulkner, William. 1951. Interview by Lavon Roscoe. *Western Review* 15: 359–68.

Ferré, Rosario. 1998. *Maldito amor*. New York: Vintage Books.

Fidzani, B.T. 1998. "Information Needs and Information-Seeking Behaviour of Graduate Students at the University of Botswana". *Library Review* 47 (7): 329–40.

Finn, Janet L., Maxine Jacobson and Jillian D. Campana. 2004. "Participatory Research, Popular Education, and Popular Theater: Contributions to Group Work". In *Handbook of Social Work with Groups*, edited by Charles D. Garvin, Lorraine M. Gutiérrez and Maeda J. Galinsky, 326–43. New York: Guildford Press.

Fong, Mary. 2004. "Multiple Dimensions of Identity". In *Communicating Ethnic and Cultural Identity*, edited by Mary Fong and Rueyling Chuang, 19–35. Lanham, MD: Rowman and Littlefield.

Forbes, Curdella. 2005. *From Nation to Diaspora: Samuel Selvon, George Lamming and the Cultural Performance of Gender*. Kingston: University of the West Indies Press.

Foucault, Michel. 1980. *Power/Knowledge: Selected Interviews and Other Writings 1972–1977*. Edited by Colin Gordon. London: Harvester.

Gajar, Rosemarie. 1998. "GB not on a racist head". *Independent*, 28 November.

García, Cristina. 1994. *Dreaming in Cuban*. New York: Ballantine Books.

Gee, J.P. 1999. *An Introduction to Discourse Analysis: Theory and Method*. London: Routledge.

Geertz, Armin W., and Jeppe S. Jensen, eds. 2011. *Religious Narrative, Cognition and Culture: Image and Word in the Mind of Narrative*. London: Equinox.

Gibbs, Raymond W., Jr., and Gerard J. Steen, eds. 1997. *Metaphor in Cognitive Linguistics: Selected Papers from the 5th International Cognitive Linguistics Conference*. Amsterdam: John Benjamins.

Gilbert, Jeremy. 2012. "Culture and Cultural Studies in a Postdemocratic Age". Paper presented at the 9th International Crossroads in Cultural Studies Conference. Paris, 2–6 July.

Gilroy, Paul. 1993. *The Black Atlantic: Modernity and Double Consciousness*. London: Verso.

Ging, Debbie. 2004. "The Politics of Sound and Image". In *The Montage Principle: Eisenstein in New Cultural and Critical Contexts*, edited by Jean Antoine-Dunne and Paula Quigley, 67–96. Amsterdam: Rodopi.

Glissant, Édouard. 1981. *Le Discours Antillais*. Translated by J. Michael Dash. Paris: Seuil.

———. 1989. *Caribbean Discourse: Selected Essays*. Translated by J. Michael Dash. Charlottesville: University Press of Virginia.

———. (1997) 2000. *Poetics of Relation*. Translated by Betsy Wing. Ann Arbor: University of Michigan Press.

Goffman, Erving. (1961) 1990. *Asylums: Essays on the Social Situation of Mental Patients and Other Inmates*. New York: Anchor Books; New York: Doubleday.

Golafshani, Nahid. 2003. "Understanding Reliability and Validity in Qualitative Research". *Qualitative Report* 8 (4): 597–607.

Gray, Ann. 2003. *Research Practice for Cultural Studies: Ethnographic Methods and Lived Cultures*. London: Sage.

Griffin, Gabriele. 2005. *Research Methods for English Studies*. Edinburgh: Edinburgh University Press.

Griffith, Glyne A. 1996. *Deconstruction, Imperialism and the West Indian Novel*. Kingston: University of the West Indies Press.

Hall, Stuart. 1991. "Myths of Caribbean Identity". Walter Rodney Memorial Lecture. Centre for Caribbean Studies, University of Warwick, 1–13 October.

———. 1994. "Cultural Identity and Diaspora". In *Colonial Discourse and Post-Colonial Theory: A Reader*, edited and introduced by Patrick Williams and Laura Chrisman, 392–403. New York: Prentice Hall/Harvester Wheatsheaf.

———. 1996. "Cultural Studies and Its Theoretical Legacies". In *Stuart Hall: Critical Dialogues in Cultural Studies*, edited by David Morley and Kuan-Hsing Chen, 262–75. London: Routledge.

———. 1997a. "The Meaning of New Times". In *Stuart Hall: Critical Dialogues in Cultural Studies*, edited by David Morley and Kuan-Hsing Chen, 223–38. London: Routledge.

———. 1997b. "New Ethnicities". In *Stuart Hall: Critical Dialogues in Cultural Studies*, edited by David Morley and Kuan-Hsing Chen, 443–49. London: Routledge.

———. 2002. "Introduction: Who Needs Identity". In *Questions of Cultural Identity*, edited by Stuart Hall and Paul du Gay, 1–17. London: Sage.

Hall, Stuart, and Paul du Gay. 1992. "The Question of Cultural Identity". In *Modernity and Its Future*, edited by Stuart Hall, D. Held and T. McGrew, 274–316. Cambridge: Polity.

———, eds. 1996. *Questions of Cultural Identity*. London: Sage.

Hanisch, Carol. (1969) 1979. "The Personal is Political". In *Feminist Revolution*, 204–5. England: Random House. Accessed June 2011, http://www.carolhanisch.org/CHwritings/PIP.html.

Harcourt Brace and Company. 2009. *Harbrace College Handbook*. Fort Worth: Harcourt Brace College.

Harricharan, Michelle. 2008. "Culture Collision and Hybridity in Selected Works of J.R.R. Tolkien". MPhil thesis, University of the West Indies, St Augustine.

Harris, Wilson. 1967. *Tradition, the Writer and Society*. London: New Beacon.

———. 1970. "History, Fable and Myth in the Caribbean and the Guianas". In *Edgar Mittelhölzer Memorial Lectures*. Volume 3, part 4, 152–66. National History and Arts Council. Austin: University of Texas.

———. 1999. *The Unfinished Genesis of the Imagination: Selected Essays of Wilson Harris*. Edited by Andrew Bundy. London: Faber and Faber.

———. 2003. *The Mask of the Beggar*. London: Faber and Faber.

Hassanali, Liza. 1998. "Monarch, Composer to Share Prize Car". *TnT Mirror*, 1 March.

Hearne, John. 1982. *The Sure Salvation*. New York: St. Martin's Press.

Henry, Frances, and Pamela Wilson. 1975. "The Status of Women in Caribbean Societies: An Overview of the Social, Economic and Social Roles". *Social and Economic Studies* 24: 164–93.

Henry, Paget. 2000. *Caliban's Reason: Introducing Afro-Caribbean Philosophy*. New York: Routledge.

Heritage, John, and Paul Drew. 1993. *Talk at Work: Interaction in Institutional Settings*. Cambridge: Cambridge University Press.

Higman, B.W. 1999. *Writing West Indian Histories*. London: Macmillan.

———. 2008. *Jamaican Food: History, Biology, Culture*. Kingston: University of the West Indies Press.

Hodge, Merle. 1970. *Crick Crack, Monkey*. London: Deutsch.

——. 1993. *For the Life of Laetitia*. New York: Farrar, Straus and Giroux.

——. 1997. *The Knots in English: A Manual for Caribbean Users*. Wellesley: Calaloux.

——. 2007. "A Study of Language in Trinidad and Tobago Prose Fiction of the Twentieth Century with Special Reference to the Works of Earl Lovelace". PhD diss., University of the West Indies, St Augustine.

——. 2008. "The Language of Earl Lovelace". In *A Place in the World*, edited by Funso Aiyejina, 97–101. San Juan, Trinidad and Tobago: Lexicon.

Hoggart, Richard. 1957. *The Uses of Literacy: Aspects of Working Class Life*. London: Chatto and Windus.

Holmes, James. (1972) 2004. "The Name and Nature of Translation Studies". In *The Translation Studies Reader*, edited by Lawrence Venuti, 180–92. Oxon: Routledge.

Holmes, Janet. 1995. *Women, Men and Politeness*. London: Longman.

Homer. 1996. *The Odyssey*. Translated by Robert Fagles. New York: Penguin Books.

Hopkinson, Nalo. 2000. *Midnight Robber*. New York: Warner Books.

Hulme, Peter. 1996. "A Response to Kamau Brathwaite". *Wasafiri* 23 (Spring): 49–50.

Hymes, Dell. 1972. "Models of the Interaction of Language and Social Life". In *Directions in Sociolinguistics: The Ethnography of Communication*, edited by J. Gumperz and D. Hymes, 35–71. New York: Holt, Rhinehart and Winston.

——. 1974. *Foundations of Sociolinguistics: An Ethnographic Approach*. Philadelphia: University of Pennsylvania Press.

Ismond, Patricia. 2001. *Abandoning Dead Metaphors: The Caribbean Phase of Derek Walcott's Poetry*. Kingston: University of the West Indies.

James, C.L.R. 1963. *Beyond a Boundary*. London: Hutchinson.

Jay, Gregory S., and David L. Miller, eds. 1985. "The Role of Theory in the Study of Literature". In *After Strange Texts: The Role of Theory in the Study of Literature*, 1–28. Tuscaloosa: University of Alabama Press.

Jekyll, Walter H., ed. 1907. *Jamaican Song and Story*. London: Nutt.

Johnson, R. Burke, and Anthony J. Onwuegbuzie. 2004. "Mixed Methods Research: A Research Paradigm Whose Time Has Come". *Educational Researcher* 33 (7): 14–26.

Jones, Bridget, and Sita E. Dickson Littlewood. 1997. *Paradoxes of French Caribbean Theatre: An Annotated Checklist of Dramatic Works, Guadeloupe, Guyane, Martinique from 1900*. London: Roehampton Institute.

Joseph, E.L. (1838) 2000. *Walter Arundell*, edited by Lise Winer, Bridget Brereton, Rhonda Cobham, Mary Rimmer. Kingston: University of the West Indies Press.

Kanhai, Rosanne. 1999. *Matikor: The Politics of Identity for Indo-Caribbean Women*. Trinidad: School of Continuing Studies, University of the West Indies.

Khan, Aisha. 2001. "Journey to the Center of the Earth: The Caribbean as Master Symbol". *Cultural Anthropology* 16 (3): 271–302.

Kincaid, Jamaica. (1985) 1997. *Annie John*. New York: Farrar, Straus and Giroux.

——. 1988. *A Small Place*. New York: Farrar, Straus and Giroux.

——. 1997. *My Brother*. New York: Farrar, Straus, Giroux.

——. 2002. *Lucy*. New York: Farrar, Straus, Giroux.

King, Gary. 1993. "The Methodology of Presidential Research". In *Researching the Presidency: Vital Questions, New Approaches*, edited by George Edwards III, Bert A. Rockman and John H. Kessel, 387–412. Pittsburgh: University of Pittsburgh Press.

King, Stephen. 2000. *On Writing: A Memoir of the Craft*. New York: Pocket Books (Simon and Schuster).

Kipling, Rudyard. 1892. "The English Flag". *National Observer*, 4 April 1992. (Collected 1892, *Barrack Room Ballads*.)

Kundera, Milan. 1988. *The Art of the Novel*. Translated by Linda Asher. New York: Grove Press.

Labov, William. 1966. *The Social Stratification of English in New York City*. Washington, DC: Center for Applied Linguistics.

———. 1972. *Language in the Inner City*. Philadelphia: University of Pennsylvania Press.

———. 1980. "Objectivity and Commitment in Linguistic Science". *Language in Society* 11: 165–201.

Labov, William, and Joshua Waletzky, 1967. "Narrative Analysis: Oral Versions of Personal Experience". In *Essays on the Verbal and Visual Arts*, edited by J. Helm, 12–44. Seattle: University of Washington Press.

Lakoff, George, and Mark Johnson. 1981. *Metaphors We Live By*. Chicago: University of Chicago Press.

Lalla, Barbara. 1981. "Quaco Sam: A Relic of Archaic Jamaican Speech". *Jamaica Journal* 45: 20–29.

———. 1996. *Defining Jamaican Fiction: Marronage and the Discourse of Survival*. Tuscaloosa: University of Alabama Press.

———. 1998a. *Arch of Fire*. Kingston: Kingston Publishers.

———. 1998b. "Registering Woman: Senior's Zig-Zag Discourse, and Code-Switching in Jamaican Narrative". *A Review of International English Literature* 29 (4): 83–98.

———. 2005. "Virtual Realism and the Inscriber's Dilemma: Representing the Caribbean Voice". Society for Caribbean Linguistics, Occasional Paper.

———. 2008. *Postcolonialisms: Caribbean Rereading of Medieval English Discourse*. Kingston: University of the West Indies Press.

———. 2010. *Cascade: A Novel*. Kingston: University of the West Indies Press.

———. Forthcoming. "The Facetiness Factor: Theorizing Caribbean Space in Narrative". In *Caribbean Literary Discourse: Voice and Cultural Identity in Jamaica and Other Territories of the Anglophone Caribbean*, edited by Barbara Lalla, Jean D'Costa and Velma Pollard. Tuscaloosa: University of Alabama Press.

Lamming, George. (1960) 2004. *The Pleasures of Exile*. Ann Arbor: University of Michigan Press.

———. 1979. *In the Castle of My Skin*. London: Longman.

———. 1992. "Culture and Sovereignty". In *Conversations with George Lamming: Essays, Addresses and Interviews 1953–90*, edited by Richard Drayton and Andaiye, 283–92. London: Karia Press.

———. 1995. *Coming Coming Home: Conversations II*. St Martin: House of Nehesi.

———. 2004. "The Sovereignty of the Imagination". Kingston: Arawak; 2009. In *Conversations III*. St Martin: House of Nehesi.

———. 2009. "Language and the Politics of Ethnicity". In *Beyond Borders: Cross-Culturalism and the Caribbean Canon*, edited by Jennifer Rahim with Barbara Lalla, 17–33. Kingston: University of the West Indies Press.

Larsen, Neil. 2001. *Determinations: Essays on Theory, Narrative and Nation in the Americas*. London: Verso.

Lazarus-Black, Mindie. 2007. *Everyday Harm: Domestic Violence, Court Rites and Cultures of Reconciliation*. Urbana, IL: University of Illinois Press.

Leech, Geoffrey, and Mick Short. 1981. *Style in Fiction: A Linguistic Introduction to English Fictional Prose*. London: Longman.

Le Page, R.B., and Andrée Tabouret-Keller. 1985. *Acts of Identity*. Cambridge: Cambridge University Press.

Lerner, Betsy. 2001. *The Forest for the Trees: An Editor's Advice to Writers*. New York: Riverhead Trade.

Lewis, Matthew G. ("Monk"). 1834. *Journal of a West Indian Proprietor*. London: Murray.

Lovelace, Earl. (1988) 2003. "Joebell and America". In *A Brief Conversion and Other Stories*. 111–32. New York: Persea Books.

———. 2011. *Is Just a Movie*. London: Faber and Faber.

Lowenthal, David. 2000. "Stewarding the Past in a Perplexing Present". In *Values and Heritage Conservation: Research Report*, edited by E. Avrami, R. Mason and M. de la Torre, 22–30. Los Angeles: Getty Conservation Institute. http://www.getty.edu/conservation/publications_resources/pdf_publications/valuesrpt.pdf.

Macedo, Lynn. 2003. *Fiction and Film: The Influence of Cinema on Writers from Jamaica and Trinidad*. Chichester, UK: Dido.

Magritte, René. 1950. *The Art of Conversation*. Oil on Canvas.

Mahabir, Joy. 2006. *Jouvert*. Bloomington, IN: AuthorHouse.

Mah-Chamberlain, Karen. In progress. "It Divide Up in Little Worlds: Dialogue and Discourse Analysis of Selected Novels by Samuel Selvon". PhD diss., University of the West Indies.

Maltz, D., and R.A. Borker. 1982. "A Cultural Approach to Miscommunication". In *Language and Social Identity*, edited by J. Gumperz. Cambridge: Cambridge University Press.

McCormack, Donna. 2011. "Multisensory Poetics and Politics in Shani Mootoo's *The Wild Woman in the Woods* and *Valmiki's Daughter*". *The Journal of West Indian Literature* 19 (2) April: 9–33.

Merriam, Alan P. 1951. "Songs of Afro-Bahian Cults". PhD diss. Northwestern University, Evanston, IL.

Metz, Christian. 1974. *Film Language: A Semiotics of the Cinema*. Chicago: University of Chicago Press.

———. 1986. *The Imaginary Signifier: Psychoanalysis and the Cinema*. Bloomington: Indiana University Press.

Meuris, Jacques. 2009. *René Magritte. 1898–1967.* Hong Kong: Taschen.

Mohammed, Patricia. 2002. *Gendered Realities: Essays in Caribbean Feminist Theory.* Kingston: University of the West Indies Press.

———. 2009. *Imaging the Caribbean: Culture and Visual Translation.* Oxford: Macmillan.

Moise, Myriam. In progress. "Can the Subaltern Speak? African Caribbean Women Writers in the Diaspora". PhD diss., University of the West Indies and Université Paris III – Sorbonne Nouvelle.

Mooneeram, Roshni. 2009. *From Creole to Standard: Shakespeare, Language and Literature in a Postcolonial Context.* Amsterdam: Rodopi.

Mootoo, Shani. (1996) 2001. *Cereus Blooms at Night.* London: Granta; New York: Perennial.

———. 2008. *Valmiki's Daughter.* Toronto: House of Anansi Press.

Morgan, Paula, and Valerie Youssef. 2006. *Writing Rage: Unmasking Violence through Caribbean Discourse.* Kingston: University of the West Indies Press.

Morgan, Robin. 1984. *Sisterhood Is Global: An Anthology of the International Women's Movement.* New York: Anchor Press/Doubleday.

Mulvey, Laura. (1975) 2001. "Visual Pleasure in Narrative Cinema". In *Visual and Other Pleasures,* 14–26. London: Macmillan.

Munday, Jeremy. 2008. *Introducing Translation Studies: Theories and Applications,* 2nd ed. New York: Routledge.

Naipaul, V.S. (1961) 1966. *A House for Mr Biswas.* London: Andre Deutsch; reprint, Harmondsworth: Penguin.

———. (1962) 1978. *The Middle Passage: Impressions of Five Societies – British, French and Dutch – in the West Indies and South America.* Harmondsworth, UK: Penguin.

———. (1981) 1998. *Among the Believers: An Islamic Journey.* New York: Alfred Knopf; New York: Random House.

———. 1987. *The Enigma of Arrival.* Harmondsworth, UK: Penguin.

———. 2001. *The Loss of El Dorado.* London: Picador.

———. 2002. *The Mystic Masseur: A Novel.* New York: Vintage Books.

———. 2010. *The Masque of Africa: Glimpses of African Belief.* New York: Knopf.

Nesbitt, Nick. 2003. *Voicing Memory: History and Subjectivity in French Caribbean Literature.* Charlottesville: University of Virginia Press.

———. 2008. *Universal Emancipation: The Haitian Revolution and the Radical Enlightenment.* Charlottesville: University of Virginia Press.

Nettleford, Rex. 1978. *Caribbean Cultural Identity: The Case of Jamaica: An Essay in Cultural Dynamics.* Kingston: Institute of Jamaica.

———. 1984. Introduction to *Culture, Race and Class in the Commonwealth Caribbean,* M.G. Smith, vii–x. Kingston: School of Continuing Studies, University of the West Indies.

Nichols, Grace. 1983. *I Is a Long Memoried Woman.* London: Caribbean Cultural International.

Nourbese-Phillip, Marlene. 2008. *Zong!* Middletown, CT: Wesleyan University Press.

Nunez, Elizabeth. 2006. *Prospero's Daughter.* New York: Ballantine Books.

O'Callaghan, Evelyn. 1993. *Woman Version: Theoretical Approaches to West Indian Fiction by Women*. London: Macmillan.

———. 1998a. "'Compulsory Heterosexuality' and Textual/Sexual Alternatives in Selected Texts by West Indian Women Writers". In *Caribbean Portraits: Essays on Gender Ideologies and Identities*, edited by Christine Barrow, 294–319. Kingston: Ian Randle.

———. 1998b. "Jumping into the Big Ups' Quarrels: The Hulme/Brathwaite Exchange". *Wasafiri* 28 (Autumn): 34–36.

———. 2001. "The 'Pleasures' of Exile in Selected West Indian Writing Since 1987". In *Bucknell Review: Caribbean Cultural Identities*, edited by Glyne Griffith, 73–103. Lewisburg, PA: Bucknell University Press.

Ogunlade, Nandi, ed. 2006. *The Progress of Winsford Devine: A Collection of Caribbean Lyrics*. New York: Mayaro.

Oxford University. 2009. *Oxford Thesaurus of English*. Oxford: Oxford University Press.

Paul, Annie. 2011. "Log On: Towards Social and Digital Islands". In *The Routledge Companion to Anglophone Caribbean Literature*, edited by Michael A. Bucknor and Alison Donell, 626–35. London: Routledge.

Pearsall, Judy, ed. 1999. *The Concise Oxford Dictionary*, 10th ed. New York: Oxford University Press.

Perkins, Cyrus Francis. 2003. *Busha's Mistress or Catherine the Fugitive: A Stirring Romance of the Days of Slavery in Jamaica*, edited by Paul E. Lovejoy, Verene Shepherd and David Trotman. Kingston: Ian Randle.

Persaud, Lakshmi. 1990. *Butterfly in the Wind*. Leeds: Peepal Tree.

Pollard, Charles W. 2004. *New World Modernisms: T.S. Eliot, Derek Walcott, and Kamau Brathwaite*. Charlottesville: University of Virginia Press.

Pouchet Paquet, Sandra. (1960) 2004. Foreword to *The Pleasures of Exile*, George Lamming, vi–xxvii. Ann Arbor: University of Michigan Press.

———. 1998. "The Thematics of Diaspora and the Intercultural Identity Question". *Caribbean Writer* 12: 229–37.

———. 2008. "Self-Fashioning in Earl Lovelace's *Growing in the Dark*". In *A Place in the World: Essays and Tributes in Honour of Earl Lovelace @70*, edited by Funso Aiyejina, 59–71. San Juan, Trinidad and Tobago: Lexicon.

Powell, Patricia. (1994) 2003. *A Small Gathering of Bones*. Boston: Beacon Press.

Probyn, Elspeth. 2007. "The Politics of Experience". In *Centre for Contemporary Cultural Studies: Selected Working Papers*, vol. 1, edited by Ann Gray, Jan Campbell, Mark Erickson, Stuart Hanson and Helen Wood, 425–33. New York: Routledge.

Puri, Shalini. 2004. *The Caribbean Postcolonial: Social Equality, Post-Nationalism, and Cultural Hybridity*. New York: Palgrave Macmillan.

Radway, Janice. 1981. *Reading the Romance: Women, Patriarchy and Popular Culture*. Chapel Hill: University of North Carolina Press.

Ramchand, Kenneth. (1970) 1983. *The West Indian Novel and Its Background*. London: Heinemann.

———. 1970. "Concern for Criticism". *Literary Half-Yearly* 11 (2): 151–61.

———. 1976. *An Introduction to the Study of West Indian Literature*. Kingston: Nelson.

———. 1991. "Acts of Possession: The New World of West Indian Writers". Dr Eric Williams Memorial Lecture Series, 4 May.

———. 1997. "The Same Ship, the Same Trip". *Trinidad Guardian,* 5 February, 9.

Rampersad, Sheila. 2002. "Merle Hodge's Revolutionary Dougla Poetics". In *Centre of Remembrance: Memory and Caribbean Women's Literature*, edited by Joan Anim-Addo, 147–63. London: Mango.

Reddock, Rhoda, ed. 2004. *Interrogating Caribbean Masculinities: Theoretical and Empirical Analyses*. Kingston: University of the West Indies Press.

Regis, Louis. 1999. *True Opposition: The Political Calypso in Trinidad and Tobago 1962–1987*. Kingston: University of the West Indies Press; Gainesville: University Press of Florida.

Reiss, Timothy. 2002. *Against Autonomy: Global Dialectics of Cultural Exchange*. Stanford, CA: Stanford University Press.

Rhys, Jean. 1966. *Wide Sargasso Sea*. Harmondsworth: Penguin; 1968. Translated by Raquel Costa as *El vasto Mar de los Sargazos* (Havana: Casa de las Américas, 1981). Translated by Andrés Bosch as *Ancho Mar de los Sargazos* (Barcelona: Bruguera, 1982). Translated by Elizabeth Power as *Ancho Mar de los Sargazos* (Madrid: Cátedra, 1998; London: Penguin, 2000).

Riley, Denise. 2000. *The Words of Selves: Identification, Solidarity, Irony*. Stanford, CA: Stanford University Press.

Robinson, Jean-Louis. 2011. "El tratamiento de la variación lingüística y las referencias culturales en la película 'El curandero místico'". MA thesis, Universitat Autònoma de Barcelona, Barcelona.

Rodden, John. 2001. *Performing the Literary Interview: How Writers Craft Their Public Selves*. Lincoln: University of Nebraska Press.

Rogers, Rebecca. 2004. *An Introduction to Critical Discourse Analysis in Education*. Hillsdale, NJ: Lawrence Erlbaum.

Rohlehr, Gordon. 1990. *Calypso and Society in Pre-Independence Trinidad*. Port of Spain, Trinidad: Gordon Rohlehr.

———. 1991. "Researching Calypso". *Pastoral Bulletin* (St Augustine, Trinidad and Tobago) 3 (2): 12–19.

———. 1992a. *My Strangled City and Other Essays*. Port of Spain, Trinidad and Tobago: Longman Trinidad.

———. 1992b. *The Shape of That Hurt*. Port of Spain, Trinidad and Tobago: Longman Trinidad.

———. 2006. "Drum and Minuet: Music, Masquerade, and the Mulatto of Style". In *Caribbean Literature in a Global Context*, edited by Funso Aiyejina and Paula Morgan, 256–303. San Juan, Trinidad and Tobago: Lexicon Trinidad.

———. 2007a. "George Lamming and Kamau Brathwaite: Nationalist, Caribbean Regionalist, Internationalists". In *Transgression, Transition, Transformation: Essays in Caribbean Culture*, edited by Winston Hackett, Raymond Ramcharitar and Gordon Rohlehr, 392–409. San Juan, Trinidad and Tobago: Lexicon Trinidad.

———. 2007b. "Humour, Fantasy, Picong and Smut. From Attila to the Seventies". Audio and video recordings. Canboulay, Trinidad and Tobago.

———. 2010a. *Ancestories*. San Juan, Trinidad and Tobago: Lexicon.

———. 2010b. "From Apocalypse to Awakenings". Interview with Paula Morgan. St Augustine, Trinidad and Tobago: Faculty of Humanities and Education, University of the West Indies. Video.

Ross, George. 1800. Diary. MS in Fourah Bay College Library, Freetown, Sierra Leone, from which extract reproduced in Lalla and D'Costa, *Voices in Exile*, 20–24.

Rouse-Jones, Margaret D. 2003. *Guide to Manuscripts, Special Collections and Other Research Resources for Caribbean Studies at the University of the West Indies, St Augustine Campus Libraries*. St Augustine, Trinidad and Tobago: University of the West Indies.

Ryan, Selwyn. 1999. *The Jhandi and the Cross: The Clash of Cultures in Post-Creole Trinidad and Tobago*. St Augustine, Trinidad and Tobago: Institute of Social and Economic Research, University of the West Indies.

Sacks, Harvey, E. Schegloff and G. Jefferson. 1974. "A Simplest Systematics for the Organization of Turn-taking for Conversation". *Language* 50: 696–735.

Said, Edward W. 1983. *The World, the Text, and the Critic*. Cambridge, MA: Harvard University Press.

———. (1986) 1998. *After the Last Sky*. Photographs by Jean Mohr. New York: Columbia University Press.

Salomon, Joshua, Ajay Tandon and Christopher Murray. 2004. "Comparability of Self-Rated Health: Cross Sectional Multi-Country Survey Using Anchoring Vignettes". *BMJ* 328: 258–61.

Sanderson-Cole, Karen. 2003. "The Politics of Perspective: Interrogating Popular Romance with Special Reference to *Ti Marie*". MPhil thesis, University of the West Indies, St Augustine.

Saukko, Paula. 2003. *Doing Research in Cultural Studies: An Introduction to Classical and New Methodological Approaches*. London: Sage.

Saunders, Patricia. 2007. *Alien-Nation and Repatriation: Translating Identity in Anglophone Caribbean Literature*. Lanham, NY: Lexington.

Scott, Lawrence. 1998. *Aelred's Sin*. London: Allison and Busby.

Selby, Aimee, ed. 2009. *Art and Text*. London: Black Dog.

Selvon, Samuel. (1956) 1985. *The Lonely Londoners*. Harlow, UK: Longman.

———. (1975) 1984. *Moses Ascending*. Caribbean Writers Series 31. London: Heinemann.

Shakespeare, William. 1968. *The Tempest*, edited by Ann Righter. Harmondsworth: Penguin; London: Arden, 1999.

Shattuck, Roger. 1984. *The Innocent Eye: On Modern Literature and the Arts*. New York: Farrar, Straus and Giroux.

Shepherd, Rajendra. 2010. "The Write Way: Constructing the PM in the Media of Trinidad and Tobago". Postgraduate seminar presentation, University of the West Indies, St Augustine, Trinidad and Tobago, September.

Shields-Brodber, Kathryn. 2001a. "Contrapuntal Conversations and the Performance Floor". In *Due Respect: Papers on English and English-Related Creoles in the Anglophone Caribbean in Honour of Professor Robert Le Page*, edited by Pauline Christie, 208–18. Kingston: University of the West Indies Press.

———. 2001b. "Is the Pain in Your Belly Bottom?" In *Exploring the Boundaries of Caribbean Creole Languages*, edited by Hazel Simmons McDonald and Ian Robertson, 188–210. Kingston: University of the West Indies Press.

Sibley, Inez. 1978. *Dictionary of Place Names in Jamaica*. Kingston: Institute of Jamaica.

Silverman, David, and Anssi Peräkylä. 1990. "AIDS-counselling: The Interactional Organization of Talk about 'Delicate' Issues". *Sociology of Health and Illness* 12: 293–318.

Simon, Sherry. 2005. *Gender in Translation: Cultural Identity and the Politics of Transmission*. London: Routledge.

Skeete, Geraldine. 2007. "Development of a Discourse of Alternative Sexuality in Literature of the Anglophone Caribbean". PhD diss., University of the West Indies, St Augustine.

Smith, Ian. 1999. "Critics in the Dark". *Journal of West Indian Literature* 8 (2): 2–9.

Snell-Hornby, Mary. 1988. *Translation Studies: An Integrated Approach*. Amsterdam: John Benjamins.

Spivak, Gayatri Chakravorty. 2003. *Death of a Discipline*. New York: Columbia University Press.

Stam, Robert, and Allesandra Raengo. 2005. *A Guide to the Theory and Practice of Film Adaptation*. London: Blackwell.

Sumillera, Rocío. 2008. "Postcolonialism and Translation: The Translation of *Wide Sargasso Sea* into Spanish". *New Voices in Translation Studies* 4: 26–41.

Tajpal, Tarun J. 2011. "What Writing Can Do That Nothing Else Can". Sir V.S. Naipaul at THiNK. http://www.youtube.com/watch?v=TPjxZX8qMAM.

Tannen, Deborah. 1996. *Gender and Discourse*. Oxford: Oxford University Press.

Thackeray, William Makepeace. (1877) 1994. *Vanity Fair*. London: Penguin.

Thelwell, Michael. 1980. *The Harder They Come*. London: Pluto.

Thompson, Krista. 2006. *An Eye for the Tropics: Tourism, Photography and Framing the Caribbean Picturesque*. Durham, NC: Duke University Press.

Tolkien, J. R. R. 1937. *The Hobbit*. London: Allen and Unwin.

Twyman, Michael. 2008. "The Long-Term Significance of Printed Ephemera". *RBM: A Journal of Rare Books, Manuscripts, and Cultural Heritage* 9 (1): 19–57.

University of the West Indies. 1998. *Thesis Guide: A Guide to the Preparation of Theses, Research Papers and Project Reports*. St Augustine, Trinidad and Tobago: University of the West Indies.

———. 2001. *Graduate Studies Guide for Students and Supervisors at the University of the West Indies*. St Augustine, Trinidad and Tobago: University of the West Indies.

van Dijk, Teun. 1998. "Opinions and Ideologies in the Press". In *Approaches to Media Discourse*, edited by Allan Bell and Peter Garrett. Oxford: Blackwell.

———. 2000a. *Ideology: A Multidisciplinary Approach*. London: Sage.

———. 2000b. "New(s) Racism. A Discourse Analytical Approach". In *Ethnic Minorities and the Media*, edited by Simon Cottle, 33–49. Maidenhead, UK: Open University Press.

Venuti, Lawence. 1995. *The Translator's Invisibility: A History of Translation.* London: Routledge.

Walcott, Derek. 1973. *Another Life.* London: Jonathan Cape.

———. 1980. *Remembrance and Pantomime: Two Plays.* New York: Farrar, Straus and Giroux.

———. 1981. *Selected Poetry.* Oxford: Heinemann.

———. 1990. *Omeros.* London: Faber and Faber.

———. 1993. *The Antilles: Fragments of Epic Memory.* London: Faber and Faber.

———. 1998. "The Muse of History". In *What the Twilight Says*, 36–64. New York: Faber and Faber.

———. 2000. *Tiepolo's Hound.* New York: Farrar, Straus and Giroux.

———. 2004. *The Prodigal.* New York: Farrar, Straus and Giroux.

Walk, Kerry. 1998. "For the Writing Center at Harvard University". http://www.fas .harvard.edu/~wricntr/documents/CompAnalysis.html.

Walmsley, Anne. 1992. *The Caribbean Artists Movement 1966–1972.* London: New Beacon.

Warner, Keith. 2000. *On Location: Cinema and Film in the Anglophone Caribbean.* London: Macmillan.

Warner-Lewis, Maureen. (1984) 2003. "Samuel Selvon's Linguistic Extravaganza: Moses Ascending". In *Critical Issues in West Indian Literature*, edited by E. Smilowitz and R. Knowles, 101–11. Parkersburgh: Caribbean Books. In *Something Rich and Strange: Selected Essays on Sam Selvon*, edited by Martin Zehnder, 65–66. Leeds, UK: Peepal Tree Press.

———. 2005. "The Oral Tradition in the African Diaspora". Cultural Studies Distinguished Public Lecture, University of the West Indies, St Augustine, 22 September.

Williams, Emily Allen. 2002. *Anglophone Caribbean Poetry, 1970–2001: An Annotated Bibliography / Emily Allen Williams.* Westport, CT: Greenwood Press.

Williams, Raymond. 1983. "Culture". *Keywords: A Vocabulary of Culture and Society, Revised Edition.* 242–43. New York: Oxford University Press. http://pubpages.unh .edu/~dml3/880williams.htm#N_1_.

Wilson, George. 1986. *Narration in Light: Studies in Cinematic Point of View.* Baltimore: Johns Hopkins University Press.

Winer, Lise. 2009. *Dictionary of the English/Creole of Trinidad and Tobago.* Montreal: McGill-Queens University Press.

Wodak, R. 1996. *Disorders of Discourse.* London: Longman.

Wood, Beverley A., and Barbara A. Chase. 2007. "Ephemera and the Academic Library: The Response of the Main Library, the University of the West Indies, Cave Hill, Barbados". In *Caribbean Libraries in the 21st Century: Changes, Challenges, and Choices*, edited by Cheryl Peltier-Davis and Shamin Renwick, 79–94. Medford, NJ: Information Today.

Woolf, Virginia. (1927) 1987. *To the Lighthouse*. England: Hogarth Press; London: Penguin.

Wynter, Sylvia. 1973. "Creole Criticism: A Critique". *New World Quarterly* 5 (4): 12–36.

———. 1990. "Afterword: Beyond Miranda's Meanings: Un/Silencing the 'Demonic Ground of Caliban's Woman'". In Boyce Davies and Fido, *Out of the Kumbla: Caribbean Women and Literature*, 355–72.

Young, Timothy G. 2003. "Evidence: Towards a Library Definition of Ephemera". *RBM: A Journal of Rare Books, Manuscripts, and Cultural Heritage* 4 (1): 11–26.

Youssef, Valerie. 1993. "Marking Solidarity across the Trinidad Speech Community: The Use of 'an ting' in Medical Counselling to Break Down Power Differentials". *Discourse and Society* 4 (3): 292–306.

———. 1996. "Varilingualism: The Competence behind Code-Mixing in Trinidad and Tobago". *Journal of Pidgin and Creole Languages* 11 (1): 1–22.

———. 2001. "Working Out Conversational Roles through Questioning Strategies". In *Due Respect: Papers on English and English-Related Creoles in the Anglophone Caribbean in Honour of Professor Robert Le Page*, edited by Pauline Christie, 219–46. Kingston: University of the West Indies Press.

———. 2009a. "Less Blame, More Action: Media Depiction of Unresolved Child Abuse". Paper presented at Criminology Conference, Developing a Caribbean Criminology, Institute of Critical Thinking, University of the West Indies, St Augustine, 8–9 April.

———. 2009b. "The News Depiction of Crimes against Children". Paper presented at "First They Must Be Children", Cultural Studies Conference, University of the West Indies, St Augustine, 21–22 May.

———. 2009c. "Who Says What to Whom, and in What Circumstances? Negotiating Affective Encounters in a Second Language Context". Paper presented at the Modern Languages Symposium, University of the West Indies, St Augustine, 26 May.

Youssef, Valerie, and Pauline Russell-Brown. 2001. "When 'Same Sex' Talk Works: Issues of Communicative Success on a Telephone Response Service". *Illness, Crisis and Loss* 9 (2): 209–27.

Youssef, Valerie, and David Silverman. 1992. "Normative Expectations for Medical Talk". *Language and Communication* 12 (2): 123–31.

Zepetnek, Steven Tötsöy de. 1998. *Comparative Literature: Theory, Method, Application*. Volume 18 of *Textxet: Studies in Comparative Literature*. Amsterdam: Rodopi.

Zobel, Joseph. (1950, 1974, 1983, 1984) 1997. *La Rue Case-Nègres*. Paris: J. Froissart; Paris: Présence Africaine.

Filmography

Antoine-Dunne, Jean. 2011. Walcott documentary.

Black, Stephanie. 2001. *Life and Debt.*

Duigan, John. 1993. *Wide Sargasso Sea.*

Gilkes, Michael. N.d. *Sargasso.*

Henzell, Perry. 1972. *The Harder They Come.*

Lovelace, Asha. 2005. *Joebell and America.*

Maher, Brendan. 2006. *Wide Sargasso Sea* (television).

Mootoo, Shani. 1993. *The Wild Woman in the Woods.*

Newell, Mike. 2007. *Love in the Time of Cholera.* New Line Cinema.

Solomon, Francis-Anne. 1990. *I Is a Long Memoried Woman.*

Contributors

Barbara Lalla is Professor Emerita, Language and Literature, University of the West Indies, St Augustine, Trinidad and Tobago. Her publications include *Postcolonialisms: Caribbean Re-reading of Medieval English Discourse; Defining Jamaican Fiction: Marronage and the Discourse of Survival*; and (with Jean D'Costa) *Language in Exile: Three Hundred Years of Jamaican Creole and Voices in Exile*. She is also author of the novels *Cascade* and *Arch of Fire*.

Nicole Roberts is Senior Lecturer, Department of Modern Languages and Linguistics, University of the West Indies, St Augustine, Trinidad and Tobago. Her publications include *Main Themes in Twentieth Century Afro-Hispanic Caribbean Poetry: A Literary Sociology* and *Border Crossings: A Trilingual Anthology of Short Narrative by Caribbean Women Writers* (co-edited with Elizabeth Walcott-Hackshaw).

Elizabeth Walcott-Hackshaw is Senior Lecturer in French and Francophone Literatures, Department of Modern Languages and Linguistics, University of the West Indies, St Augustine, Trinidad and Tobago. Her publications include *Border Crossings: A Trilingual Anthology of Caribbean Women Writers* (co-edited with Nicole Roberts); *Echoes of the Haitian Revolution 1804–2004* and *Reinterpreting the Haitian Revolution and Its Cultural Aftershocks* (co-edited with Martin Munro); and *Four Taxis Facing North*, a collection of short stories.

Valerie Youssef is Professor of Linguistics, Department of Modern Languages and Linguistics, University of the West Indies, St Augustine, Trinidad and Tobago. Her publications include *The Languages of Tobago: Genesis and Perspectives* (co-authored with Winford James) and *Writing Rage: Unmasking Violence in Caribbean Discourse* (co-authored with Paula Morgan).

Jean Antoine-Dunne is Senior Lecturer, Department of Literatures in English and co-designer of the BA in film, University of the West Indies, St Augustine, Trinidad and Tobago. She is co-editor of *The Montage Priniciple: Eisenstein in*

New Cultural and Critical Contexts and editor of *Where Is Here? Remapping the Caribbean*, a special issue of the *Journal of West Indian Literature*. She has also edited a collection of essays on Derek Walcott, *Interlocking Basins of a Globe*.

Béatrice Boufoy-Bastick is Senior Lecturer in French and TESOL, Department of Modern Languages and Linguistics, University of the West Indies, St Augustine, Trinidad and Tobago. Her publications include *The International Handbook of Cultures of Professional Development for Teachers: Collaboration, Reflection, Management and Policy*; *Preserving National Unity: Culturometric Rapid Appraisals of Ethnic Inequalities*; and *Academic Attainments and Cultural Values*.

Jairo Sánchez-Galvis is Lecturer in Spanish, Department of Modern Languages and Linguistics, University the West Indies, St Augustine, Trinidad and Tobago. His publications include *A Translation Manual for the Caribbean / Un manual the traducción para el Caribe*.

Merle Hodge is retired Senior Lecturer, Faculty of Humanities, University of the West Indies, St Augustine, Trinidad and Tobago. Her publications include the novels *Crick Crack, Monkey* and *For the Life of Laetitia* and the textbook *The Knots in English: A Manual for Caribbean Users*.

Paula Morgan is Senior Lecturer, Department of Literary, Cultural and Communications Studies, University the West Indies, St Augustine, Trinidad and Tobago. Her publications include *Language Proficiency for Tertiary Level*; *Writing about Literature* (co-authored with Barbara Lalla); and *Writing Rage: Unmasking Violence in Caribbean Discourse* (co-authored with Valerie Youssef).

Jennifer Rahim is Senior Lecturer in Literature, Department of Liberal Arts, University of the West Indies, St Augustine, Trinidad and Tobago. Her publications include *Beyond Borders: Cross-culturalism and the Caribbean Canon* and *Created in the West Indies: Caribbean Perspectives on V.S. Naipaul* (both co-edited with Barbara Lalla). Her poetry and fiction publications include *Between the Fence and the Forest*, *Approaching Sabbaths* and *Songster and Other Stories*.

Louis Regis is Head of the Department of Literary, Cultural and Communication Studies, University of the West Indies, St Augustine, Trinidad and Tobago. His publications include *Black Stalin Kaisonian* and *The Political Calypso: True opposition in Trinidad and Tobago 1962–1987.*

Geraldine Skeete is Lecturer of Literatures in English, Department of Literary, Cultural and Communication Studies, University of the West Indies, St Augustine, Trinidad and Tobago. She is co-editor (with Giselle Rampaul) of *The Child and the Caribbean Imagination.*

Glenroy Taitt is Senior Librarian I and Head, West Indiana and Special Collections Division, Alma Jordan Library, University of the West Indies, St Augustine, Trinidad and Tobago.

www.ingramcontent.com/pod-product-compliance
Lightning Source LLC
Chambersburg PA
CBHW030629110726
47901CB00002B/386